Beginning Syntax

A coherent introduction to generative syntax by a leader in the field, this textbook leads students through the theory from the very beginning, assuming no prior knowledge. Introducing the central concepts in a systematic and engaging way, it covers the goals of generative grammar, tacit native-speaker knowledge, categories and constituents, phrase structure, movement, binding, syntax beyond English and the architecture of grammar. The theory is built slowly, showing in a step-by-step fashion how different versions of generative theory relate to one another. Examples are carefully chosen to be easily understood, and a comprehensive glossary provides clear definitions of all the key terms introduced. With end of chapter exercises, broader discussion questions, and annotated further reading lists, *Beginning Syntax* is the ideal resource for instructors and beginning undergraduate students of syntax alike. Two further textbooks by Ian Roberts, *Continuing Syntax* and *Comparing Syntax*, will take students to intermediate and advanced level.

IAN ROBERTS obtained a BA in Linguistics with a French minor from the University of Bangor in 1979. From 1981 to 1985 he attended the University of Southern California, obtaining a PhD in Linguistics in 1985. He took up his current post as Professor of Linguistics at the University of Cambridge in 2000. In 2007 he became an Ordinary Fellow of the British Academy. He has published eight monographs and three textbooks, and has edited several collections of articles. He was Joint Editor of *Journal of Linguistics*, the journal of the Linguistics Association of Great Britain, for 1994–8.

T0371132

CAMBRIDGE TEXTBOOKS IN LINGUISTICS

General editors: U. ANSALDO, P. AUSTIN, B. COMRIE, R. LASS,
D. LIGHTFOOT, K. RICE, I. ROBERTS, S. ROMAINE, M. SHEEHAN,
I. TSIMPLI

Beginning Syntax
An Introduction to Syntactic Analysis

In this series:

R. CANN *Formal Semantics*

J. LAVER *Principles of Phonetics*

F. R. PALMER *Grammatical Roles and Relations*

M. A. JONES *Foundations of French Syntax*

A. RADFORD *Syntactic Theory and the Structure of English: A Minimalist Approach*

R. D. VAN VALIN JR AND R. J. LAPOLLA *Syntax: Structure, Meaning and Function*

A. DURANTI *Linguistic Anthropology*

A. CRUTTENDEN *Intonation* Second edition

J. K. CHAMBERS AND P. TRUDGILL *Dialectology* Second edition

C. LYONS *Definiteness*

R. KAGER *Optimality Theory*

J. A. HOLM *An Introduction to Pidgins and Creoles*

G. G. CORBETT *Number*

C. J. EWENH. VAN DER HULST *The Phonological Structure of Words*

F. R. PALMER *Mood and Modality* Second edition

B. J. BLAKE *Case* Second edition

E. GUSSMAN *Phonology: Analysis and Theory*

M. YIP *Tone*

W. CROFT *Typology and Universals* Second edition

F. COULMAS *Writing Systems: An Introduction to Their Linguistic Analysis*

P. J. HOPPER AND E. C. TRAUGOTT *Grammaticalization* Second edition

L. WHITE *Second Language Acquisition and Universal Grammar*

I. PLAG *Word-Formation in English*

W. CROFT AND A. CRUSE *Cognitive Linguistics*

A. SIEWIERSKA *Person*

A. RADFORD *Minimalist Syntax: Exploring the Structure of English*

D. BÜRING *Binding Theory*

M. BUTT *Theories of Case*

N. HORNSTEIN, J. NUÑES AND K. GROHMANN *Understanding Minimalism*

B. C. LUST *Child Language: Acquisition and Growth*

G. G. CORBETT *Agreement*

J. C. L. INGRAM *Neurolinguistics: An Introduction to Spoken Language Processing and Its Disorders*

J. CLACKSON *Indo-European Linguistics: An Introduction*

M. ARIEL *Pragmatics and Grammar*

R. CANN, R. KEMPSON AND E. GREGOROMICHELAKI *Semantics: An Introduction to Meaning in Language*

Y. MATRAS *Language Contact*

D. BIBER AND S. CONRAD *Register, Genre, and Style*

L. JEFFRIES AND D. MCINTYRE *Stylistics*

R. HUDSON *An Introduction to Word Grammar*

M. L. MURPHY *Lexical Meaning*

J. M. MEISEL *First and Second Language Acquisition*

T. MCENERY AND A. HARDIE *Corpus Linguistics: Method, Language and Practice*

J. SAKEL AND D. L. EVERETT *Linguistic Fieldwork: A Student Guide*

A. SPENCERA. LUÍS *Clitics: An Introduction*

G. CORBETT *Features*

A. MCMAHON AND R. MCMAHON *Evolutionary Linguistics*

B. CLARK *Relevance Theory*

B. LONGPENG *Analyzing Sound Patterns*

B. DANCYGIER AND E. SWEETSER *Figurative Language*

J. BYBEE *Language Change*

S. G. THOMASON *Endangered Languages: An Introduction*

A. RADFORD *Analysing English Sentences* Second edition

R. CLIFT *Conversation Analysis*

R. LEVINE *Syntactic Analysis*
I. PLAG *Word-Formation in English* Second edition
Z. G. SZABÓ AND R. H. THOMASON *Philosophy of Language*
J. PUSTEJOVSKY AND O. BATIUKOVA *The Lexicon*
D. BIBER AND S. CONRAD *Register, Genre, and Style* Second edition
F. ZÚÑIGA AND S. KITTILÄ *Grammatical Voice*
Y. MATRAS *Language Contact* Second edition
T. HOFFMANN *Construction Grammar*
W. CROFT *Morphosyntax: Constructions of the World's Languages*
I. ROBERTS *Beginning Syntax: An Introduction to Syntactic Analysis*

Earlier issues not listed are also available.

Beginning Syntax
An Introduction to Syntactic Analysis

IAN ROBERTS

Downing College, University of Cambridge

Shaftesbury Road, Cambridge CB2 8EA, United Kingdom

One Liberty Plaza, 20th Floor, New York, NY 10006, USA

477 Williamstown Road, Port Melbourne, VIC 3207, Australia

314–321, 3rd Floor, Plot 3, Splendor Forum, Jasola District Centre,
New Delhi – 110025, India

103 Penang Road, #05–06/07, Visioncrest Commercial, Singapore 238467

Cambridge University Press is part of Cambridge University Press & Assessment,
a department of the University of Cambridge.

We share the University's mission to contribute to society through the pursuit of
education, learning and research at the highest international levels of excellence.

www.cambridge.org
Information on this title: www.cambridge.org/9781316519493

DOI: 10.1017/9781009023849

First published 2023

A catalogue record for this publication is available from the British Library

*A Cataloging-in-Publication data record for this book is available from the Library
of Congress*

ISBN 978-1-316-51949-3 Hardback
ISBN 978-1-009-01058-0 Paperback

Contents

Preface   *page* xiii
List of Abbreviations   xv

Introduction: What Linguistics Is About and
What Syntax Is About   1
    What Is (a) Language?   3
        What Is Language? vs What Is a Language?   3
        Natural Language vs Artificial Languages   4
    Language and Languages   7
    Natural Language   9
    Exercises   12
    For Further Study and/or Discussion   13
    Further Reading   13

1 Tacit Knowledge (or: Several Things You Didn't Know
You Knew about English)   15
  1.1   Introduction   15
  1.2   Some Fish   15
  1.3   More Fish and Some Relative Clauses 22
  1.4   Really Challenging Fish   25
  1.5   Conclusion: What the Fish Have Taught Us   31
  Exercises   32
  For Further Study and/or Discussion   33
  Further Reading   34

2 Constituents and Categories   35
  2.1   Introduction and Recap   35
  2.2   Categories   36
      2.2.1 Introduction: Lexical and Functional Categories   36
      2.2.2 Morphological Diagnostics for Categories   38
      2.2.3 Syntactic Diagnostics for Categories   39
      2.2.4 Phonological Diagnostics for Categories   42
      2.2.5 Semantics and Categories   42
      2.2.6 Conclusion   44
  2.3   Constituent Structure   44
      2.3.1 Phrasal Constituents   44
      2.3.2 Hierarchical Relations among Constituents   45
  2.4   Conclusion   47

Exercises   48
Further Reading   49

3 Phrase-Structure Rules and Constituency Tests   51
    3.1   Introduction   51
    3.2   Phrase-Structure Rules   52
    3.3   Recursion   55
    3.4   Constituency Tests   59
    3.5   Summary and Conclusion   75
    Exercises   76
    For Further Discussion   77
    Further Reading   77

4 X′-theory   78
    4.1   Introduction   78
    4.2   Possible and Impossible PS-Rules   78
    4.3   Introducing X′-theory   80
    4.4   X′-theory and Functional Categories: The Structure of the Clause 87
    4.5   Adjuncts in X′-theory   95
    4.6   Conclusion   96
    Exercises   97
    For Further Discussion   98
    Further Reading   98

5 Movement   99
    5.1   Introduction and Recap   99
    5.2   Types of Movement Rules   100
    5.3   Wh-Movement: The Basics   104
    5.4   Subject Questions, Indirect Questions and Long-Distance
           Wh-Movement   112
    5.5   The Nature of Movement Rules   118
    5.6   Limiting Wh-Movement   122
    5.7   Conclusion   126
    Exercises   127
    For Further Discussion   128
    Further Reading   128

6 Binding   130
    6.1   Introduction and Recap   130
    6.2   Pronouns and Anaphors   130
    6.3   Anaphors   132
    6.4   Pronouns   142
    6.5   R-expressions   143
    6.6   The Binding Principles   144
    6.7   Variables, Principle C and Movement   146
    6.8   Conclusion   153

Exercises   154
For Discussion   154
Further Reading   155

7 Syntax beyond English   156
   7.1   Introduction and Recap   156
   7.2   Approaching Universal Grammar   156
   7.3   Verb Positions in French and English   157
   7.4   Word Order and X′-theory   160
   7.5   A Case Study: German   165
   7.6   The Wh-Movement Parameter   171
   7.7   Conclusion   174
   Exercises   176
   For Further Discussion   178
   Further Reading   178

8 The Architecture of Grammar   179
   8.1   Introduction and Recap   179
   8.2   A Model of Grammar   179
   8.3   The Lexicon   180
   8.4   D-structure   187
   8.5   S-structure   190
   8.6   Phonological Form (PF)   195
   8.7   Logical Form (LF)   203
   8.8   Conclusion   211
   Exercises   212
   Further Reading   214

Conclusion   215

Glossary   219
Index   234

Preface

The purpose of this book is to present the essential elements of the theory of syntax, presupposing no prior knowledge of either syntax or linguistics more generally. The first chapter introduces the thinking behind modern formal linguistics, defining the core background concepts. The second chapter is an extended demonstration of linguistic competence, revealing to an English speaker their tacit, untutored knowledge of the intricacies of the syntax of the language. The next four chapters introduce the core technical concepts of syntax: phrase structure, constituency, movement rules and construal rules. Chapter 7 is a very brief introduction to comparative syntax, illustrating how the theory developed in the earlier chapters can apply to languages other than English. Finally, Chapter 8 discusses the overall architecture of grammar, introducing several levels of representation, including the interface levels of Phonological Form and Logical Form.

The book is based on a first-year lecture course I have taught at Cambridge for most of the past ten years, called 'Structures'. That course has successfully laid the groundwork for more advanced study; several professional syntacticians had their first exposure to the subject in that context.

I do not attempt to review either the history or the state of the art in contemporary generative syntax. Instead, the book is intended to provide a solid basis from which the student can move on to more advanced topics. In the decades since its inception, generative theory has yielded a range of core insights and concepts which can be studied independently of the details of a given framework and which form the core of any formal approach to syntax (and core background to the formal study of other areas of linguistics, in particular semantics). These are the focus of this introduction, where the theoretical orientation of the book is most clearly set out. This volume is intended as the first in a series; future volumes will build on the material presented here, as well as both adding an explicitly comparative and typological dimension and engaging more directly with the minimalist programme for linguistic theory. The overall aim of the series is to provide a complete course in syntax, taking the student from beginner level to being able to engage with contemporary research literature.

This volume is intended for students starting out in syntax and assumes no prior knowledge. As mentioned above, it corresponds to a first-year course taught at Cambridge. It can be taught over a single term or semester with tutorial support (as I have done at Cambridge) or over an entire year as a lecture course. The book tries to introduce the main concepts of syntactic theory in an engaging way with a minimum of technicalities. Each chapter features exercises, some straightforwardly testing the material covered in the chapter, others raising further questions for reflection and discussion (e.g. in tutorials), as well as suggestions for further reading. Model answers are provided separately for the first type of exercise. The second type presupposes student participation in discussions. Chapter 1 is somewhat different from the others in that it introduces some fairly complex data; the point at this stage of the exposition is to demonstrate tacit knowledge, i.e. native-speaker competence; the technical issues are, as appropriate, revisited and introduced more gradually later. Instructors may wish to skip over some of this material and/or revisit it later (for example, the Italian data can supplement the material covered in Chapter 7).

I would like to thank the other people who have taught this course in whole or in part over the years: Dora Alexopoulou, Theresa Biberauer, Craig Sailor and Jenneke van der Wal, as well as the many doctoral students, postdocs and others who have given tutorials for the course. Most of all, I'd like to thank the students themselves: you ultimately make everything happen. Thanks also to Bob Freidin and Dalina Kallulli for comments on early drafts. And of course, thanks to the two Helens at Cambridge University Press: Helen Barton and Helen Shannon, whose tolerance of missed deadlines fully matches my capacity to bring them about.

Abbreviations

AAVE	African-American Vernacular English
ACC	accusative case
Agr	agreement
A(P)	adjective (phrase)
Adv(P)	adverb (phrase)
ASL	American Sign Language
Aux(P)	auxiliary (phrase)
BSL	British Sign Language
C(P)	complementiser (phrase)
CNPC	Complex NP Constraint
Comp	complementiser
Conj	conjugation
D(P)	determiner (phrase)
GEN	genitive case
LBC	Left Branch Condition
LF	Logical Form
M	mood
Mod	modifier
Neg(P)	negation (phrase)
NOM	nominative case
N(P)	noun (phrase)
NSL	Nicaraguan Sign Language
NUM	number
OV	object-verb
OSV	object-subject-verb
OVS	object-verb-subject
PF	phonological form
Pl	plural (preceded by an Arabic numeral, denotes the relevant person, e.g. 3Pl = third-person plural)
P(P)	preposition(al phrase)
Perf(P)	perfect (phrase)
Pres	present
Prog(P)	progressive (phrase)
PST	past

Q	Question
QR	Quantifier Raising
S	sentence
SASL	South African Sign Language
Sg	singular (preceded by an Arabic numeral, denotes the relevant person, e.g. 3Sg = third-person singular)
SOV	subject-object-verb
SVO	subject-verb-object
Spec	specifier
TOP	topic (marker)
T(P)	tense (phrase)
UG	Universal Grammar
VO	verb-object
V(P)	verb (phrase)
VOS	verb-object-subject
VSO	verb-subject-object
WALS	*World Atlas of Language Structures* (Haspelmath et al. 2013)

Introduction: What Linguistics Is About and What Syntax Is About

This book is an introduction to one part of the general subject of linguistics: **syntax** (words which are boldfaced are either technical terms or names of languages and language families which may not be familiar; at the end of the book you can find a glossary where these terms are defined). Syntax is the study of the structure of sentences, how these sentences arise and how speakers of a language are able to use and understand sentences by having a mental representation of their structure. In this book, the language we focus on is English, not because there is anything particularly special about English, but just because that's the one language I can be sure you know, since you're reading this book.

Syntax is one of the central sub-disciplines of modern linguistics. The other central areas of linguistics are **phonology** (the study of sounds and sound systems) and **semantics** (the study of meaning). There are many other aspects to linguistics (e.g. **morphology**, the study of the form of words), but these three form the core of language: the fundamental thing about language is that it connects sound and meaning through sentences. Phonology deals with the sounds, semantics deals with the meanings and syntax deals with the sentences. Syntax is the bridge between the sound and the meaning of sentences. We'll have plenty more to say about this in the chapters to follow, but first let's look at linguistics more broadly.

Modern linguistics is the scientific study of language. The education systems in many parts of the world make a major distinction between sciences (like biology, physics and chemistry) and arts or humanities (like history, music or literature). Languages are almost always classified on the arts/humanities side, so it might seem odd to talk about looking at language and languages scientifically. 'Science' conjures up visions of men (mostly) in white coats carrying out experiments using various kinds of specialised equipment, all of which seems a far cry from reading Shakespeare, learning French verbs or trying out Spanish conversation.

But really, looking at something scientifically means two main things. First, it means observing things as part of nature (rocks, stars or slugs, for example). Language is so much a part of us that it can be difficult to think of it as a natural object, the way rocks, stars and slugs obviously are. But imagine you were a Martian observing planet Earth: you'd see rocks, slugs, plenty of insects and a featherless biped building machines (including spacecraft), in control of everything, and making noises with its breathing and eating apparatus. As an intelligent Martian, you'd soon recognise that there is some connection between the bipeds' noises, their ability to build machines and their control over all the other species. You'd also notice that only the featherless bipeds make these noises and that the young of the species spontaneously start making the noises when they're very small and still dependent on their parents for survival. After abducting some bipeds and looking inside their brains, you'd realise that there's just a couple of areas of the biped brain which seem to control the noise-making ability. The noises are language (Martians would probably first notice phonology, but being super-intelligent they'd quickly realise that there was more to language than just that). By looking at ourselves through Martian 'eyes' (which might of course be infrared heat sensors attached to their feet, but never mind), we can appreciate language as a natural object.

The second thing about science is that it's not just about observing things; it's also about putting the observations together to make a theory of things. One of the most famous of all scientific theories is Einstein's Theory of Relativity. This is hardly the place to go into that, but the point is that Einstein and other physicists wanted to construct a general understanding, based on observation, of certain aspects of nature: the Theory of Relativity is mostly about space, time and gravity. A good theory, like relativity, makes sense of the observations we have already made and also predicts new ones that we should be able to make.

So saying linguistics is scientific doesn't necessarily mean that we have to put on white coats and start a laboratory. But it does mean that we should try to make observations about language and put those observations together to make a theory of language. Since we're going to focus on syntax, we're going to make observations about syntax and make a theory of syntax. So the goal of this book is to present a particular theory of syntax, a scientific theory of what it is that links sound and meaning (as you can imagine, there are separate but connected theories of phonology and semantics). The theory that I will introduce here is called **generative grammar**. The reasons for that name will emerge over the next couple of chapters.

Approaching language, or syntax, in this way means that there are aspects of the more traditional, humanities-style approaches to language that we leave behind, since they do not contribute to the goal of making observations and building theories. First, it implies that the goal of linguistics is not to set standards of 'good' speaking or writing. This is not to imply that such standards should not be set, or that linguists, or others with particular expertise in language, should not be those responsible for setting them. Instead, it means that setting these standards falls outside the scientific study of language, since doing this doesn't involve making observations about what people say, write or understand but involves recommending that people should speak or write in a certain way. Zoologists don't tell slugs how to be slimy; linguists don't tell people how to speak or write. Ideas of 'good' syntax have no place here. **Prescriptive grammatical** statements of a kind once common in the teaching of English in schools in most of the English-speaking world (see below for some examples) are similarly irrelevant to our concerns here.

A second consequence of leaving behind the traditional humanities-style approach to the study of language and adopting a scientific approach instead is that we do not evaluate language aesthetically. This does not mean that the aesthetic appreciation of language, in particular literary language, is without interest or value as a study in itself, merely that this represents a different way of studying (and enjoying) language from the scientific one. Botanists may appreciate the beauty of flowers as much as anybody else, and zoologists no doubt admire the beauty of slugs, but the scientific study of flowers and slugs leaves aside any aesthetic response to them. Similarly, linguists may well appreciate the beauty and power of great works of literature, but the goal of modern linguistics is not to explicate our reaction to such works; that is for our colleagues in the literature departments.

There is also a third aspect of a scientific approach to a field of investigation, a really basic one. That is to begin by defining our terms, so let us start in this way. If linguistics is the scientific study of language, then we should start by defining language itself. That, as we shall see, is not as simple as might first appear.

What Is (a) language?

What Is language? vs What Is a Language?

First of all, it is useful to distinguish language as a general concept from individual languages. Our definition of linguistics makes reference to this general concept and, as such, tells us that linguistics is concerned with this general concept rather than with the study of individual languages (and hence tells us that linguistics is not about acquiring proficiency in individual languages; this is another aspect of the traditional humanities approach to language that modern linguistics leaves aside). It is very difficult to give an adequate general definition of language, especially in advance of the first steps in constructing any kind of theory of language or its subparts. For the moment, let us define language as the communicative and cognitive capacity that, as far as we know, most clearly distinguishes humans from other animals; this is what the Martians saw when they observed terrestrial featherless bipeds making noises. All human societies and cultures that have ever been discovered have language, most commonly spoken language; current estimates are that there are over 7,000 languages spoken in the world (www.ethnologue.com), although individual languages are hard to count, and we will see below that there are reasons to question whether English, French, etc., are really natural objects. On the other hand, no non-human animal has a linguistic or communicative capacity comparable to ours. This is not to deny that communication systems of various kinds are easy to observe in other species, but none of these systems seem to have the structural complexity we can observe in human language; as we shall see, the nature of the syntax of human language may lie behind the gulf between human language and animal communication. Indeed it could be argued that language is not just unique to our species, but a defining property of it. The official biological name of our species (in the **Linnean taxonomy**) is *Homo sapiens*, Latin for 'wise man'. Since a glance at a history book or a newspaper leads one to question the wisdom of our species, one could think that *Homo loquens* ('talking man') might have been a better term to define us.

As just mentioned, the general concept of language, roughly defined above, should be distinguished from individual languages. An individual language can be taken to be a specific variant of the uniquely human capacity defined above, usually part of a given culture: English, **Navajo**, **Warlpiri**, **Basque**, etc. Concepts such as 'English' are thus, at least in part, cultural concepts. The distinction between language (in general) and languages (individual languages as partly cultural entities) distinguishes two variants of a single word in English. This is rather like the way we can distinguish the general concept of cheese from individual cheeses such as Brie, Cheddar, Parmigiano Reggiano and so on. *Language* and *cheese* are mass nouns; they denote general concepts. Individual cultures in different parts of the world produce their local variants of the general thing, associated with countable versions of the same nouns, i.e. individual languages and cheeses. In several European languages, different words are used to make the distinction between language and languages. French distinguishes *langage* (language in general) from *langue* (individual languages); in Italian *linguaggio* is distinguished from *lingua* in a similar way, and Spanish distinguishes *lenguaje* from *lengua*.

Natural Language vs Artificial Languages

A very important distinction in the context of defining the object of study of scientific linguistics is that between natural languages and artificial languages. Natural languages are natural objects (like slugs, etc., as we have seen), and so they can be the object of scientific study. Natural languages are languages spoken as native languages (they are almost always somebody's mother tongue) and are intrinsically capable of fulfilling a full range of communicative functions (making statements, asking questions, giving orders, etc.). Moreover, the origins of natural languages are obscure in that we are unable to fix a specific time or place for where they began. For example, handbooks on the history of the English language typically date the beginning of English to the arrival of the Angles, Saxons and Jutes in the British Isles starting in the fifth century CE. The Angles, Saxons and Jutes spoke closely related **Germanic** dialects which originated where they themselves originated, in what is now Southern Denmark and Northern Germany. As far as we know, nothing changed about their language when it was transplanted, along with its speakers, from the mainland to the offshore islands. Hence, the date attached to the 'beginning of English' reflects a random aspect of external history and almost certainly does not reflect any linguistic change at all. English is a direct continuation of the Germanic dialects spoken on the continent before the fifth century by the Angles, Saxons and Jutes.

These dialects were in turn a continuation of one dialect of **Indo European**, which was originally spoken (as far as we know) three or four millennia earlier in either the Pontic-Caspian steppe region of what is now Ukraine or in Central Anatolia (modern Turkey). Again, the beginnings and endings of 'English', 'Germanic' and 'Indo European' are arbitrarily chosen historical events. The languages themselves simply continue; what came before Indo European is uncertain, and this further illustrates the point that natural languages have an essentially unknown origin. All we can be sure of is that our capacity for language must have evolved at some stage in the history of our species, but this event is lost in the mists of time many millennia before Indo European or its precursors.

Artificial languages, on the other hand, are languages designed for some specific purpose and restricted in terms of their functions. We can usually say when and by whom they were invented. As such, they are not natural objects. So, for example, **logic**, which can be thought of as an artificial language, was invented by Aristotle *ca* 400 BCE, and the various computer-programming languages in use today and in recent years were all invented after roughly 1950, when modern computers themselves were invented. Semaphore, Morse code and other signalling systems are also artificial languages of this general kind, and also highly restricted in function. Artificial languages are of less interest for our purposes here, since they are not natural objects. So I will leave them aside in what follows.

In this context, we should mention other kinds of language and languages. **Sign language** is of great interest. In fact, sign language is not a single linguistic entity: there are various different Sign Languages, e.g. British Sign Language (BSL), American Sign Language (ASL), Nicaraguan Sign Language (NSL), South African Sign Language (SASL) and many others in many parts of the world. Sign languages are primarily used by Deaf communities. It is now an established finding of modern linguistics that sign languages are natural languages in precisely the sense defined above: they are natural objects. Sign languages serve the full range of communicative functions and their origins are obscure. Most importantly, sign languages are not manual versions of the spoken or written language used by the hearing communities around them. For example, BSL is the creation of the British Deaf community. Its history goes back to accounts in the fifteenth century describing deaf people using signs. The first description of those signs appears in the Marriage Register of St Martin's, Leicester, in 1576, describing the vows signed by Thomas Tillsye, who 'was and is naturally deafe and also dumbe, so that the order of the forme of marriage used usually amongst others which can heare and speake could not for his parte be observed' (www.ucl.ac.uk/british-sign-language-history/beginnings/marriagecertificate-thomas-tillsye).

The only difference between sign language and familiar languages such as English is that sign languages use a different medium, the gestural/visual medium, while familiar languages use the oral/aural medium (and of course writing). One of the striking features of natural languages, both spoken and signed, is that their salient structural properties are independent of their medium of transmission: sign-language syntax, for example, has the same structural properties as English, French and other spoken languages.

Constructed languages, or conlangs, are also relevant here. Conlangs are of two main kinds. First, there are languages which were deliberately constructed as 'ideal' languages intended to serve for more efficient communication than could be afforded by seemingly imperfect already existing languages. Esperanto is probably the best known, although far from the only, language of this kind. Esperanto was invented by L. L. Zamenhof in 1887, at a time when there was no clear international lingua franca in the Western world (since 1945, English has played this role; at earlier times Latin and French did). The vocabulary of Esperanto is a mixture of Romance, Germanic and Slavic elements, and the grammatical system is a highly simplified and artificially regularised. The system is, however, closely based on various European, principally Romance, languages. As such it is arguably a natural language, which happens to have a particular origin and purpose. It is debatable, however, whether Esperanto has any true native speakers, although it is certainly used as a second language by up to 2 million people all around the world (compare this with the estimated 2 billion second-language speakers of English). Many other invented languages (**Interlingua**, **Volapük**, etc.) have the same status as Esperanto, although these days they are hardly spoken at all.

The other principal kind of constructed languages are those invented for fictional purposes, in order to give linguistic realism to invented worlds and their denizens. Among the best-known examples are the languages invented by J. R. R. Tolkien in his extensive mythological writings (*The Lord of the Rings*, *The Hobbit*, *The Silmarillion*, etc.). Tolkien was a professional philologist, and so the languages he constructed have an air of authenticity. Like Esperanto, however, they are largely based on existing, mainly European, languages. They are thus natural languages which are unusual in their origin and purpose; they are also barely spoken at all and certainly have no native speakers. Above all for this last reason, we leave such languages aside here; our interest is in languages which are acquired naturally.

Two other kinds of 'language' should also be mentioned. First, there is 'body language': frowning, shaking or nodding one's head, crossing one's arms or legs, etc. Body language can certainly communicate various attitudes or emotional states (friendliness, aggression, etc.), but it is not a language in the sense that it lacks the structural properties of natural, spoken and signed, languages; it has no discernible syntax, for example. Second, there is music. Music is often said to be a language, and indeed it has been shown to have structural, syntactic properties which are akin to, perhaps even identical to, natural language. However, although music may have a profound emotional impact, it lacks a clear propositional semantics, in that it cannot communicate true or false statements. It may be that music is a cognitive capacity which shares some, but not all, of the properties of natural languages. Certainly, music appears to be both universal across human cultures and unique to humans; in these important respects, it resembles natural language.

To sum up, our focus here is on natural language. Modern linguistics is really about natural language in the sense described at the beginning of this section and, henceforth, I will restrict the discussion along these lines. Linguists thus believe that it makes sense to study natural language in general and not just individual languages. If natural language forms a coherent object of study, and if individual languages are specific variants of language in general, then this implies that all individual languages must have something in common. Hence, a major focus of linguistic research, particularly since the middle of the twentieth century, but with much older historical roots, has been the following question: what are the common properties of natural languages not shared by other systems of communication?[1] One of the central goals of modern linguistic theory is the attempt to answer this question, and we will address this question as it applies to syntax in much of what follows.

Language and Languages

Once we define natural language in the way we have done so far, its study can still be approached from various perspectives. As we mentioned earlier, one approach, which comes from the traditional humanities, is the prescriptive one. This involves defining precepts of 'good' English, in principle independently of how native speakers might actually speak or write the language. This has led to the formulation of precepts such as 'Don't use two negatives, since that makes a positive.' In many varieties of non-standard English all over the English-speaking world, it is easy to observe people saying things like *I don't like no-one* or *Mick can't get no satisfaction*, and so on. Here two negatives are used, but the result is not a positive. Invoking an artificial kind of logic, which does not correspond to the facts we can observe about the syntax and the meanings of these sentences, is not in line with the scientific approach to language we are adopting here. Such artificial 'rules' mostly originate in the eighteenth and nineteenth centuries and reflect little of substance about the true nature of English or any other language.[2] So I will say no more about 'rules' of this kind (although negative sentences of the kind shown above are very common in many languages of the world, including French; they illustrate a phenomenon known as **negative concord**).

---

[1] See R. Robins (1967), *A Short History of Linguistics from Plato to Chomsky*, London: Longman, and V. Law (2003), *The History of Linguistics in Europe*, Cambridge: Cambridge University Press, for discussion.

[2] See R. Freidin (2020), *Adventures in English Syntax*, Cambridge: Cambridge University Press, for a very illuminating discussion.

Another perspective is a teleological one. This is certainly relevant for the study of individual languages with the goal of attaining proficiency in speaking and/or writing them, another important aspect of the traditional way of studying language and languages. If I say *I am learning to speak Catalan*, then 'speaking Catalan' here is defined as a goal I am striving towards. It does not correspond to any currently existing knowledge or ability I have. But this is clearly something distinct from studying Catalan, or any other individual language, with the goal of understanding its structure; in particular, understanding its structure in relation to the general question of the possible structural commonalities of all natural languages, as discussed in the previous section. Hence, the teleological approach to the study of individual languages, although of course worthwhile, falls outside of modern linguistics as we understand it here.

Still another perspective on language is the sociopolitical one. One very important distinction in this connection is that between a dialect and a 'standard' language. Despite the social and political importance of this distinction, if we consider individual languages and dialects to be variants of the more general notion of language, then we are led to consider all natural-language systems as equal, whatever their social or political status (or that of the people who speak them). If we consider language to be a single coherent entity, then we expect to find the same general structural characteristics in all individual languages and dialects; this, of course, is the initial hypothesis that we intend to investigate and, if possible, substantiate.

Moreover, all natural languages and dialects appear to be of roughly the same level of complexity. Although this point is hard to assess and verify in detail and in a fully satisfactory way, there does not appear to be any reason to assert that one or another language or dialect is 'simpler' or 'more basic' or 'more primitive' than another. In structural terms, then, there is no reason to privilege one language or dialect over any other; the fact that one particular variety may have emerged as a standard is usually just a historical accident. For example, Standard (British) English emerged in the fifteenth and sixteenth centuries as English became the main language of commerce and correspondence. Standard English came to predominate as the written form of the language and came to be taught in schools as the 'correct' or 'standard' form. The emergence of Standard English was a consequence of social and political factors; it had nothing to do with the structural features of that variety of English, and there is accordingly no reason to think that that particular variety is in any way intrinsically superior to any other.

So, from the point of view we adopt here, the distinction between dialects and standard languages is an artificial one, extrinsic to the structural features of the varieties in question. When we look at language variants as natural objects, we see that the language vs dialect distinction is spurious; it comes from culture, not nature. Back in 1945, the American sociolinguist Max Weinreich captured this point by saying that 'a language is a dialect with an army and a navy'. Political, economic and military power confer prestige on standard languages, but from a purely linguistic point of view, they are not distinct from dialects.

We can take this line of thought further. The notion of a standard language is really a type of idealisation, one specially constructed by language planners and educationalists often interested in telling people what to do. In many countries, one of the goals of teaching the standard language is teleological, in the sense discussed above. In reality, nobody really speaks the ideal standard language; everybody speaks some form of dialect. One very clear result of the scientific study of the social aspects of language (the field known as sociolinguistics) is that no language is homogeneous. Everybody, including people who consider themselves speakers of 'Standard English', actually speaks a slightly different variant of the language, approximating an ideal standard in slightly different ways (which, in practice, one may hardly ever have cause to notice). As pointed out well over a century ago by the German historical linguist Hermann Paul, 'we must in reality distinguish as many languages as there are individuals'. No two speakers of a given language actually know precisely the same things about that language or use it in precisely the same way. Alongside dialects, then, we recognise **idiolects**, the variety of a language employed by a particular person. We may also want to recognise **sociolects** (varieties associated with particular social classes), **ethnolects** (varieties associated with particular ethnic groups) and so on.

All of this may leave you feeling perplexed. If all speakers have different idiolects, is there a notion of an individual language that can really be usefully defined at all? Atkinson (1992:23) gave the following definition of an English speaker:

> The person in question has an internal system of representation … the overt products of which (utterance production and comprehension, grammaticality judgements), in conjunction with other mental capacities, are such that that person is judged (by those deemed capable of judging) to be a speaker of English.[3]

We can see from this that defining 'a language' isn't as simple as we might have at first thought.

Leaving aside the social, cultural and political dimensions (which are evident in Atkinson's definition), we can try to understand what 'language' is so that we can then define 'a language' as a specific variant (token) of this more general entity (type). In this way, we take the everyday terms for individual languages (English, French, etc.) to be primarily sociocultural. Strictly speaking, these terms are not, in fact, part of scientific linguistics, since they designate cultural rather than natural objects.

Natural Language

Leaving aside the sociocultural dimensions, then, we concentrate on looking at natural language from a scientific perspective. More precisely, we

---

[3] M. Atkinson (1992), *Children's Syntax*, Oxford: Blackwell.

will look at language from a cognitive perspective. This approach treats language as a form of knowledge; the central idea is that our uniquely human language capacity is part of our cognitive make-up. Language is really a kind of instinct humans, and no other species, are pre-programmed with (in fact, *The Language Instinct* is the title of an influential and important book by Stephen Pinker in which this approach is explained in detail; see Further Reading at the end of this Introduction). This is the view that forms the basis of the theory of generative grammar and so this is the view I will adopt here. This approach, and most of the concepts introduced in this section, are due to Noam Chomsky (see Further Reading at the end of the Introduction for more details).

The cognitive approach treats our capacity for language as an aspect of human psychology which is ultimately rooted in biology. In this way, it clearly treats language, and our capacity for language, as natural objects. On this view, there are **three factors in language design**. The first is contributed by genetics: an innate aptitude for language that is unique to our species, our 'language instinct'. The second factor is experience, particularly in early life. The language we are exposed to as children represents the crucial linguistic experience; when I was growing up in England, everyone around me spoke English and so I acquired English. My great-grandfather was surrounded by Welsh speakers when he was growing up in nineteenth-century North Wales, so he acquired Welsh. Whichever language, or languages, we are exposed to as small children, our innate language-learning capacity is brought to bear on this experience in such a way as to result in our competence as native speakers of our first language (I will say more about **language acquisition** below). Third, general cognitive capacities, not specific to language and perhaps not specific to humans, clearly play a role in shaping our knowledge and use of language, although the exact role these capacities play and how they interact with (and can be distinguished from) the language-specific aspects of our linguistic capacities are difficult questions. Together, these three factors constitute the human **language faculty**. It can be extremely difficult to distinguish the specifically linguistic aspects that contribute to forming the language faculty from more general cognitive abilities, but the distinction can certainly be made in principle and is of course very important for our general cognitive theory of language.

In these terms, **Universal Grammar (UG)** is the theory of the first factor which makes up the language faculty: our innate genetic endowment for language. As already mentioned, UG is assumed to play a central role in language acquisition. It is also vital in helping us to understand how we can make sense of the idea that specific languages are actually variants of a single type of entity, language. Our goal here, then, is to look at one part of UG: how words combine to form sentences. In so doing, we will construct the theory of syntax.

We can now make an important distinction. Language can be seen from an internal, individual perspective, **I-language**, or it can be seen as external to the individual, **E-language**. Here we are going to focus on I-language, which arises from the interaction of the three factors just introduced. This is a natural approach, given our interest in how syntactic structures arise in the mind. E-language is in fact a more complicated notion, involving society, culture, history and so on. Concepts like 'English' and 'French' in their everyday senses are E-language concepts; it is for this reason that they do not, strictly speaking, form part of our object of study. I-language is a natural object; E-language is not.

Taking I-language as the central notion treats language as part of individual psychology. This is a cognitive theory of language, because it intrinsically involves the human mind. In fact, this theory of language could be part of an overall theory of the mind. However, we would really like our theory of language to be part of an overall theory of the brain; being an obviously physical object, the brain is a natural object, and it is a clearer notion than 'mind' (in fact, philosophers have worried for centuries about whether 'mind' is something physical, but we don't need to). Unfortunately, though, at present our understanding of how brain tissue supports cognitive processes such as language, thought and memory is extremely limited, and so we are unable to say very much about the relation between the physical brain and cognitive processes. That's why I will continue to use the older, strictly speaking vaguer, term 'mind'.

What does it mean to say our theory is a formal theory? A formal approach to any kind of problem or phenomenon assumes discrete, systematic ways of forming complex things out of simple things. For example, the alphabet is formal: its twenty-six letters can be combined in various different, but more or less systematic, ways to form a very large number of words. Arithmetic is a formal system combining numbers of various kinds and functions such as addition, subtraction, multiplication, etc.

In formal syntax and formal semantics, we combine simple elements (roughly words and their meanings) to form more complex elements (sentences and their meanings). The modes of combination must be systematic and precise; as we will see, this is a major part of the challenge of constructing such a theory.

A further natural question to ask is why we want a formal and cognitive theory. The answer to this lies in certain general trends of thought both in psychology and in philosophy of mind (at least in the English-speaking world). It is widely believed that the best way to understand the mind is to think of it as a kind of computer. Computers manipulate symbols according to formal instructions, i.e. algorithms and programs. We can think of I-language in these terms as a piece of cognitive software, a program run on the hardware of the brain (this raises the intriguing question, which I will not go into here, of who or what wrote the program). Therefore, our theory of I-language must be a formal theory. What we are interested in is how our knowledge of I-language is represented in our mind. If we can get an idea of this, which I believe we can from studying syntax, then we gain a very important insight into the human mind; what it is to be human, what it is to be you.

To conclude this general discussion, we will concentrate here on developing one aspect of a formal, cognitive theory of I-language: the theory of syntax. As already mentioned, syntax is concerned with how relatively simple units, words, are combined to form more complex units, sentences. This is taken to be a cognitive capacity all humans have, as a reflex of their genetic endowment which includes UG. UG interacts with linguistic experience in early life, and with domain-general 'third factors' as described above, to give rise to mature adult **competence** in one's native language. This competence manifests itself in the ability to produce and understand an unlimited number of sentences, and to make judgements regarding both the syntax and the semantics of those sentences. In the next chapter, we will look in detail at a concrete example of this competence in action, for native speakers of English.

Just a final note: given what I've said, strictly speaking I shouldn't talk about 'English', as it is not a scientific term since it does not designate a natural object. Instead of talking about 'English speakers', I should really say something like 'individuals who identify themselves and are identified in their cultural milieu as possessing an I-language which corresponds to the E-concept "English"'. For brevity I will gloss over this more accurate formulation and continue to talk about 'English speakers'; the same goes for other E-language names (Italian, etc.). More generally, the term 'language' will refer to that aggregate of I-languages whose speakers recognise themselves and each other as belonging to the same E-language community.

Now we can move from the rather general matters we have been considering here to actually starting out on the study of syntax. As we delve more and more into the detailed and intricate nuts and bolts of the theory of syntax in the chapters to follow, the background issues we have discussed here should be kept in mind as they form the overall conceptual underpinning to the theory we'll develop.

But now for the nuts and bolts. Or, actually, the fish.

Exercises

1.   Write a short paragraph (not more than half a page as an absolute maximum; ten–twelve lines per concept would be ideal) to explain *in your own words* what the following notions mean to linguists:

   - The language faculty
   - Formal approaches to the study of language
   - 'Language' vs 'languages'
   - English

2.   You are Martian Space Cadet λxCloverx231057. Write a report to Martian Mission Control describing your observations having abducted a featherless terrestrial biped with the aim of understanding more about its noise-making capacities.

3.   'Children are very good imitators and are able to learn when their mistakes are corrected by their elders.' How could you go about refuting these claims about language acquisition?

4.   Martian Space Cadet λxCloverx231057 has discovered that the ter-
            restrial featherless bipeds can communicate by means additional to
            the noises produced by their vocal apparatus. Report these discover-
            ies to Mission Control.

For Further Study and/or Discussion

1.   No two people speak the same language.
2.   Could we understand an alien language?
3.   Are conlangs 'real' languages?

Further Reading

Adger, D. 2019. *Language Unlimited*. Oxford: Oxford University Press.
Pinker, S. 1994. *The Language Instinct*. New York: Harper Perennial Modern Classics.
Roberts, I. 2017. *The Wonders of Language, or How to Make Noises and Influence
          People*. Cambridge: Cambridge University Press.

These three books all provide general introductions to language and linguistics assuming no prior knowledge on the reader's part. Each book has its own perspective: Adger
concentrates on how syntax is fundamental to human language and cognition, and so is
perhaps most in line with our concerns here. Pinker is a classic; it is a witty and engaging
introduction to linguistics with the emphasis on the relation between language and mind.
Roberts offers a comprehensive introduction to several different subfields of linguistics,
ranging from phonetics to historical linguistics; syntax is covered in Chapter 4.
      Larson, R. 2010. *Grammar as Science*. Cambridge, MA: MIT Press, Unit 1. This book
is an introduction to syntax whose central idea is to present the field as an exercise in the
construction of a scientific theory. In this first unit, the central ideas regarding knowledge
of language and Universal Grammar are introduced in an attractive and original way.
      Carnie, A. 2013. *Syntax: A Generative Introduction*. Oxford: Blackwell, Chapter 1.
Another very sound and well-written introduction to generative grammar. This first
chapter presents the central ideas behind syntactic theory, along with a section on different approaches to syntax (something I do not attempt here). Isac, D. & C. Reiss.
2008. *I-language*. Oxford: Oxford University Press, Chapters 1 and 3.
      As the title suggests, the focus of this book is on the I-language approach to linguis-
tics and syntax. The first chapter starts with a presentation of linguistic data in order
to illustrate the approach. The third chapter considers different notions of language,
similar to what has been presented here but with a different overall slant; reading that
chapter will complement this one nicely.
      Freidin, R. 2012. *Syntax: Basic Concepts and Applications*. Cambridge: Cambridge
University Press, Chapter 2. This chapter contains an excellent introduction to I-language,
the nature of grammaticality, native speakers' ability to recognise deviant sentences as
an indication of knowledge of language, language acquisition and the argument from
the poverty of the stimulus, and, in particular, language production and comprehension.

Adger, D. 2003. *Core Syntax: A Minimalist Approach*. Oxford: Oxford University Press, Chapter 1. This chapter also gives an excellent introduction to the central concepts behind generative grammar, including the notions of grammaticality and acceptability, tacit knowledge, recursion, poverty of the stimulus and I-language.

Other good general introductions to the goals and assumptions of generative grammar include the following:

Anderson, S. & D. Lightfoot. 2002. *The Language Organ*. Cambridge: Cambridge University Press, Chapters 1 and 2.

Radford, A. 2016. *Analysing English Sentences*. Cambridge: Cambridge University Press, Chapter 1.

Smith, N. 2005. *Chomsky: Ideas and Ideals*. Cambridge: Cambridge University Press, Chapter 1.

1   Tacit Knowledge (or: Several Things You Didn't Know You Knew about English)

1.1   Introduction

In this chapter, we begin our study of the theory of syntax. As we will see later, there is no end to syntax. It is also rather difficult to discern where it begins. Here we will make a start by doing two things. First, you'll find out some rather surprising facts about your knowledge of English, things you didn't know you knew. This will give you a concrete illustration of your competence in English. Second, by carrying out a little translation exercise, we'll get a first glimpse of what makes languages similar to one another and what makes them differ.

We begin with very simple sentences (see (1)) and build up to rather strange and complex ones. It's not necessary to follow every detail of the discussion here; all the technical ideas are presented again in later chapters. Our goal here is to demonstrate the nature of your tacit knowledge of English syntax. We can do it with just one word: *fish*. This chapter can also be skipped and returned to later (e.g. after Chapter 7).

1.2   Some Fish

Let's start with a single, rather banal-looking English word. We'll see that we can build some quite striking and intriguing sentences with it. The word is *fish*.[1] So our first sentence is:

(1)   Fish!

Like quite a few basic words in English, *fish* is actually ambiguous. It can be understood either as a **verb** or as a **noun**. As a noun, it refers to a class of aquatic animals; as a verb, it refers to the activity of hunting those aquatic animals. We indicate this ambiguity in the standard way, by surrounding the word with square brackets, and writing the 'category label' (Noun/Verb) as a subscript to the left bracket. So, the sentence in (1) actually has two distinct representations:

---

[1] Thanks to my good friend and colleague Professor Robert Freidin of Princeton University for these examples. The implications of the fish sentences are discussed and explored in more detail in Chapter 1 of Freidin (2012). Freidin's discussion is more detailed than here, although it focuses exclusively on English. The exercises given there are also well worth trying.

(2) a.   [_{Noun} Fish]
     b.   [_{Verb} Fish]

The brackets are just a way of saying 'what is inside here is a Noun/Verb'. A representation like that in (2) is called a **labelled bracketing**.

The fact that *fish*, like many other words including *cook*, *book*, *police*, *report*, *promise* and many others, is ambiguous between a verb and a noun is a consequence of the fact that English has very few **inflectional endings** to mark grammatical information of various kinds. If we compare English with a more richly inflected language such as Italian, we see that the two versions of *fish* correspond to two differently inflected words:

(3) a.   [_{Noun} fish] = Italian *pesce*
     b.   [_{Verb} fish] = Italian *pescare*

It is quite easy to see that the Italian words share the root *pesc-* and distinct inflections: *-e*, indicating a singular noun; and *-are*, indicating the infinitive of a first-conjugation verb (the infinitive is the basic form of a verb with no tense marking; 'first conjugation' refers to an arbitrary morphological class of verbs in Italian: there are four conjugations altogether, as we will see below). To cut a very long historical story short, English has largely lost its equivalents of *-e* and *-are*, and so we are left with the equivalent of the ambiguous root *pesc-* (you may also note a family resemblance between *pesc-* and *fish*; this is because both are ultimately derived from an ancient root in the common ancestor language of English and Italian, Indo European).

The ambiguous single word in (1) and (2) constitutes an entire sentence on its own. More precisely, each interpretation of *fish* constitutes a sentence, so really there are two distinct sentences here. We can represent them as follows (here, again following standard conventions, 'Noun' is abbreviated as N and 'Verb' as V, and S stands for 'Sentence'):

(4) a.   [_S [_N Fish]]
     b.   [_S [_V Fish]]

Interpreted as in (4a), the sentence draws attention to the presence of a single fish or group of fish (note that *fish* is one of a relatively small group of English nouns that is identical in the singular and the plural: the plural form *fishes* exists, but it denotes several species of fish, not several individual fish of the same species). Interpreted as in (4b), it is an imperative, indicating an order given to go fishing. Here there is an implicit **second-person pronoun**, since an order is naturally understood as being addressed to an interlocutor, so we could elaborate (4b) as in (5):

(5)   [_S [_N ~~You~~] [_V fish]]

Here the pronoun (a kind of noun, hence N) is 'understood'; we take that to mean that it is present in the syntactic and semantic representations of the sentence, but not in the phonological representation, what you actually hear or say. This is our first indication that there is more to syntax than meets the ear.

Two occurrences of the word *fish* also make up a grammatical sentence:

(6)   Fish fish.

The natural interpretation of this sentence is to treat the first *fish* as a noun and the second one as a verb, the combination again forming a sentence. We represent this as in (7):

(7)   [s [N fish] [v fish]]

In this sentence, the noun *fish* is the subject, understood as carrying out the action performed by the verb. The verb *fish* indicates the action the subject carries out. So the sentence means "Fish fish stuff". As this rough gloss indicates, there is an implicit direct object here, indicating, somewhat vaguely, what is being fished for, what undergoes the action of fishing.

Alternatively, we can understand the first *fish* as a verb, and the second *fish* as a noun. This is easier to see if we add an exclamation mark to (6) (*Fish fish!*), corresponding to a different intonation pattern in speech. Then the sentence has the structure in (8):

(8)   [s [v fish] [N fish]]

Here, as in the verbal interpretation of the single-fish example in (1), the verb is understood as an imperative and so there is a deleted second-person pronoun (*you*) as subject:

(9)   [s ~~You~~N [v fish] [N fish]]

The second *fish*, the noun, is an explicit direct object, indicating that fish are what is fished.

In Italian, where the ambiguities of the English roots are clarified by inflectional endings, the two interpretations of (6) can be rendered as in (10):

(10) a.   I pesci pescano.   (= (7))
     b.   Pesca pesci!   (= (8/9))

In addition to disambiguating the English sentence in (6), these translations show us that there might be more silent material in the English examples than just the deleted pronoun in (8/9). The first word of (10a), *i*, is the masculine plural form of the **definite article**, i.e. 'the'. It is obligatory in this context in Italian. What it shows us is that the subject is more than just a noun, but a **phrasal category** of which the noun is the most important member: a **Noun Phrase**, or NP. The basic function of the definite article in both English and Italian is to indicate that the noun refers to some unique known existing entity, in this case what philosophers would call the '**natural kind**' fish. Since there is no fundamental meaning difference between (6) with the structure and interpretation in (7) and (10a) (in other words, since (10a) is a reasonable translation of the English sentence), the noun *fish* in (7) also denotes the unique, known, existing, natural kind fish. So we could posit a silent "the" in the subject of (7) and, correspondingly, an NP rather than just an N. Then (7) lines up exactly with (10a):

(11)   [s [NP ~~the~~ fish] [v fish]]
         [s [NP I pesci] [v pescano]]

Why go to this trouble to line up English and Italian in this way? There are two reasons. First, the English and the Italian sentences mean the same thing. Although we tend in our everyday lives to pay more attention to cultural differences than to cognitive similarities, it seems reasonable to assume that English speakers and Italian speakers are cognitively alike (we could perhaps say that English speakers and Italian speakers are I-alike but E-different, thinking of the distinction made in the previous section between I-language and E-language). In that case, the semantic representations of the two sentences ought to be the same. It therefore simplifies the connection (more technically, the 'mapping') between the syntax and the semantics if the respective syntactic representations 'line up', as in (11). Secondly, we are attempting to develop a theory of Universal Grammar (UG, see the Introduction); we therefore want our syntactic representations of comparable (i.e. semantically matching, or at least highly similar) sentences in different languages to be as uniform as possible. Of course, it is not always possible to achieve a parallel as straightforward as that depicted in (11), but we should strive towards this goal as part of the UG project. Ideally, then, we would want (a) the semantic representations of sentences which mean the same thing to be identical across languages, (b) the syntactic representations of such sentences to be as uniform as possible across languages while, of course, recognising (c) that their phonological and phonetic shapes, including the linear order of the words in a sentence, are different. The syntax and semantics are 'externalised' with different phonologies in different languages, but the syntax is (near-)uniform and the semantics entirely uniform. We will come back to these issues in Chapters 7 and 8.

The Italian sentence in (10a) tells us two more interesting things. First, the noun *pesci* is plural: it has the plural ending *-i* (compare the singular *pesce* in (3a)). In the English version, *fish* is plural too; we have already noted that *fish* has no overt plural ending. If we substitute a more regular noun, one which forms its plural with *-s*, we can see this:

(12)   Boys fish.

Second, the verb *pescano* consists of the root *pesc-* and the ending *-ano* (again compare the infinitive ending *-are* in (3b)). This is not the place to go into the full details of Italian verbal morphology, but this ending contains the information that the verb is first **conjugation, present tense, indicative mood** (it makes a statement of fact) and **third-person plural** ('they'). That's quite a bit of information in just three overt phonemes. The *-a-* part of the ending recurs in the infinitive ending, and this can be seen as the marker of first conjugation. The *-no* part of the ending shows up in many other tenses and is clearly marking third-person plural. Present tense and indicative mood are arguably just 'understood'. As we have already seen, saying something is 'understood' is a way of saying that it is part of the semantic representation of the sentence, where there is no pronounced element that represents it. In order to simplify the syntax–semantics connection, we want the syntactic representation to reflect the semantic interpretation as fully as possible. Since we have silent syntactic elements, perhaps we can also have silent morphological elements. So we are led to think that *pescano* has the structure in (13):

(13)   pesc-a- ~~Indicative~~ - ~~Present~~ -no

Furthermore, we can, and for the sake of consistency must, put labelled brackets around each part of the structure:

(14)   [$_V$ [$_V$ pesc-] [$_{Conj}$ -a-] [$_M$ ~~Indicative~~] [$_T$ ~~Present~~] [$_{Agr}$ -no]]

The labels are fairly straightforward: 'V' indicates that both the root and the whole thing form a verb, 'Conj' indicates the conjugation-class marker, 'M' indicates mood (the traditional grammatical category indicating whether a sentence describes a state of affairs believed to be true or not), 'T' indicates tense and 'Agr' indicates agreement: the verb is third-person plural because the subject, *i pesci*, is third-person plural.

Now, if the Italian verb has a structure like (14), and the Italian sentence in (10a) is an accurate translation of the English sentence in (7) and our assumption that English and Italian verbs should be minimally different means that we want structures to 'line up' across languages, our logic leads us to posit something like (15) as the structure of the verb *fish* in (7):

(15)   [$_V$ [$_V$ fish-] [$_{Conj}$ ~~??~~] [$_M$ ~~Indicative~~] [$_T$ ~~Present~~] [$_{Agr}$ ~~3Pl~~]]

Here, Conj, M, T and Agr are all silent. But our logic leads us to conclude that they are all structurally present. Now we come up against the limits to this lining-up-in-the-name-of-UG approach. It seems reasonable to take the verb *fish* in (7) to be indicative in mood, present in tense and third-plural in agreement, but the conjugation-marking seems to impose an idiosyncracy of Italian morphology onto English, moreover an idiosyncracy that appears to have no semantic correlate. So perhaps we should eliminate 'Conj' from (15). The other silent endings are, however, justified by the semantics and our universalising methodology.

Both tense and agreement endings do audibly appear on English verbs (mood may too, but this is a little trickier and so I'll leave it aside). If we make the subject of our example in (12) singular, but keep the present tense, we have:

(16)   The boy fishes.

Here the verb has the ending *-es*. If we make the verb past tense, we have:

(17)   The boy fished.

Here the verb has the ending *-ed*. So we could give the verbs in (16) and (17) the structures in (18a) and (18b) respectively:

(18) a.   [v [v fish-] [M ~~Indicative~~] [T ~~Present~~] [Agr -es]]
      b.   [v [v fish-] [M ~~Indicative~~] [T -ed] [Agr ~~3Sg~~]]

Here, we have dropped the Italocentric Conj, for the reasons given above; Mood remains silent, but T is realised as *-ed* in the past tense and Agr is realised as *-es* in the third-person singular (agreeing with the third-person singular subject *the boy*) in the present tense. So there is justification for lining up these aspects of English verbal inflection with Italian. The fundamental difference between English and Italian has already been mentioned: in the history of English many markers of inflection have lost their overt phonological representation, while their Italian counterparts have retained most of theirs. So English has more silent inflections than Italian. Semantics and UG together lead us to postulate those inflections nonetheless.

  We can also observe another interesting parallel between English and Italian brought out in (16). Here, unlike in (12) where *boys* is plural, an article must appear with *boy*. Compare:

(19)   *Boy fishes.

The article doesn't have to be definite. In fact, a range of determiners of various kinds can appear here:

(20)   A/This/That/One/Every/Each/No/Some boy fishes.

The fact that where *boys* is plural as in (12) no audible determiner is required, combined with the unique, known, existing 'natural kind' interpretation assigned to *boys* here, supports the idea that there is a silent determiner. This in turn supports the lining-up of English and Italian seen in (11).

  We can now replace (11) with a fuller lined-up, (nearly) uniform English and Italian structure, in which the determiners, silent and overt, are represented by the category D:

(21)   [s [NP [D ~~the~~] [N [N fish-[Num ~~Pl~~]]] [v [v fish-]   [M ~~Indicative~~] [T ~~Present~~]
            [Agr ~~3Pl~~]]]
            [s [NP [D I] [N [N pesc-[Num i]]] [v [v pesc-] [Conj -a-] [M ~~Indicative~~] [T ~~Present~~]
            [Agr -no]]]

Here I've added the specification of number on the noun (the ending Num); plural number is silent in the case of *fish* in English as we have observed. We could add further specifications: Person on the noun (3rd here), number marking on the Italian article *i* (implying, by our now-familiar reasoning, that English *the* has a silent plural ending). Furthermore, the Italian articles show gender marking: article *i* is masculine. So we should add that specification to the Italian sentence. Should we add it to the English one? The Italian gender is grammatical, not semantic. *Pesce* is a masculine noun, but not all fish are male (or there would be no more fish, since they reproduce sexually). In Italian, all nouns have masculine or feminine gender, and this has no semantic basis at all in many cases: 'sun' is masculine (*il sole*); 'moon' is feminine (*la luna*), 'sincerity' is

feminine, 'feminism' is masculine, 'violence' is feminine, 'socialism' is masculine and so on. Try as one might, it is hard to find the slightest metaphorical or
cultural basis for this: the words are just arbitrarily assigned to two distinct morphological classes. Hence gender-marking has no consequences for the semantic representation. So perhaps, as with the Conj-ending on verbs, it would be
Italocentric of us to impose Italian genders on English nouns or articles.

One last point on the structure in (21): are M, T and Agr part of the verb V,
as indicated there, or, analogously to D, part of the Verb Phrase, VP? We could
think that V and N each have their 'satellite categories' which carry grammatical
information often realised as inflection or as 'little words' like the articles *the*
and *i*: the satellites of N are D and Num, and the satellites of V are M, T and
Agr. Semantically, though, Mood and Tense arguably modify the sentence, by
indicating whether it makes a true statement and relating the time of the situation
described to the speech time (this is what Tense does). So M and T look like
they belong to S. Agr seems to connect the subject NP and the verb; as such, this
too looks like a sentence-level, rather than a verb-level, property. We leave the
question of the status of M, T and Agr open for now; later we will see that M
and T are indeed parts of S, while Agr may be a relation rather than a category.

Let us now go back to the structure in (9), which I repeat here for convenience:

(9)   [$_S$ ~~You~~$_N$ [$_V$ fish] [$_N$ fish]]

We saw the Italian translation of (9) in (10b):

(10b)   Pesca pesci!

The full representations of both examples, with silent endings indicated, are
given in (22):

(22) a.   [$_S$ ~~[$_{NP}$ you]~~ [$_{VP}$ [$_V$ [$_V$ fish-] [$_M$ ~~Imperative~~] [$_T$ ~~Present~~] [$_{Agr}$ ~~2~~]] [[$_D$ ~~some~~]
             [$_N$ [$_N$ fish-[$_{Num}$ ~~Pl~~]]

     b.   [$_S$ ~~[$_{NP}$ tu]~~ [$_V$ [$_V$ pesc-] [$_{Conj}$ -a-] [$_M$ ~~Imperative~~] [$_T$ ~~Present~~] [$_{Agr}$ ~~2Sg~~]]]
             [$_{NP}$ [$_D$ ~~i~~] [$_N$ [$_N$ pesc-[$_{Num}$ i]]]

Both examples have an understood second-person subject. English *you* can be
either singular or plural, and so (8/9) can be interpreted as giving an order to a
single person or to a group of people. The Italian subject is singular, as the verbal ending shows (the plural is *pescate*), and the understood subject is the singular pronoun *tu*. M is specified as Imperative: these sentences do not make factual
statements but give orders. Imperative is the 'ordering Mood', while, as we saw,
Indicative is the 'stating Mood'. The object NPs are similar to the subject NPs
in (21), except for the Ds. The Italian example does not have a definite article
and the English silent D is 'some'. Both of these points are related to the fact
that the object here has a subtly different interpretation from the subject in (21).
In (21), the subject names a unique, known, existing 'natural kind'; this interpretation is known as the **generic** reading of the NP. The object does not denote
a natural kind; it merely denotes some arbitrary, not necessarily known and not

necessarily existing group of fish (the fishing expedition could be completely unsuccessful with no fish at all actually being caught). This is an **indefinite** interpretation of the NP. Hence the definite D, silent in English, overt in Italian, does not appear. I have glossed the silent indefinite D as 'some' in English.

From the above, we can see that our simple two-fish sentence in (6) has a great deal more to it than meets the eye, or ear. The Italian translations are very revealing, especially when we try to line them up as closely as we can to their English counterparts. We see that both verbs and nouns have satellite categories which may be realised as inflectional endings or as articles such as *the* and *i*, and are frequently silent. We also see that not all satellite categories are universal: Italian has grammatical gender on nouns and Conj-marking on verbs, but there is no reason to posit counterparts to these in English. Of course, a very natural, and, it turns out, very difficult question is whether the other categories such as D, M, T and Agr are universal. We are in no position to answer this question at the moment, but we can observe that it seems reasonable to take these categories to be shared by Indo-European languages such as Italian and English.

So we see that simple sentences like English (6) and Italian (10) can tell us a lot. In the next section, we'll take this line of thought a bit further, with some more complicated sentences (but still using the same English word).

1.3   More Fish and Some Relative Clauses

In this section, we'll look at three-, four- and five-fish sentences. These sentences are simultaneously silly and serious; they're silly because they describe rather unlikely situations (which you can nonetheless imagine), and they're serious because they can reveal a lot about our linguistic competence.

So let's look at what happens when we combine three occurrences of *fish*:

(23)   Fish fish fish.

The Italian translation of (23) is (24):

(24)   I pesci pescano pesci.

Both of these are full sentences where the first 'fish' is the subject, the second the verb and the third the direct object. Clearly, what is added to the two-fish examples discussed above is an explicit direct object, compared to (7), and an explicit subject, compared to (9). Traditional grammars tell us that a complete sentence consists of a subject, what the sentence is about, and a **predicate**, which says something about the subject. The predicate contains the main verb and the direct object. Thus we could represent (23) as follows (leaving aside for the moment the representation of the silent inflections):

(25)   [s [N Fish] [Predicate [v fish] [N fish]]]

Since the verb is the most important part of the predicate, we can give a more strictly categorial representation of (25) as follows:

(26)   [s [N Fish] [VP [V fish] [N fish]]]

Here VP, the Verb Phrase, is the category which functions as the predicate.[2]

The 'full' representations for (23) and (24), complete with specification of silent inflections and other satellite categories, are shown in (27):

(27) a.   [s [NP [D ~~the~~] [N [N fish-[Num ~~Pl~~]]] [VP [V [V fish -] [M ~~Indicative~~] [T ~~Present~~]
            [Agr ~~3Pl~~]] [NP [D ~~some~~] [N [N fish-[Num ~~Pl~~]]]]

    b.   [s [NP [D I] [N [N pesc-[Num i]]] [V [V pesc-] [Conj -a-] [M ~~Indicative~~] [T ~~Present~~]
            [Agr -no]] [NP [D ɨ] [N [N pesc-[Num i]]]]

These representations are almost exactly the expected combination of (21) with an explicit direct object as in (22). Again, the subject and object have different structures and interpretations, with the subject being generic and the object indefinite.

Now let's try four fish:

(28)   Fish fish fish fish.

This sentence is both grammatical and interpretable, but, unlike the two-fish and three-fish examples it requires a little thought. The intonation with which it is to be read is important: it should be 'fish FISH fish [short pause] FISH', with stress on the second *fish* and the strongest stress on the final *fish*. The structure here is significantly more complex than our earlier examples. For this reason, from now on I will mainly give simplified representations of these more complex examples, leaving aside the silent inflectional material (although we should not forget that it is there).

What does (28) mean and what is its structure? Again, the Italian translation can give us an important clue:

(29)   I pesci che i pesci pescano pescano.

We have seen that *pesci* is unambiguously a noun and *pescano* is unambiguously a verb. At the absolute minimum, then, (29) has the structure *N che N V V*. The English example in (28) lines up with this, except that there is no counterpart to *che*. The Italian word *che* usually translates as *that*. We can add *that* to (28), to get:

(30)   Fish that fish fish fish.

The markers *that* and *che* introduce a **relative clause**, a **clause** which modifies a noun; for our purposes, the only real difference between *that* and *che* is that *che* appears obligatorily in this context, while *that* can be 'dropped' (i.e. silent). So

---

[2] We will look in detail at the relation between grammatical categories like NP and VP and grammatical functions like subject and predicate in Chapter 2 of Volume II.

the second two *fish*, the sequence noun-verb, constitute a relative clause modifying the first noun *fish* (known as the head of the relative). The fourth *fish* is the verb of the main clause, with an implicit direct object just as in the two-fish example with the structure in (7). We can thus make a first pass at a structure for (28) as follows:

(31)   [s [N fish] [Relative clause fish fish] [VP [v fish]]]

The relative clause is a kind of subordinate clause. In fact, we can tell that the first *fish* inside the relative clause is the subject and the second *fish* is the verb of the predicate. So we have an NP-VP structure here (remember that the presence of the overt definite article in Italian shows us that the subject is an NP, not just a noun):

(32)   [s [N fish] [Relative clause [NP [N fish]] [VP [v fish]]] [VP [v fish]]]

The main clause, i.e. the independent clause containing the relative clause, indicated as S here, must also have a subject NP, not just N. This NP includes the relative clause, since the relative clause modifies the noun, so we have (33):

(33)   [s [NP [N fish] [Relative clause [NP [N fish]] [VP [v fish]]]] [VP [v fish]]]

Both the main clause and the relative have a subject and a predicate. Identifying predicates with VP again, (33) tells us that each VP contains just the verb *fish*. In the case of the main clause, this may be correct, since the object here is implicit and has a rather vague interpretation (roughly 'stuff'). But the object of the relative has a completely different, and very precise, interpretation: 'fish'. Here we see an important characteristic of relative clauses: there is always something missing, often referred to as a 'gap', which corresponds semantically to the head of the relative (which we could then call the 'filler'). Since we know that syntactic representations contain silent elements (actually, we are beginning to see that they *mostly* contain silent elements) and we want to keep the syntax-semantics mapping as straightforward as possible, the best way to account for the interpretation of the gap is that it is a silent copy of the filler. So we replace (33) with (34):

(34)   [s [NP [N fish] [Relative clause [NP [N fish]] [VP [v fish] [NP [N fish]]]]] [VP [v fish]]]

We said above that English *that*, unlike its Italian counterpart *che*, can be 'dropped'. This implies that sentences with and without *that* are synonymous: *that* and *che* are just meaningless syntactic markers (saying 'what comes next is a relative clause' in our examples). However, (30) has another interpretation that (28) doesn't have. In (28) the gap inside the relative clause is the direct object, as (34) shows; it means 'fish that get fished fish stuff'. But (30) allows a further interpretation, where the gap can be interpreted as the subject of the relative clause: 'fish that fish other fish fish stuff'. This example has the following structure:

(35)   [s [NP [N fish] that [Relative clause [NP [N fish]] [VP [v fish] [NP [N fish]]]]] [VP [v fish]]]

Here it is the subject of the relative that is the silent copy of the head, and the marker *that* is obligatory. The Italian translation of this English sentence is unambiguous and should be compared to the one in (29):

(36)   I pesci che pescano pesci pescano.

It is now easy to interpret a five-fish example:

(37)   Fish fish fish fish fish.

As we saw, the four-fish example in (28) had an implicit direct object in the main clause ('Fish fish fish fish stuff'). The five-fish example in (37) has an explicit direct object in the main clause. We can therefore give the structure as in (38), and the Italian translation in (39):

(38)   [$_S$ [$_{NP}$ [$_N$ fish] [$_{Relative\ clause}$ [$_{NP}$ [$_N$ fish]] [$_{VP}$ [$_V$ fish] [$_{NP}$ [$_N$ fish]]]] [$_{VP}$ [$_V$ fish]
            [$_{NP}$ [$_N$ fish]]]]

(39)   I pesci che i pesci pescano pescano pesci.

By now we may begin to wonder just how many repetitions of the word *fish* (in the phonology, the subpart of the syntactic structure that is actually pronounced) can give rise to a grammatical, interpretable sentence. It is clear that the step from three fish to four fish, involving as it did the introduction of a relative clause into the structure, places a burden on comprehension. But this burden can be readily overcome and the sentence is fully comprehensible; in fact we can recognise that it describes a rather odd state of affairs, the very silliness of the sentence proves that we can understand it. We see, then, that the comprehension burden does not increase linearly as we add extra words; the structural complexity of the four-fish sentence is significantly greater than the three-fish one, and this is reflected in our initial hesitation in understanding it.

In the next section, we'll see some really challenging examples as we increase the number of fish still further.

1.4   Really Challenging Fish

Here we're going to look at six- and seven-fish sentences. These are really hard to understand, especially the six-fish one (it's harder than seven, as we'll see). You don't have to follow every detail of the analysis of these sentences here, as long as you get the main point, which comes after (54). Skip ahead to that discussion if the fish tire you out. Or, fish-like, just go with the flow.

The non-linear increase in comprehension difficulty becomes very sharp indeed when we move from five fish to six fish. Here is the six-fish example:

(40)   Fish fish fish fish fish fish.

Most people are completely stumped by this sentence at first sight; it appears to be simply a random repetition of the word *fish* with no meaning (and so, perhaps, no structure) at all. But in fact this isn't true, as we'll see below. What is striking though is that seven *fish* is easier to interpret than six:

(41)   Fish fish fish fish fish fish fish.

We know from (28) that a sequence of three *fish* can be a relative clause with an object gap, 'fish that are fished by other fish'. In (28), the relative clause is in the subject position. But relative clauses can be in object position too (in fact, (28) can be interpreted that way too, a point that was left aside above). So (41) has the approximate structure in (42a), given in fuller detail in (42b) (where RC stands for relative clause, and the structure is presented as a tree diagram, as this makes it easier to see the relations among the fish; we'll look at tree diagrams more systematically in the next chapter):

(42) a.   [[Fish fish fish] [fish [fish fish fish]]]

b.

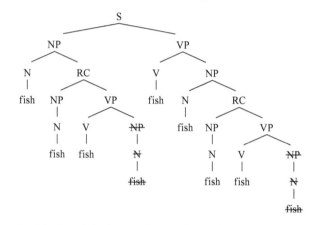

Pronounced with the right intonation ('Fish FISH fish [pause] fish fish FISH fish'), this example is fairly easy to understand, especially in the light of the four- and five-fish examples. But none of this makes (40), with just six fish, any easier to understand.

In order to see what the structure, and hence the interpretation of (40) is, we must go back to our earlier, simpler examples. Here, once again, is the two-fish example with noun-verb interpretation, repeated from (7):

(7)   [s [N fish] [v fish]]

Of course, we now know that N and V here are contained in their respective NPs and VPs. Relative clauses are really a kind of sentence, as we pointed out above. So let us label them as S from now on. We go from two fish to four fish by putting the structure in (7) inside the subject NP:

(43)   [s [NP [N fish] [s [N fish] [v fish]]] [vp [v fish]]]

Actually it's not quite accurate to say we put (7) inside the subject NP; really, we put the three-fish sentence, with the structure seen in (26), inside the subject NP and make the object a silent version of the head of the relative:

(44)   [s [NP [N fish] [s [NP [N fish]] [vp [v fish] [NP [N fish]]]]] [vp [v fish]]]

On the basis of (44), we can add two more pronounced *fish* by inserting a relative clause inside the subject NP of the relative clause, i.e. after the second [~N~ *fish*]. This gives the string of six *fish* in (41), and shows us what the structure is:

(45)   [~S~ [~NP~ [~N~ fish] [~S~ [~NP~ [~N~ fish [~S~ [~NP~ [~N~ fish] [~VP~ [~V~ fish] ~[NP [N fish]]~]]]]] [~VP~ [~V~ fish] ~[NP [N fish]]~]]]] [~VP~ [~V~ fish]]]

If we add some relative markers, preferably *which* (another relative marker in English alongside *that*), we can just about start to make sense of (45):

(46)   Fish which fish which fish fish fish fish.

So (41) is, despite initial appearances, a grammatical and interpretable sentence: the string is *N N N V V V*. It might be easier to see this if we use some different, and more varied, vocabulary. Let's start with (47):

(47)   The mouse the cat chased died.

By now, we know a relative clause when we see one. The essential structure of (47) has a relative clause inside the subject containing an object gap:

(48)   [~S~ [~NP~ the mouse [~S~ [~NP~ the cat [~VP~ chased ~[the mouse]~]]]] [~VP~ died]]

(48) is quite easy to understand. The analogue to (41), but with different words, is (49):

(49)   [~S~ [~NP~ the mouse [~S~ [~NP~ the cat [~S~ [~NP~ the dog [~VP~ bit ~[NP the cat]~]]]]] [~VP~ chased ~[NP the mouse]~]]]] [~VP~ died]]

Again, the jump from (48) to (49), caused by simply adding another relative clause modifying *the cat*, poses severe difficulties of comprehension. Adding some relative markers (*that* again) makes (49) considerably easier to understand:

(50)   The mouse that the cat that the dog bit chased died.

This phenomenon is known as **centre-embedding**; it seems that embedding more than one relative clause inside another without an overt relative marker creates real comprehension difficulties. Nonetheless, such sentences are in fact grammatical and interpretable. The rules of English syntax allow us to embed relatives inside one another and, under the right conditions, to 'drop' relative markers. The fact that embedding more than one relative clause inside another causes comprehension difficulties is a matter of **performance**; our short-term memory seems unable to 'keep track of' the structure. But since these sentences are generated by the rules of English syntax they are grammatical; so we designate them as grammatical, but, because of the comprehension load they impose, unacceptable. Grammaticality is a competence notion, while **acceptability** is a performance notion. Most of the time, grammaticality and acceptability coincide, but in cases like centre-embedding we can see the distinction. Another famous example where the two notions come apart is the sentence *Colourless* *green ideas sleep furiously*; most people find this sentence unacceptable for the perfectly good reason that it doesn't make any sense. It is, however, syntactically well-formed, as its exact formal counterpart *Revolutionary new ideas spread quickly* shows. Both sentences are grammatical in that they conform to the rules of English syntax; the first one is semantically anomalous (in fact, it is self-contradictory) and so unacceptable. This contrast also shows that syntax and semantics are distinct in that a sentence can be syntactically well-formed but semantically ill-formed; we will see more examples of this type in Section 8.3.

Of course, examples with centre-embedding like (50) become still more difficult to understand when the same phonological word occurs six times over, as in (40). There is, in principle, no difference in grammaticality between (40) and (50) but a real difference in acceptability (they just go from bad to worse). But now we can line (40) up with the variant of (50) without the relative markers, and we can see how (40) works, and see that it is in fact grammatical:

(40)   Fish   fish   fish   fish fish   fish.

(51)   The mouse the cat the dog bit   chased died.

Finally, here are the easier versions complete with the relative pronouns *which* and *that* inserted in the appropriate places:

(46)   Fish   which fish   which fish   fish fish   fish.

(50)   The mouse that   the cat that   the dog bit chased died.

These examples have the structures shown in (45) and (49) respectively.

Relative clauses can be put one inside another without limit. They can just go on and on. Consider (52):

(52)   This is [NP1 the guy [S1 who loved [NP2 the girl [S2 who befriended [NP3 the boy [S3 who lived]]]]]].

For those familiar with the Harry Potter stories, each NP here describes one of the central protagonists by means of modification by a relative clause, each relative clause is inside the NP it modifies, and each NP – except NP1 – is embedded in the next relative clause. NP3 describes Harry Potter himself, *the boy who lived*. NP2 describes Hermione Granger, *the girl who befriended the boy who lived*, and NP1 describes Ron Weasley, *the guy who loved the girl who befriended the boy who lived*. Relative clauses give language a great deal of its expressive power, by making it possible to modify nouns using modifiers that can be as complicated as we want: in principle, there is no upper limit to the number of times one relative clause can be embedded inside another. This is reflected in nursery rhymes like 'The House that Jack Built': *the dog who bit the cat who ate the rat who lived in the house that Jack built*. Centre-embedded relatives can also, in principle, be constructed without limit. The problem is that, in practice, as we have seen, they quickly become very hard to understand.

Compare the following centre-embedded sequence with the excerpt from 'The House that Jack Built' just given:

(53)   [The rat [the cat [the dog [bit]] [ate]] [lived in the house that Jack built]

All of this leads us to three questions:

(54) a.   What is the highest number of repetitions of the word *fish* alone that constitutes a grammatical English sentence?

   b.   Have you seen these sentences before?

   c.   Where did you learn these facts about English?

To answer (54a), we could keep on trying longer and longer fish sentences. There is certainly no reason to take seven, the most we have seen here (see (41) and the structures in (42)), to be an upper limit. If we look at the examples with even numbers of fish, (28) and (40), we see that they have the general form in (55):

(55) a. $N_1 + N_2 + V_2 + V_1$ (four fish, (28))

   b. $N_1 + N_2 + N_3 + V_3 + V_2 + V_1$ (six fish, (40))

(This is not their exact structure, as we have seen, but these simplified representations make our point here.) Each pair $N_n + V_n$, for $n = n$ forms a relative clause modifying N_{n-1}. Hence, as Freidin (2012:13) points out 'any sentence containing an even number of *fish* from four onwards will have at least one grammatical representation'. Furthermore, although each relative clause (i.e. each pair $N_n + V_n$ in (55) for $n > 1$) has an object gap, as we saw above (see (44) and (45)), V_1 does not have an object. But of course it could have, and this object could be *fish*. This is what got us from four *fish* to five *fish* and from six *fish* to seven *fish*. To quote Freidin (2012:13) again: 'As this procedure [adding an object to V_1, IR] can be applied to any sentence with an even number (n) of *fish*, there will be a corresponding sentence with an odd number (n+1) of *fish* ... Hence any number of *fish* will correspond to a sentence of English.' In principle, then, a sentence containing any number of repetitions of the word *fish* is grammatical. Our linguistic competence allows us to understand such sentences, although more than five iterations, with the exception of seven, give rise to sentences that are difficult to understand in practice, i.e. sentences which may be unacceptable to varying degrees. We are able to assign syntactic representations, more technically known as **structural descriptions**, to the sentences, and from there recover the meaning. The full representations of these sentences, as we saw in our discussion of the Italian counterparts of the two- and three-fish examples, are quite complex. The full representation of the seven-fish example in English would be (56):

(56)   [$_S$ [$_{NP}$ [$_D$ ~~the~~] [$_N$ [$_N$ **fish**-[$_{Num}$ ~~Pl~~]]] [$_S$ [$_{NP}$ [$_D$ ~~the~~] [$_N$ [$_N$ **fish**-[$_{Num}$ ~~Pl~~]]] [$_{VP}$ [$_V$ [$_V$ **fish**-] [$_M$ ~~Indicative~~] [$_T$ ~~Present~~] [$_{Agr}$ ~~3Pl~~]] ~~[$_{NP}$ [$_D$ the] [$_N$ [$_N$ fish-[$_{Num}$ Pl]]]~~]] [$_{VP}$ [$_V$ [$_V$ **fish**-] [$_M$ ~~Indicative~~] [$_T$ ~~Present~~] [$_{Agr}$ ~~3Pl~~]] [$_{NP}$ [$_D$ some] [$_N$ [$_N$ **fish**-[$_{Num}$ Pl]]] [$_S$ ~~[$_{NP}$ [$_D$ the] [$_N$ [$_N$ fish-[$_{Num}$ Pl]]]~~] [$_{VP}$ [$_V$ [$_V$ **fish**-] [$_M$ Indicative] [$_T$ Present] [$_{Agr}$ 3Pl]] [$_{NP}$ [$_D$ the] [$_N$ [$_N$ fish-[$_{Num}$ Pl]]]]]]]

You don't need to pick your way through all the details of this representation in order to see two things. First, most of the structure is silent. Second, sentences of this kind are highly complex objects. But remember, and this is the really important thing, we quite unconsciously compute such complex sentence structures all the time.

Concerning question (54b), it is highly unlikely that anyone would come across sentences of this kind (outside of a linguistics class). But, as we have seen, they can be fairly readily understood. It is extremely difficult to see how any account of linguistic knowledge based on simply imitating, learning and generalising routines (perhaps through processes of stimulus, response and reinforcement, as in behaviourist psychology) could account for our general capacity to produce and understand, mostly instantaneously, sentences we have never heard before and which may never have been uttered before.

Question (54c) is the question that goes to the heart of the matter. As native speakers of English, we have very rich tacit knowledge, of even the silliest and most awkward sentences, which we were almost certainly never 'taught' in any meaningful sense of the word. Our experience in early childhood, combined with our cognitive capacities (both language-specific and not), has made it possible for us to perform the kinds of mental computations required to extract structure and meaning from what appear to be merely strings of repetitions of the same word. Of course, this ability is not restricted to native speakers of English: native speakers of Italian can just as easily make sense of sentences like (24), (29), (36) and (39), and the same exercise can be repeated, in principle, with any speaker of any language.

The fish sentences clearly illustrate the distinction between competence and performance. As we have mentioned, competence refers to a state of knowledge, knowledge of an I-language, that a native speaker of a given language (in roughly the 'E'-sense as discussed in the Introduction) possesses. Performance refers to the application of I-language in a given situation: combined with other cognitive and social capacities, performance makes normal speaking and comprehension possible. Freidin's conclusion that 'any number of *fish* will correspond to a sentence of English' clearly concerns competence; the rules of English syntax are such that sentences of this kind can exist, but of course, owing to performance limitations, no actual speaker could produce or understand a sentence consisting of an infinite number of occurrences of the word *fish* and nothing else. Since placing an upper bound on the number of times one relative clause could be embedded in another would be arbitrary, we regard the rules of English (and other languages) as allowing for this in principle. Of course, the same applies to numbers: no individual can ever write out an infinite number, although our mathematical competence tells us, and this can of course be proved, that the series of natural numbers is infinite. In Chapters 3 and 4, we will see the precise structure-building mechanisms that achieve this result.

1.5   Conclusion: What the Fish Have Taught Us

In this chapter we have tried to outline and illustrate, with the concrete help of the fish sentences, what linguistic theory investigates. The central goal is to elucidate what it means to be a competent speaker of a language. In other words, linguistic theory is primarily about knowledge: what is it that a person described as a native speaker of English (for example) knows? What are the properties of individual I-languages and what are the properties of UG that underlie them? Clearly this must involve the operations that are capable of producing the kinds of structures we saw in relation to the fish examples. A further central question is where this knowledge comes from: how do children acquire their first language? Related to this is the question of how similar and different languages are. We saw that we can 'line up' English and Italian quite well, especially if we assume that English has a number of silent inflectional 'satellite' categories many of whose Italian counterparts are overtly pronounced. In language-acquisition terms, this suggests that children are looking for evidence – semantic, syntactic, morphological or phonological – for the presence of these categories. Many complex issues arise as we try to pursue these ideas, but we saw in connection with the Italian fish examples that the combination of semantic evidence and UG predispositions of various kinds can lead us to significantly limit the differences between English and Italian. As we said there: semantics is universal, syntax is near-universal and languages differ primarily in their morphophonologies. We will return to these ideas repeatedly in the chapters to follow.

This is a formal, cognitive theory of linguistic knowledge. Each individual over the age of five or so has a specific I-language which makes possible their competence in their native language. This I-language corresponds more or less to a sociocultural E-language construct such as English, Italian and so on. We also saw that English and Italian speakers are I-alike but E-different: the I-languages may turn out to be quite similar to each other, while many aspects of the cultures borne by the corresponding E-languages are strikingly different (in ways that people generally find fascinating). Given how little we understand about the brain, as well as ethical restrictions on what kinds of experiments we can do on healthy children or adults, we can only find out about what is inside the mind, how an individual's grammatical system works, from the observed outputs of the I-language. This includes, quite simply, the things we say and hear (language production and comprehension) along with judgements about grammaticality, interpretation and so on.

We saw in the Introduction that there are three factors that make an I-language. These are, first, the genetic endowment. Here we take this to be UG, containing the various kinds of rules and systems of rules that build and interpret syntactic, semantic and phonological representations. The details of what constitutes UG will occupy us for much of what follows. The second factor is experience, in particular linguistic experience: exposure to a language as a small child. This happens to almost everyone, and the nature of the early linguistic experience will determine which E-language group an individual belongs to, in part determined by the I-language which develops from the interaction of the linguistic experience, UG and the third factors. The third factors cover a range of different things, but among the most important are general cognitive abilities, not specific to language. As we mentioned in the Introduction, it can be very difficult in certain cases to distinguish general cognitive abilities from language-specific abilities (which we would attribute to UG unless they clearly stem from experience).

All the above remarks apply to linguistic theory, conceived as here, in general: to semantics, syntax, morphology and phonology. The goals of syntactic theory in particular are above all to investigate the nature of the adult's tacit competence in the native language, i.e. to investigate I-language. This is done by discovering and describing grammatical and ungrammatical structures (which, as we saw, mostly but not always correspond to acceptable and unacceptable sentences according to native-speaker judgements); these observations are systematized as a model for that knowledge. In the chapters to follow, we will see how this is done. This model is then tested and adapted against further language data; if we are looking at UG, we may look at data from a range of languages. The rule systems are grounded in the three factors discussed above. So three really fundamental, and in this approach, intertwined questions are:

(57) a.   how does a given I-language relate to UG?
     b.   how does adult I-language result from acquisition?
     c.   how is I-language related to general cognition and the third factors?

Each of these questions relates I-language to one of the three factors in language design that underlies it. In this connection, our fish sentences are very important. They show us that syntactic structures are potentially infinite and yet built out of very simple elements. In particular, the structures are formed by repeating the same operations again and again. The next few chapters, as well as much of Volume II, are devoted to demonstrating this in full detail. The fish have given us a first inkling of the nature of the syntactic component of I-language, but now it is time to look more systematically into the details.

Exercises

1.   Consider again the four-fish example in (28), repeated here as (i):

      (i)   Fish fish fish fish.

      We assigned the structure in (34), here (ii), to this sentence:

      (ii)   [s [NP [N fish] [Relative clause [NP [N fish]] [VP [V fish] [NP [N fish
                ]]]]] [VP [V fish]]].

We also observed that inserting the relative marker *that* between the first two *fish* made possible a different interpretation, which we gave in (35) (= (iii)):

(iii)   [s [NP [N fish] that [Relative clause ~~[NP [N fish]]~~ [VP [v fish] [NP [N fish]]]]] [VP [v fish]]].

In all of (i–iii) there is an implicit main-clause object, meaning something vague like 'stuff'. It is, however, possible to interpret (i) as having an overt object. Try to see that interpretation, indicate its structure (in a rough way, along the lines of (ii) and (iii)), its interpretation and, if you can, its approximate intonation. (HINT: look again at the ambiguity of the two-fish example discussed in (7–9)).

2.   Now look again at the five-fish example from (37) (= (i)):

(i)   Fish fish fish fish fish.

We said that (i) is the four-fish example plus an overt direct object for the main-clause verb, giving the structure in (38) (= (ii)):

(ii)   [s [NP [N fish] [Relative clause [NP [N fish]] [VP [v fish] ~~[NP [N fish]]~~]]] [VP [v fish] [NP [N fish]]]]

But in fact (i) has a further interpretation, where the main-clause object is a relative clause. Give the structure for this interpretation of (i).

     Furthermore, the relative clauses in both interpretations can be marked with *that*, and in each case this gives rise to a further ambiguity inside the relative clause. Explain the ambiguity and give the relevant structures.

3.   Give the structure for the six-fish example in (40) (= (i)):

(i)   Fish fish fish fish fish fish.

Now try to add a further level of embedding to (40), using any lexical items you like (except perhaps *fish*). This will correspond to an eight-fish sentence; give the structure for this one.

For Further Study and/or Discussion

1.   If you speak a language other than English or Italian, translate the fish sentences into your language as best you can; if you don't speak any other language, ask a friend who does (preferably a patient friend). Try to assign structures along the lines of (27) to your sentences. What difficulties arise in the translations? How similar to or different from English or Italian are your translations? Which of the satellite categories we identified do you need? Do you need other ones?

2.   Google Translate gives (i) as the Italian translation of the three-fish
             English sentence:

             (i)   Pesce pesce pesce.

             This is not a grammatical sentence but rather obviously just the
             Noun *pesce* repeated three times. As we saw in (24), the correct Ital-
             ian translation of the three-fish English sentence is (ii):

             (ii)   I pesci pescano pesci.

             What does an Italian speaker have that Google Translate lacks?

Further Reading

R. Freidin. 2012. *Syntax: Basic Concepts and Applications*. Cambridge: Cambridge
       University Press.

2   Constituents and Categories

2.1   Introduction and Recap

In the last chapter we saw, using the fish sentences, that syntactic structures are potentially infinite and are built out of very simple elements by repeating the same operations on structure again and again. We also defined the goals of linguistic theory, construed as a formal, cognitive theory, as being primarily to discover what it is that people know when they know a language, i.e. what is I-language competence? A further central question is how this knowledge is acquired.

Our focus henceforth will be on elucidating the nature of I-language in relation to syntax. As we have seen, syntax is a central aspect of language, in that it relates sound and meaning over an infinite domain, so clearly any theory of syntax will be a central part of UG. We continue to take UG to be universal innate knowledge, one of the three factors making up the language faculty. We will therefore develop the theory of I-language syntax, taking this, like the rest of the language faculty, to arise from the three factors in language design: UG, exposure to language in early life and domain-general third factors (as described in the Introduction).

The fundamental notion in syntax is **constituent structure**, i.e. the way in which words group together into intermediate units (or phrases) of various categories, ultimately forming whole sentences. Some groupings of words, which we hear as different ordered strings of words, are ill-formed, or ungrammatical; others are well-formed, or grammatical. We saw in Chapter 1 that grammaticality and acceptability generally coincide: almost all of the examples we consider from now on are of this kind. So when I use the terms 'grammatical/ungrammatical' (or 'well-formed/ill-formed'), these will refer to examples which are correspondingly acceptable or unacceptable, i.e. native-speaker judgements consistently correspond to what is generated, or not, by the rules of grammar. Consider, for example, the following fairly simple ten-word English sentence:

(1)   Goona hopes that Vurdy will be ready for his dinner.

There are ten! = 3,628,800 possible orders for this ten-word sentence, the vast majority of which are ungrammatical, such as the following:

(2) a.   *Hopes Goona that Vurdy will be ready for his dinner.
    b.   *Hopes that Goona Vurdy will be ready for his dinner.

Our theory must make the distinction between grammatical and ungrammatical strings and structures; it must tell us how and why (1) is grammatical
while the examples in (2) are ungrammatical. Furthermore it should tell us
when two sentences consisting of different words (and therefore meaning
different things) have the same structure. This is true for (1) and the examples in (3):

(3) a.   Ron said that Hermione would be happy with her homework.
    b.   Boris thinks that Emile must be angry with his behaviour.
    c.   Alex believes that Eric should be worthy of a medal.

The basic notions we use to do this are those of **categories** and **constituents**,
which we now look at in turn.

2.2   Categories

2.2.1   Introduction: Lexical and Functional Categories

Like many approaches to morphology and syntax, including traditional grammar, we make a first distinction between two main types of categories, which we will call **lexical categories** and **functional categories**.

The principal lexical categories correspond to some of the 'parts of speech'
of traditional grammar: they are noun, verb, **adjective**, **adverb** and **preposition**,
abbreviated standardly as N, V, Adj, Adv and P (we saw nouns and verbs in
our fish examples in Chapter 1). These lexical categories are open: people can
and do invent nouns and verbs all the time, and even the most up-to-date online
dictionaries struggle to keep up. Words belonging to these categories have clear
non-linguistic semantic content: as we saw, *fish*, as a noun, denotes a certain
class of aquatic animals, while *fish*, as a verb, denotes the activity of hunting
these animals. New adjectives and adverbs are less readily coined, but they do
arise, e.g. *downloadable*, *googlable*, etc. Prepositions are the one lexical class it
is difficult to add to; in this and certain other respects, prepositions are more similar to functional categories. We will return below to the possibility of defining
syntactic categories semantically.

Furthermore, lexical categories do not vary greatly across languages. The distinction between nouns and verbs, in particular, seems to recur in all known
languages (although there is some debate about this in certain cases). Adjectives
are not found in every language; some indigenous languages of North America
may lack them, for example. In other languages, e.g. the West African languages
Hausa and Igbo, they form a small, closed class. In languages where the class
of adjectives is small or non-existent, the semantic work of adjectives, roughly
describing qualities, is usually done by relative clauses (*a bus which reds*). It
is probable that prepositions are not universal: the *World Atlas of Language
Structures (WALS)* lists thirty languages lacking adpositions (a cover term
for pre- and postpositions), including several indigenous languages of North

America such as Blackfoot, Cree and Kiowa.[1] English is comparatively rich in prepositions (although they do not really constitute an open class, unlike the other lexical categories; to some degree, prepositions straddle the border between lexical and functional categories).

Functional categories include the 'satellite words' we introduced in the discussion of the Italian fish sentences in Chapter 1; some of these, e.g. determiner (or article), correspond to traditional parts of speech, but many of the others would be treated in traditional grammar as parts of words rather than as syntactic categories (a consequence of the fact that the traditional parts of speech were designed for the description of Greek and Latin, both highly inflected languages). There we saw D, Num, Mood, Tense and Agr(eement). Functional categories tend to constitute small classes of, typically, rather small words; they may also be realised as inflectional endings or, indeed, have no overt realisation at all, as we saw for several cases in English in Chapter 1. English auxiliaries (e.g. *must, be, do, have,* etc.) represent several functional categories, notably Mood and Tense. English is particularly rich in auxiliaries and they play a central role in many aspects of English syntax, as we will see. Further functional categories of English include determiners (D: *the, a, this, my,* etc.) and Number (represented by the plural inflection *-s*). There are other functional categories, e.g. complementisers, or C, the words which introduce subordinate clauses of various kinds: *if, that, for,* etc. (these are known in traditional grammar as subordinating conjunctions).

Functional categories are closed classes: it is seemingly impossible to consciously invent new ones. Furthermore, their semantic content is either highly abstract, as in the case of Mood, Tense and determiners, or perhaps non-existent: for example, what is the meaning of the complementiser *that* in (1)? It seems that it can be left out without affecting the meaning of the sentence at all. Furthermore, functional categories appear to vary quite a lot from language to language. Here we have given examples from English. Even in languages fairly closely related to English, the auxiliary system is less rich, and various semantic notions indicated by auxiliaries in English (e.g. future tense *will*) may be indicated by inflections instead, as in several of the Romance languages for example. In Chapter 1 we saw that Italian is much more richly inflected than English: Mood, Tense and Agreement (M, T and Agr) are mostly realised by verbal inflections in Italian and the other Romance languages but often not realised at all or realised by auxiliaries in English (although English does have a little bit of tense and agreement inflection, as we saw). In a radically non-inflecting language such as Chinese or Thai, Mood and Tense are indicated by invariant (non-inflecting) 'sentence particles' and agreement is entirely absent. One of the major issues in developing the theory of UG is understanding the extent to which functional categories can vary, both in their realisation (as inflections, separate words, or silence) and in their existence (recall our discussion of Conj-marking in English and Italian in Chapter 1). We will gradually develop this

[1] *WALS* Map/Feature 85A, https://wals.info/feature/85A#2/16.3/153.1.

theme over the coming chapters, and return to it armed with more empirical and theoretical knowledge in Volume III.

How can we distinguish the various categories? This is quite a tricky matter, and there are no absolute hard-and-fast diagnostic tests. For lexical categories in particular, we can make use of four kinds of properties, relating to the main areas of linguistic structure. Hence we can distinguish categories on the basis of their morphology, their syntax, their phonology and aspects of their meaning. Let us look at each of these in turn.

2.2.2   Morphological Diagnostics for Categories

The morphological criteria are arguably the easiest to see. We can distinguish lexical categories in terms of the typical inflections and other endings they can have. So, for example, regular count nouns in English can have the plural marker -s (as in *boys* but not *fish*, as we saw in Chapter 1). There is a handful of nouns with irregular plurals: *children, mice, men, feet* and a few more. Mass nouns such as *milk, water, air, bread* denote uniform quantities of stuff rather than countable individuals, and as such do not have plurals. Many of them can, however, be 'coerced' into acting like count nouns and thereby forming plurals: for example, *beer* is a mass noun, but one can say *I drank two beers*, meaning two units (glasses, pints or types) of beer.

English verbs inflect for past tense and third-person singular (3Sg) agreement in the present, as we saw in Chapter 1. The regular form of the past tense is -*ed*, although there are about 150 irregular verbs in Modern English: *sang, brought, drove, took*, etc. All verbs (as opposed to auxiliaries) take the regular 3Sg present-tense ending: the only irregularities are *says*, which is pronounced 'sez' (IPA /sɛz/) rather than 'says' by most people and *does*, pronounced /dʌz/ not /duːz/ whether used as a main verb or an auxiliary.

As we saw in Chapter 1, languages with richer inflections offer more morphological ways of distinguishing categories. We saw that in Italian *fish* the noun is *pesce*, while *fish* the verb is *pescare*. This distinction reflects the prevalent pattern in Italian, making verbs and nouns very easy to distinguish in terms of their inflections (and all but eliminating fully ambiguous forms comparable to English *fish*). Nouns mainly fall into one of three classes, which can be distinguished by their singular endings: one class ends in -*a*, forms the plural in -*e* and is feminine in gender (e.g. *mela/mele* 'apple(s)'); a second class ends in -*o*, forms the plural in -*i* and is masculine in gender (e.g. *gatto/gatti* 'cat(s)') and the third class, illustrated by *pesce*, ends in -*e* in the singular and forms its plural in -*i*; this last class may be either masculine or feminine. Verbs largely fall into one of four conjugation classes marked by a characteristic vowel immediately following the root. The first conjugation is marked by -*a*-, as in *pescare* (this is the truly open, productive conjugation; for example, a fairly recent innovation is *googlare*, 'to google'); the second conjugation is marked by unstressed -*e*-, as in *leggere* ('to read'), the third by stressed -*e*- as in *vedere* ('to see') and the fourth by -*i*- as in *dormire* ('to sleep'). In all cases, the infinitive ending is -*re*. Italian verbs have a large number of tense and agreement endings, far too many to list here.

All of this makes it very easy to identify verbs in terms of their morphology. What we see in Italian is typical of the Romance languages, and, with variations, common across the Indo-European languages as a whole. Some languages show case marking on nouns, which indicates the function of the noun (or really of the NP) in the clause: **nominative** case marking typically marks **subjects**, **accusative direct objects**, **dative indirect objects**, etc. So in Latin *dominus* ('master') has the *-us* ending for nominative singular (in this class of nouns, known as the second **declension**), *-um* for accusative singular, *-o* for dative singular and in fact three more cases. In languages of this type, nouns can be identified by case marking (adjectives agree with the nouns they modify, so they can too).

In Modern English, common adjectives can be identified by their ability to form the comparative with the ending *-er* (*tall – taller*) and the superlative in *-est* (*tallest*). This applies only to adjectives of two syllables or less; hence there is no comparative *beautifuller* or superlative *beautifullest*. This constraint applies to the root form of adjectives, so *unhappier* exists, since the root is the two-syllable *happy*. As usual, there is a handful of irregular adjectives, e.g. *good – better – best*, *bad – worse – worst*.

Regular adverbs are formed from the corresponding adjective by adding *-ly*, e.g. *beautifully, happily, badly*. There are some irregular adverbs, e.g. *well*, and some which simply do not add *-ly*, e.g. *fast*. Conversely, there are some adjectives which end in *-ly*, e.g. *friendly*. Prepositions are invariant: they do not inflect at all in English.

So morphological criteria can identify lexical categories in English. In most of the Romance and the other Germanic languages, where there is typically more inflection than in English, these criteria are correspondingly more useful and reliable. As we saw with our fish sentences in Chapter 1, English allows many apparently inflectionless, and hence morphologically ambiguous, forms (we suggested that this may be due to a large amount of silent inflection in English).

2.2.3 Syntactic Diagnostics for Categories

Given the paucity of overt inflection in English, syntactic criteria may provide better diagnostics for categories, especially functional categories (which tend either to show irregular inflection or to be invariant). Typical syntactic tests rely on the **distribution** of categories, identifying positions in the sentence which are reserved for words of a given category; each category thus has its characteristic distribution. For example, only auxiliaries invert in direct yes/no questions, so alongside the declarative in (4a) we have the yes/no interrogative (so-called because it invites the answer 'yes' or 'no') in (4b):

(4) a.   Cambridge will flood as a consequence of global warming.
     b.   Will Cambridge flood as a consequence of global warming?

In (4a), the declarative has the order *Subject – Auxiliary – Verb …* . In (4b), the interrogative shows the 'inverted' order of subject and auxiliary. Here the auxiliary is *will*, indicating (roughly) future tense. If there is no auxiliary in the

declarative sentence, the seemingly meaningless, 'dummy' auxiliary *do* appears
in the 'inverted', pre-subject position in the interrogative. This can be seen in (5):

(5) a.   Cambridge flooded after all the heavy rain last spring.
    b.   Did Cambridge flood after all the heavy rain last spring?

In the declarative (5a), there is no auxiliary and past tense is marked by the -*ed*
ending on the verb. In (5b), the auxiliary *do* appears, marked for past tense as
did, and precedes the subject, while the verb has no ending. Placing the inflected
verb in front of the subject is ungrammatical (indicated by the asterisk * preceding the sentence):

(6)   *Flooded Cambridge after all the heavy rain last spring?

This way of forming interrogatives is characteristic of Modern English. Until
roughly the seventeenth century, verbs could also 'invert' with the subject. So
we find examples like the following in Shakespeare:

(7)   Looks it not like the king? (*Hamlet* Act One, Scene I)

For this reason, readers familiar with Shakespeare and other writers from the
seventeenth century or earlier may find that examples like (6) have a certain
Shakespearean ring to them, but they are not really part of Modern English.
    Following traditional grammar, we have said that clauses are divided into a
subject and a predicate. The predicate is usually a Verb Phrase, VP. Other categories are able to function as predicates, though, providing we include the auxiliary *be*. We can see this in examples like the following, where the predicative
category is labelled in the way we saw for the fish sentences in Chapter 1 (AP
stands for Adjective Phrase, PP for Prepositional Phrase):

(8) a.   John is [AP nice].
    b.   John is [AP interesting].
    c.   John is [PP in a bad mood].
    d.   John is [NP a nice person].
    e.   John is [VP sleeping].

In (8e), the verb *sleep* appears in its '**progressive**' form marked with -*ing*, indicating an ongoing situation.
    In addition to following *be*, predicative categories can also follow certain
verbs, such as *seem*.
    An important distributional property of VPs is that, unlike predicative APs,
PPs or NPs, they are unable to directly follow verbs like *seem*, as the ungrammaticality of (9e) shows:

(9) a.   John seems [AP nice].
    b.   John seems [AP interesting].
    c.   John seems [PP in a bad mood].
    d.   John seems [NP a nice person].
    e.   *John seems [VP sleeping].

So this test picks out VPs, since only VPs are ungrammatical following *seem*.

One important distributional test which picks out NPs is that only NPs can be subjects. Thus only an NP (which may consist of just a single noun or pronoun) can appear in the blank in (10):

(10)   ___ can be a pain in the neck.

From (10), we can form the sentences in (11a) by inserting a single noun or pro-noun (representing a whole NP), or those in (11b) where we see more complex NPs, but not those in (11c), where the words inserted are not nouns:

(11) a.   You/kids/injections/syntax/Dave can be a pain in the neck.
     b.   Professors of Linguistics/other people's kids/injections which go wrong/ fish fish fish can be a pain in the neck.
     c.   *Walk/tall/in can be a pain in the neck.

Similarly, only VPs (which can be just a single verb) can appear between an auxiliary and a manner adverb, i.e. in the slot in (12):

(12)   Students can ___ quickly.

In (13a), we have single-verb VPs in that position and in (13b) more com-plex VPs. In (13c) the words inserted are not VPs and so the sentences are ungrammatical:

(13) a.   Students can talk/write/learn/understand quickly.
     b.   Students can dissolve in sulphuric acid/get married/conclude that you're not worth listening to/fish fish quickly.
     c.   Students can *Olly/*kids/*injections/*syntax/*tall/*in quickly.

The distributional tests we have seen so far allow us to identify NPs, VPs and auxiliaries.

Here is a distributional test for APs. Only (gradable) APs can appear in the blank slot in (14):

(14)   The students are very ___ .

In (15a) we see simple, one-adjective APs in that slot, in (15b) we have complex APs of various kinds, while (15c) shows that other categories cannot appear there:

(15) a.   The students are very intelligent/diligent/nice/eager.
     b.   The students are very much more intelligent than I expected/diligent in handing in their essays/nice to talk to/eager to please.
     c.   The students are very *from/*walk/*Olly.

Finally, a test for PPs is that they can be identified by their characteristic intensifiers such as *straight* and *right*. Thus only PPs can appear in the blank slot in (16):

(16)   John walked straight ___ .

In (17), we have the same pattern as in (11), (13) and (15). Example (17a) gives simple PPs (intransitive PPs, containing just a P); (17b) illustrates PPs of various kinds, almost always with an NP object, and (17c) shows that APs, NPs and VPs cannot appear in this slot:

(17) a. John walked straight out/on/up/in.
     b. John walked straight out of the room/on to his destiny/up the hill/into the pub.
     c. John walked straight *red/*talk/*Olly.

We see that syntactic, distributional tests can isolate the main lexical categories, NPs, PPs, VPs and APs. In an inflectionally poor language like English, these are probably the most reliable category diagnostics available.

2.2.4   Phonological Diagnostics for Categories

Phonological tests are rather limited in scope in English. However, there are some. For example, there is a small class of disyllabic words in English which, like *fish*, are ambiguously nouns or verbs in their written form. However, the categorial distinction is marked by **stress**, as the following examples illustrate:

(18) a. Apple wants to in**crease** its profits.
     b. Apple wants an **in**crease in its profits.

In (18a), *increase* is a verb and has stress on the second syllable (shown by the **bold** letters). In (18b), *increase* is a noun and is stressed on the initial syllable.

Another case where phonology indicates an aspect of syntactic structure concerns the difference between **word stress** and **phrasal stress**. Hence *blackbird*, with stress on the first syllable, is a word, in fact a compound noun. This noun denotes a particular species of bird. On the other hand, *black **bird***, with stress on *bird*, is an NP (or part of an NP; strictly speaking there should be a determiner or plural marking). This NP denotes any bird which happens to be black, following the usual rules for attributive modification in English (so, *red bus* denotes any bus which happens to be red, and so on). Thus one can say *That black **bird** is not a **black**bird* without self-contradiction, which would be impossible if the different stress patterns did not indicate different structures (NP vs N) and therefore different meanings.

2.2.5   Semantics and Categories

Turning now to semantic criteria, these are typically invoked in traditional definitions of syntactic categories (often called 'parts of speech'). Nouns are defined as naming a person, place or thing, while verbs name actions and adjectives qualities. Here are some typical definitions of verbs: 'A verb describes what a person or thing does or what happens' (https://en .oxforddictionaries.com/grammar/word-classes/verbs); 'A *verb* is simply a doing or action word' (www.bbc.com/bitesize/articles/zpxhdxs); '*Verbs* are words that show an action (sing), occurrence (develop), or state of being (exist)' (www.merriam-webster.com/dictionary/verb).

There is something to these definitions, although they are rather vague and limited. On their own, they scarcely suffice to identify categories. Take, for example, 'what someone does' as part of the first definition just given, or 'action' in the second and third definitions (after all, actions are what people do). The word *action* clearly denotes 'action', but it's a noun. Similarly for *occurrence*, also a noun, or 'state of being' (*existence* is a noun). Or consider the following example:

(19)   The economy worries John.

Here *worries* is a verb, but it's neither an action nor a 'state of being' (either of the economy, or of John). Is it an occurrence? That seems a rather difficult question to answer, but it's not clear that answering either way would shed much light on things. Similarly, *nothing* is a noun, but it doesn't denote a thing, and it certainly doesn't denote a place or a person.

Despite the vagueness of these definitions, we can discern some semantic component in category distinctions. This can be seen relatively clearly in English where, as we have repeatedly noted by now, words can belong to different categories without changing form. For example, consider the different meanings of *round* in the following examples:

(20) a.   the **round** church
      b.   **Round** the rugged rock the ragged rascal ran.
      c.   These cars **round** corners very nicely.
      d.   Time for another **round**.

In (20a), *round* is an adjective, making up an AP on its own, and, much in line with the traditional semantic definition of adjectives, it denotes a property of the noun it modifies, its shape. In (20b), *round* is a preposition. It denotes a path in relation to the NP following it; again, prepositions are typically defined as denoting locations or paths. In (20c), *round* is a verb. Here again, it denotes a path in relation to its object, *corners*, traversed by its subject, *these cars*; so we can roughly think of it as denoting an action or a characteristic situation involving the subject and the object. In (20d), we have *round* as a noun. Here it denotes a particular cultural convention (characteristic of English pubs) metaphorically based on a circular shape. In each case, there is the same core of meaning in *round*, involving a circular shape or path; how that notion is interpreted in relation to the other elements in the sentence depends on the word's syntactic category and, as a consequence of that, its syntactic relations with the other words. So the traditional idea that adjectives denote qualities, prepositions locations or paths, verbs actions or situations and nouns "things" has some purchase here. We saw the same with *fish*: as a noun, it denotes a category of animals (a 'thing'), as a verb it denotes the action of hunting the thing in question. The adjective *fishy*, formed by adding the characteristic adjectival suffix *-y*, denotes the quality of being 'fish-like' (and has various metaphorical extensions which are perhaps more commonly used than the basic sense). There is no prepositional variant of *fish*, and it is rather difficult to imagine what that might be.

2.2.6   Conclusion

We have now seen several different ways of identifying syntactic categories. None of them is absolutely foolproof, but taken together, they are fairly reliable. Arguably, the distributional syntactic criteria are the most reliable for English. In languages with richer inflectional morphology, such as Italian, morphology can be more informative than in English.

There is little doubt that the diagnostics for categories vary from language to language. But do the categories themselves vary? Does every language have the same category inventory? In discussing this question at the beginning of this section, we pointed out that the noun–verb distinction may be universal, while adjectives and prepositions probably are not. Moreover, there appears to be variation in the inventory of functional categories a language can have. We might want to include Gender as a functional category, a 'satellite' of N, in Italian given the presence of grammatical gender in that language, but we would probably not include it in English, since there is no grammatical gender. This reasoning might lead us to exclude quite a few familiar functional elements, determiners for example, from our grammar of Chinese. These questions remain open and, as we said above, we will revisit them in Volume III, when we have more facts and more theory to bring to bear on them. For now, we will assume that English has the lexical categories N, V, Adj, Adv and P and at least the functional categories Aux(iliary), D(eterminer) and C(omplementiser). Furthermore, our conception of the nature and inventory of the functional categories will be successively revised as we go on.

2.3   Constituent Structure

2.3.1   Phrasal Constituents

Now that we have an idea of the inventory of categories (at least for English) and how to find them using various morphological, syntactic, semantic or phonological tests, we can begin to look at how categories combine to form constituents and constituent structure. This is really the core notion of syntax; everything else flows from our conception of the structure of complex syntactic units such as phrases and sentences, and how these are made up of words (or smaller units) of various categories.

Let us start with some very simple two-word sentences:

(21) a.   Clover slept.
    b.   Vurdy grew.
    c.   Charlie laughed.
    d.   Fish fish.

Taking our cue from how we analysed (21d) in (7) of Chapter 1, we can take each of these sentences to consist of at the very minimum a noun and a verb, and assign them the labelled bracketings in (22):

(22) a.   [_Noun Clover] [_Verb slept]
    b.   [_Noun Vurdy]   [_Verb grew]
    c.   [_Noun Charlie]   [_Verb laughed]
    d.   [_Noun Fish]   [_Verb fish]

But we have seen that nouns belong in NPs. So we can substitute more complex NPs for the simple nouns in (22):

(23) a.   [_NP The fat cat]   [_Verb slept]
    b.   [_NP The boy who lived]   [_Verb smiled]
    c.   [_NP The owner of the famous dog]   [_Verb laughed]
    d.   [_NP Fish fish fish]   [_Verb fish]

These more complex categories are Noun Phrases, NPs. NPs consist of at least a noun, along with other words and phrases that depend on and/or modify that noun (adjectives/APs, PPs, relative clauses, etc.) as well as satellite functional categories such as Num and D, as we saw in Chapter 1.

Similarly, we have seen that verbs belong in VPs, so we can substitute more complex VPs for the simple verbs in (22) and (23):

(24) a.   [_NP Clover] [_VP ate a mouse].
    b.   [_NP Kate] [_VP hopes that chocolate will not get more expensive].
    c.   [_NP Beth] [_VP ate her dinner with a nice Chianti].
    d.   [_NP Fish] [_VP fish fish fish fish].

So here we see another kind of complex category: the Verb Phrase, VP. VPs consist of a verb and other words and phrases that depend on/modify that verb (objects, adverbs, adverbial phrases, subordinate clauses, PPs, etc.). We will come back to the question of the status of satellite functional categories connected to VP such as T, M and Agr in Chapter 4.

2.3.2   Hierarchical Relations among Constituents

As we saw in Chapter 1 with the fish examples, we can represent syntactic structure generally with labelled bracketings, such as the following for (24a):

(25)   [_S [_NP [_N Clover]] [_VP [_V ate] [_NP [_D a] [_N mouse]]]]

In technical terms, the labelled bracketing provides a structural description of the sentence. Another way to give the structural description of a sentence is with a **tree diagram** (or **phrase marker**):

(26)

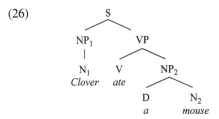

(Here NP_1, N_1, NP_2 and N_2 are numbered simply to keep them distinct; the numbers have no theoretical significance.) It is important to see that tree diagrams and labelled bracketings present exactly the same information in typographically different ways. The choice between them is a matter of convenience. However, most people find trees easier to work with, since the relations among the elements of the tree are more readily visible than in labelled bracketings. But this is just a matter of personal preference; nothing theoretical depends on it. In what follows, I will mostly use trees to represent structural descriptions.

We can now introduce some terminology that relates to the parts of the tree diagram. S, NP, VP, etc. are the **nodes** of the tree; the nodes are linked by **branches**. Branches never cross and all emanate from S, which is often referred to as the '**root**' node (in this sense the tree is in fact upside down in relation to botanical trees, since the root is depicted as being at the top; again this is purely a matter of convention). The words are **terminal nodes**; the category symbols (S, NP, VP, etc) are **non-terminal nodes**. Pursuing the tree comparison, one could think of the terminal nodes as the leaves.

The most important relations in the tree are the vertical, hierarchical ones. The two fundamental relations are **dominance** and **constituency**. A category A dominates another category B just where A is both higher up in the tree than B and connected to B. We can put this more precisely as follows:

(27)   A node A dominates another node B just where there is a continuous path of branches going down the tree from node A to node B.

In terms of (27), we can define **immediate dominance**:

(28)   Node A *immediately* dominates node B just where A dominates B and no node C intervenes on the downward path from A to B (i.e. there is no node C such that C dominates B and C does not dominate A).

Constituency is the reverse of dominance. A given category, call it B, is a constituent of another category A just where B is both lower down in the tree than A and connected to A by a continuous path of branches going up the tree from node B to node A. In parallel with immediate dominance, we now define **immediate constituency** as follows:

(29)   B is an immediate constituent of A just where B is a constituent of A and no node C intervenes on the upward path from B to A (i.e. there is no node C such that B is a constituent of C and A is not a constituent of C).

It is easy to see that (immediate) dominance and (immediate) constituency are inverse relations: dominance 'looks downward' in the tree, while constituency 'looks upward'. More generally, we can say:

(30)   A node A (immediately) dominates a distinct node B if and only if B is an (immediate) constituent of A.

Let us now apply these definitions to the tree diagram in (26), which I repeat here for convenience:

(26)

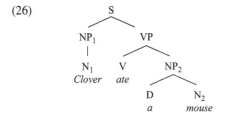

We can observe the following dominance relations in (26):

(31) a.   NP₁ and VP are immediately dominated by S.
   b.   V and NP₂ are immediately dominated by VP.
   c.   V, NP₂, D, N₂ and N₁ are dominated, but not immediately dominated, by S.
   d.   D and N₂ are immediately dominated by NP₂.
   e.   D and N₂ are dominated, but not immediately dominated, by VP.
   f.   N₁ is immediately dominated by NP₁.
   g.   NP₁ does not dominate VP or anything VP dominates.
   h.   VP does not dominate NP₁ or anything NP₁ dominates.

From (31a) and (31c), and the fact that immediate dominance entails dominance, we see that S dominates all the nodes in the tree. In fact, this is a good definition of the root node: the root node dominates all the other nodes in a tree; all the nodes in a tree are constituents of the root. Similarly, all non-terminal nodes dominate at least one distinct non-terminal or terminal node, and terminal nodes dominate nothing.

The dominance statements in (31) are exactly equivalent to the constituency statements in (32):

(32) a.   NP₁ and VP are immediate constituents of S.
   b.   V and NP₂ are immediate constituents of VP.
   c.   V, NP₂, D, N₂ and N₁ are constituents, but not immediate constituents, of S.
   d.   D and N₂ are immediate constituents of NP₂.
   e.   D and N₂ are constituents, but not immediate constituents, of VP.
   f.   N₁ is an immediate constituent of NP₁.
   g.   NP₁ is not a constituent of VP or of any constituent of VP.
   h.   VP is not a constituent of NP₁ or of any constituent of NP₁.

The relations of constituency and dominance are the most fundamental syntactic relations.

2.4   Conclusion

The central goal of the theory of syntax is to account for how words are grouped into larger units, phrases and sentences. Categories and constituents are the building blocks for analyses. In this chapter, we have seen how to test for and isolate various categories of English. None of these tests is foolproof, especially when taken alone, but taken together they do allow us to identify and distinguish categories. The second thing we have seen here are the ways in which we can present the structural description of a sentence: labelled bracketings and tree diagrams (or phrase markers). In these terms (using a tree diagram because it is more convenient), we defined the fundamental relations of dominance and immediate dominance, constituency and immediate constituency.

We take the notions of category and constituent to be part of UG (they are probably not primitives, but defined in terms of more abstract aspects of UG; nonetheless, their existence and nature are determined, perhaps indirectly, by UG). Other languages may have categories English lacks or may lack categories English has (although we have mentioned that the verb–noun distinction seems to hold up pretty well everywhere). But the notion that the words of a language fall into distinct categories, isolable by some battery of tests (which, as we saw, may relate to various other parts of the structure of language: phonology, morphology, semantics), is a hypothesis about the nature of UG which has certainly not been disproved to date.

Similarly, other languages have constituent structures that differ from those of English; not all tree diagrams represent universal structures. But, again, the fundamental ideas of (immediate) dominance and constituency are a hypothesis about the nature of UG, as are the proposals that branches never cross, all branches emanate from the root node and words are terminal nodes. As hypotheses about UG, these are ultimately hypotheses about genetically given aspects of human cognition, as we mentioned in Chapter 1.

In the next chapter, we will see ways to justify the particular constituent structures we have proposed here.

Exercises

A.   Categories

    1.   Assign the following words to a syntactic category (noun, verb, adjective, preposition), using the tests discussed in this chapter along with any others you know of. In your answer, show not only the category, but also how you apply the tests:

        cat, moon, sing, fish, to, possibly, well, dispute, round

    2.   Now do the same with the following words: *noble, ennoble, near, asleep* and *around*

B.   Constituents

    3.   Give the labelled bracketings and tree diagrams for the following examples:

        a.   Boris snorted.
        b.   The onx splooed the blarrg.
        c.   Fish fish fish fish.
        d.   Vurdy saw Goona.

e.   Clover ate the mouse.
f.   Harry met Hermione.

4.   Prepositions (invariant words typically denoting spatial or temporal relations such as *on*, *about*, *with*, *to*, *behind*, etc.) form Prepositional Phrases, or PPs, by combining with an NP, as follows:

(i)   [PP [P on] [NP the bus]]

Give the tree structure and the labelled bracketing for the following sentences, all of which contain PPs with a structure like (i):

a.   Boris talked about himself.
b.   Boris talked to the reporter about himself.
c.   Boris sent some poison to Emile.

What challenges do you encounter in the last two examples?

C.   For further discussion:

5.   What do you think might be the structure of NPs like the following? Present your hypothesis as a tree diagram.

a.   fat cat
b.   the invisible visible stars

6.   Specify all the (immediate) dominance relations in the following tree:

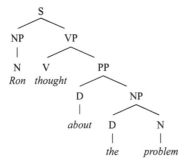

6.   How can we define terminal and non-terminal nodes in terms of constituency?

7.   S is the root of the tree. How can we define the root in terms of constituency?

Further Reading

All of the references below discuss the ways in which we can distinguish categories, using tests broadly similar to those discussed here and, as here, concentrating largely (but not exclusively) on English. All of them therefore provide useful backup, and plentiful further examples, to the ideas introduced here.

Carnie, A. 2011. *Modern Syntax: A Coursebook*. Cambridge: Cambridge University Press, Chapters 2 and 3.

Carnie, A. 2013. *Syntax: A Generative Introduction*. Oxford: Blackwell, Chapters 2, 3 and 4.

Haegeman, L. & J. Guéron. 1999. *English Grammar: A Generative Perspective*. Oxford: Blackwell, Sections 1.2.2 and 1.2.3.

Koeneman, O. & H. Zeijlstra. 2017. *Introducing Syntax*. Cambridge: Cambridge University Press, Chapter 1.

Larson, R. 2010. *Grammar as Science*. Cambridge, MA: MIT Press, Unit 9.

Radford, A. 2016. *Analysing English Sentences*. Cambridge: Cambridge University Press, Chapter 2.

Tallerman, M. 1998. *Understanding Syntax*. London: Routledge, Chapter 2.

3   Phrase-Structure Rules and Constituency Tests

3.1   Introduction

In the previous chapter, we saw the basics of the structural descriptions of sentences, the essential features of syntactic representations. Structural descriptions can be presented as labelled bracketings, as in (1a), or as tree diagrams, as in (1b):

(1) a.   [s [NP [N Clover]] [VP [V ate] [NP [D a] [N mouse]]]].
    b.

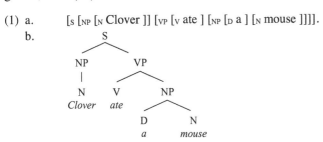

We also introduced basic tree terminology: node, root node, terminal node, non-terminal node, branch, etc., and the very important mutually definable relations of (immediate) dominance and (immediate) constituency. In addition to constituent structures, as represented in trees and labelled bracketings (i.e. structural descriptions), categories are the other fundamental notion. We illustrated the main categories of English, as well as the very important distinction between lexical and functional categories, and showed how categories can be fairly reliably isolated by a battery of syntactic, semantic, morphological and phonological tests (which vary somewhat from language to language).

The goals of this chapter are to start to describe (and explain) the difference between grammatical and ungrammatical sequences. In order to do this, we introduce the mechanisms that **generate** structural descriptions, i.e. the rules that build trees and labelled bracketings. These are the **Phrase-Structure rules**. The exact Phrase-Structure rules and the structural descriptions they generate can be justified by independent tests designed to isolate and distinguish the constituents in a tree or labelled bracketing; these are the **constituency tests**. We look first at the Phrase-Structure rules and then at some constituency tests which, for the most part, work quite well in English.

3.2   Phrase-Structure Rules

Here are some examples of ungrammatical sentences of English (in the sense that they use English words and are just about intelligible to English speakers; strictly speaking, these sentences are part of neither I-language English or E-language English):

(2) a.   *Spoke John.
    b.   *Hopes Goona that Vurdy will be on form.
    c.   *Loves the Leader of the Opposition his wife.

The question is: how do we, as speakers of English, know that these sentences are ungrammatical? Clearly we don't merely store this information for each individual sentence or we wouldn't have grammaticality judgements about novel sentences such as the fish sentences we saw in Chapter 1. What is needed is some general schema determining which are the grammatical sentences of English (that is, of the I-language of the typical native speaker of English).

To put it more technically, we need a mechanism to generate the well-formed structural descriptions of English sentences. The mechanism in question is the set of Phrase-Structure rules, PS-rules for short. PS-rules are the formal devices which generate constituent structure, by specifying all and only the possible ways in which categories can combine. An example of a basic PS-rule of English (and probably many other languages) is given in (1), where S stands for Sentence;

(3) i.   S → NP   VP

This is read as 'Rewrite the symbol S as the sequence NP VP in that order.' More generally, the rules are instructions to replace the symbol on the left of the arrow with the symbol or symbols on the right of the arrow in the linear order given. In (4) we see some more PS-rules of English:

(4) ii.   VP → V (NP) (PP)
   iii.   NP → (D) N (PP)
   iv.   PP → P NP

The brackets indicate optional categories. Strictly speaking (4ii), for example, abbreviates VP → V, VP → V NP, VP → V PP and VP → V NP PP, but we collapse these rules under (4ii) using the bracket notation. These rules can generate the structural description for the sentence *Clover ate a mouse*, given as a labelled bracketing in (1a) and a tree diagram in (1b), and similar ones.

Here is another example of a tree diagram (which we saw in the Exercises sections in the previous chapter):

(5)

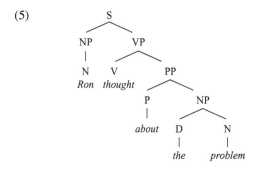

This tree can be generated by the PS-rules in (6), which combines the rules in (3) and (4):

(6)   i.   S → NP VP
      ii.   VP → V (NP) (PP)
      iii.   NP → (D) N (PP)
      iv.   PP → P NP

Each rule generates a small piece of tree, typically (but not always) a branching node and the constituents which that branching node immediately dominates. As such, each rule specifies a set of immediate dominance/constituency relations, such that the category to the left of the arrow is the label of the node which immediately dominates the constituent(s) to the right of the arrow, and the category or categories to the right of the arrow label the node(s) which is/are immediate constituent(s) of the category to the left of the arrow. So, PS-rule (6i) generates the structure in (7):

(7)
                    S
            NP   VP

PS-rule (6ii) has two categories in brackets on the right of the arrow. The brackets indicate that the categories in question are optionally immediate constituents of VP (another way to say this is to say that they are optionally part of the 'expansion of VP', given that PS-rules generally expand the category to the left of the arrow by specifying more than one category on the right). Strictly speaking, (6ii) really collapses the four distinct PS-rules seen in (8):

(8) a.   VP → V
    b.   VP → V NP
    c.   VP → V PP
    d.   VP → V NP PP

Option (8c) of rule (6ii) generates the piece of structure in (9):

(9)

```
        VP
       /  \
      V    PP
```

Rule (6iv) generates the structure in (10):

(10)

```
        PP
       /  \
      P    NP
```

Like rule (6ii), rule (6iii) collapses four rules using the bracket notation. These are given in (11):

(11) a.   NP → N
     b.   NP → D N
     c.   NP → N PP
     d.   NP → D N PP

Rule (6a) generates (12a) and rule (6b) generates (12b):

(12) a.   NP
               |
               N

     b.   NP
              / \
             D   N

The pieces of structure in (7), (9), (10) and (12a,b) combine to form the tree in (5). In (13), (5) is repeated with each part of the structure annotated giving the PS-rule which generates it:

(13)

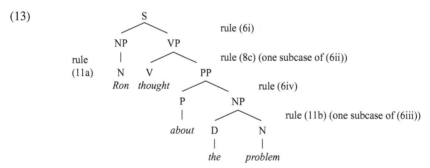

This illustrates how the structural description of the sentence is generated by the PS-rules. The tree diagram in (13) gives the structural description of the grammatical English sentence in (14):

(14)   Ron thought about the problem.

Let us now return to the ungrammatical sentences, repeated here:

(2) a.   *Spoke John.
    b.   *Hopes Goona that Vurdy will be on form.
    c.   *Loves the Leader of the Opposition his wife.

In (2a) the verb and the subject are in the wrong order for English. PS-rule (6i), $S \rightarrow NP\ VP$ states "Rewrite the symbol S as the sequence NP VP **in that order**.' Whatever expansion of VP we choose from the options in (6ii) (see (8)), V is always the first immediate constituent of VP. It follows from the combination of rules (6i) and (6ii) that the subject NP (the NP in (6i)) will precede the verb. Hence the sentences in (2) cannot be generated by our PS-rules where the immediately postverbal NP is the subject; if it is interpreted as the object, then the subject is missing and again the rules in (6) cannot generate the sentence. Our PS-rules are examples of the PS-rules of English, specifying all and only the well-formed structural descriptions of English sentences, and so the sentences in (2) are ill-formed. It is important to see that the notion 'ill-formed' here means 'not generated by the syntactic rules of English'. Our aim is to make that notion coincide as far as possible with native speakers' intuitive judgements regarding the grammaticality of English sentences, which we take to reflect their I-language competence. Here it is important to remember what we saw in our discussion of centre-embedding in Chapter 1: native-speaker judgements reflect performance, i.e. acceptability, rather than competence, i.e. grammaticality. As we mentioned there, though, most of the time grammaticality and acceptability coincide, and so most of the time matching native-speaker judgements is a good benchmark for how well our theory is doing.

As we can see from our account of the ungrammaticality of (2), PS-rules give information about the linear (left-to-right) order of nodes, including the words at the terminal nodes. They also give information about hierarchical structure, in that they specify immediate dominance and constituency relations. Finally, since the symbols they use are category symbols (S, N, V, P, etc.), they give information about the category labels of nodes. So PS-rules specify three kinds of information about structural descriptions simultaneously. We will see in Volume II that these three rather distinct kinds of information can be teased apart.

3.3 Recursion

One of the most important things our discussion of the fish sentences in Chapter 1 showed us was that the length of natural-language sentences is in principle unbounded. If infinitely long sentences are grammatical (but maybe not acceptable, as they can never be 'performed'), they should be well-formed. In other words, they should be generated by the PS-rules. Let us see how.

In fact, the rules we already have can generate infinite structures. Consider again rules (6iii) and (6iv):

(6) iii.   NP → (D) N (PP)
    iv.   PP → P NP

It is easy to see that NP appears on the left of the arrow in (6iii) and on the right of the arrow in (6iv). Given the way PS-rules work, this means NPs can appear inside other NPs, i.e. NPs can be constituents of other NPs, as illustrated in (15):

(15)

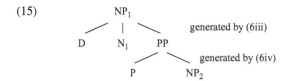

(Again, the subscript numbers on the Ns and NPs serve merely to keep the two occurrences of this category distinct; they have no theoretical significance.) Since nothing requires us to apply rules (6iii) and (6iv) in that order, after applying both rules so as to generate the structure in (15), we can go back and apply rule (6iii) again so as to expand NP$_2$ identically to NP$_1$, thereby introducing a second PP, which we can expand by rule (6iv) to give a third NP, which we can expand by rule (6iii) to give a fourth NP, which we expand by rule (6iv) to give a third PP, and so on. In principle, there is no limit to how many times we can keep applying rules (6iii) and (6iv) to their own output. The result of iterated application of these rules is complex recursive NPs of the following kind:

(16)   [NP [D the] height [PP of [NP [D the] lettering [PP on [NP [D the] covers [PP of [NP [D the] manuals [PP on [NP [D the] table [PP in [NP [D the] corner [PP of [NP [D the] room …

The ability of rules to apply to their own output is known as **recursion**, a concept that originates in mathematics and logic. Rules (6iii) and (6iv) are not individually recursive, but together they form a recursive rule system. Recursion is an extremely important concept, as it gives rise to the possibility of sentences of unlimited length and underlies the fact that human languages are able to make 'infinite use of finite means'. As we have just seen, we can construct an infinitely long NP using just rules (6iii) and (6iv). If our minds contain a recursive rule system of this kind for generating sentences in our native I-language, then our finite brains have infinite capacity. This is clearly a very important and interesting claim about human cognition, one which justifies looking at language from the formal and cognitive perspective adopted here.

In fact, we already saw recursion in action in the fish sentences in Chapter 1. Consider the structural description we gave there for the seven-fish example:

(17)   [S [NP [N fish] [RC [NP [N fish]] [VP [V fish] [NP [N fish]]]]] [VP [V fish] [NP [N fish] [RC [NP [N fish]] [VP [V fish] [NP [N fish]]]]]]]

The relative clauses introduce NPs inside other NPs and the object relative clause introduces a VP inside the main-clause VP. Since, as we said just after introducing the representation in (17), relative clauses are really sentences, i.e. of category S, we should substitute S for the RC labels in (17). Then we see that relative clauses introduce Ss inside Ss. So the reason we can have infinite fish sentences is that the PS-rules generating relative clauses are recursive. They feature occurrences of the symbols S, NP and VP on both sides of the arrow, just as rules (6iii) and (6iv) do for NP and PP.

Relative clauses are one kind of subordinate clause. I won't give the PS-rules that generate them here as certain details of their structure remain uncertain and controversial. Another kind of subordinate clause whose structure appears to be much more straightforward, however, are complement clauses. A simple complement clause is illustrated in (18):

(18)   Goona hopes [that Vurdy arrived].

Here we see a finite clause functioning as the **complement**, essentially a clausal direct object, of the verb *hope*, introduced by the complementiser (subordinating conjunction) *that*. It is easy to observe that what follows *that* in (18), *Vurdy arrived*, is a complete sentence on its own. We introduce the PS-rules in (19) to generate the complement-clause structure of (18):

(19) i.   VP → V S′
      ii.   S′ → Comp S

Rule (19i) adds to the various possible expansions of VP seen in (8). We could add '(S′)' to rule (6ii); this would subsume (19i) and predict that the sequence V NP S′ is possible (it is, as in *persuade Mary that John arrived*), the sequence V PP S′ is possible (it is, as in *say to Mary that John arrived*) and the sequence V NP PP S′ is possible (this may not be correct, but I will leave this complication aside here). In (19ii) 'Comp' abbreviates 'complementiser'. Rule (19ii) states that Comp and S are immediate constituents of the subordinate clause S′. S′ and S are not the same category: S is a clause and constitutes the root node of a tree, while S′ is the label of a subordinate clause introduced by rule (19i). Thanks to rule (19ii), we have a further case of S-recursion: S appears on the left of the arrow in rule (6i) and to the right of the arrow in rule (19ii). These rules will together generate structural descriptions with S inside another occurrence of S.

We can expand S introduced by rule (19ii) as NP VP (in fact, this is the only expansion of S our PS-rules allow as we have formulated them so far). We can then expand VP using rule (19i) and introduce S again by rule (19ii) and expand S again as NP VP, reapply rule (6i), reapply rules (19i) and (19ii), and so on without limit. Once again we see rules applying to their own output, the basic property of recursion. Recursive application of these rules in this way gives rise to unlimited sequences of subordinate clauses embedded inside one another. This is observed in English examples like (20):

(20)   Mary hopes that John expects that Pete thinks that Dave said that …

As far as competence is concerned, just as with the fish sentences and the complex NP in (16), there is no limit to the length, or to the depth of embedding, of sentences like (20). The usual performance restrictions mean that infinite sentences cannot be uttered or written down, but three PS-rules ((6i), (19i) and (19ii)) suffice to generate them.

The structural description of (18) in tree format is given in (21):

(21)

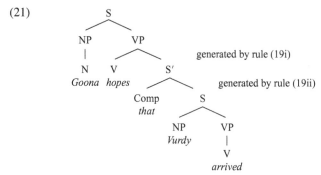

There are other complementisers in English, which introduce different kinds of subordinate clauses. As we can see in (18) and (21), *that* introduces a **finite, declarative** subordinate clause. In (22a), *whether* introduces an indirect question, and in (22b) *for* introduces an **infinitival clause**:

(22) a.   Goona wonders [s′ whether Vurdy will arrive on time].
    b.   Goona arranged [s′ for Vurdy to arrive on time].

As indicated here, both subordinate clauses are S′s, with *whether* and *for* in C. What follows *whether* in (22a) can stand alone as a complete sentence (*Vurdy will arrive on time*), and so there is no difficulty with applying rule (19ii) here. The difference with the *that*-complement in (18) is that the whole subordinate S′ stands for the direct interrogative *Will Vurdy arrive on time?* What we observe in indirect interrogatives is the absence of subject-aux inversion (briefly discussed in Chapter 2, see examples (4b) and (5b) there): in the S′ in (22a) *Vurdy* precedes *will* just as in a declarative. We also observe that the presence of *whether* contributes what we could call 'interrogative force', i.e. it makes the declarative into an interrogative.

In (22b), what follows the complementiser *for* cannot stand alone as a complete sentence: **Vurdy to arrive on time*. We clearly have a subject (*Vurdy*) and a predicate (*arrive on time*) as in (18) and (22), but what is missing is tense: there is no finite verb or auxiliary. 'Complete' clauses, those able to stand alone, must have a finite verb or auxiliary to mark tense (although the tense marker may be silent in English, as in the following complete sentences: *I/you/we/they/the boys arrive*). The particle *to* marks non-finiteness; it shows up in almost all infinitives in English. It looks as though we cannot generate **Vurdy to arrive on time* with rule (6i), since there is no place for *to*. But it seems clear *Vurdy* is the subject NP and *arrive on time* the VP. Assuming that *to* is not part of the subject NP, which seems highly unlikely, there are two possible structural descriptions for **Vurdy to arrive on time*, which are shown in the labelled bracketings in (23):

(23) a.   [s [NP Vurdy] [? to] [VP arrive on time]]
    b.   [s [NP Vurdy] [VP to arrive on time]]

Rule (6i) cannot generate (23a), but it could generate the NP VP structure in (23b). But now rule (6ii) (with its various expansions) cannot generate the VP there, which has *to* as its first constituent. In order to accommodate infinitival subordinate clauses, one of the two basic PS-rules in (6) will have to be modified. I will leave this question open here, but we will come back to it in Chapter 4 (see Section 4.4).

Combining (6) and (19), we now have the following set of PS-rules:

(24) i.   S′ → Comp S
      ii.   S → NP VP
      iii. VP → V (NP) (PP) (S′)
      iv.   NP → (D) N (PP)
      v.   PP → P NP

These rules can generate a large number, in fact, given their recursive nature, an infinite number of English sentences. However, they do not generate all the grammatical sentences of English: we have seen that there is no place for the infinitive *to* here, so we cannot generate (22b).

As we said at the end of the previous section, PS-rules give us three kinds of information: (i) information about hierarchical structure ('vertical' information, in terms of tree diagrams), information about linear precedence ('horizontal' information) and information about the category labels of nodes. These rules are very powerful formal devices which are capable of generating structural descriptions in a precise way. But how do we know that structural descriptions of the kind we have been looking at in this chapter are the right ones for English? The descriptions make very clear claims about constituent structure, but are they correct? We have also seen at least one example where it is not clear where to place a constituent in a structure: the question of where to put *to* in infinitival clauses like (22b). Which of the structures in (23) is the correct one, and why is the possibility that *to* is a constituent of the subject NP 'highly unlikely' as I said above? In the next section we will turn to questions of this kind, by showing how there are various ways of testing constituent structure, just as there are various diagnostics for categories as we saw in Section 2.2.

3.4   Constituency Tests

Let us look once more at PS-rule (6i):

(6i)   S → NP VP

This rule applies to give us the constituent structure (25b), rather than (25c), for (25a):

(25) a.   John ate the cake.
     b.   [s [np John] [vp ate the cake]]
     c.   [s [vp John ate] [np the cake]]

But why do we write the rule like this? What would be wrong with writing the rule as (6i′), which would give the constituent structure we see in (25c) for (25a)?

(6i′)   *S → VP NP

One obvious answer comes from the traditional idea that clauses consist of a subject and a predicate. But this venerable idea does not really tell us anything about phrase structure (despite what we said in Chapter 1): phrase structure represents hierarchy, order and categories, as we have seen. It does not represent grammatical functions or relations such as subject and predicate. From what we have seen up to now, these notions have no place in our theory; we may wish to build them in somehow, and we will do this in Section 5.2 (since these notions seem to be so useful for informal discussion we might want to have a theoretical way to understand them, but the fact remains that we have not actually said anything about this so far). We will look at the question of the theoretical status of grammatical functions in full detail in Chapter 2 of Volume II.

So, coming back to choosing between (6i) and (6i'), what this really amounts to is choosing between the structural description in (25b) and that in (25c) for (25a). In (25b), which is the analysis we have been assuming up to now, the verb and the direct object form a constituent that does not include the subject, while in (25c) the subject and the verb form a constituent that does not include the object. The question is: why should we prefer (25b) over (25c)? To put the question another way, what is the evidence that *ate the cake* is a constituent and *John ate* is not a constituent? The evidence is not directly audible on the basis of what we hear as (25a); this is because constituent structure, like most of syntax, is silent. The linear order in (25a) is clearly compatible with either (25b) or (25c). So we must find a way to determine what the hierarchical structure is.

The same question arises in relation to the NP P sequence in (26a) or the N A sequence in (26b):

(26) a.   They gave [NP the book] [P to] Mary.
        b.   They gave [NP Mary] [AP sweet] cookies.

We would naturally treat *to* in (26a) as a Preposition forming a PP with *Mary*. PS-rule (6iv) will generate this structure (and one version of (6ii) can generate the sequence V NP PP seen in *gave the book to Mary*). We could justify this on the grounds of the tight semantic connection between *to* and *Mary*, or on the grounds that *to* marks the indirect-object function of *Mary* here. But these are arguments based on semantics and grammatical functions, and this is not the kind of information the structural descriptions generated by PS–rules carry (at least not on the basis of anything we have seen so far). Similar considerations apply to (26b): semantic and functional considerations, i.e. the fact that *sweet* must be interpreted as modifying *cookies* and cannot be interpreted as modifying *Mary*, would lead us to group the AP *sweet* with the noun *cookies* to form an NP (which has the direct-object function). But can we find constituency-based arguments for this conclusion? If we can, then not only do we establish the constituency and have clear indications as to which set of PS-rules is the right one, we also confirm the intuition (or hunch, really) that constituent structure is closely connected to semantics, and that grammatical functions are also somehow linked to constituency relations (see Section 5.2).

Constituency tests of various kinds can show us to a large extent what the correct constituent structures are. These tests are manipulations of sentences which are sensitive to phrasal categories such as NP, VP, etc. There are several kinds of constituency tests. These involve: (a) manipulating the order of elements in such a way as to show that certain sequences of words must be manipulated together, i.e. that they constitute a phrase (these are **clefting, wh-movement** and **fronting**); (b) substituting a sequence of words with '**pro-forms**' of various kinds; (c) **ellipsis**, deleting a sequence of words in such a way that its interpretation is recoverable from the linguistic context; (d) **coordination**, conjoining two phrases of the same category with *and*, and (e) **fragments**, whether a sequence can stand alone and be in an intuitive sense 'complete', even if it is not a complete sentence. We will now look at each kind of test in turn. These operations are cases of a class of rules distinct from PS-rules, transformational rules, one type of which (wh-movement) we will focus on in Chapter 5.

Let us begin with wh-movement. Fronting a phrase containing a wh-word (i.e. the interrogative pronouns and determiners *who, what, which*, etc.; see Chapter 5) also targets constituents. This operation, known as wh-movement, is a very important one for syntactic theory, and we will introduce it fully in Chapter 5. Again, there is a gap in the sentence where the questioned phrase was, which we mark with a 't' (and which can also be taken as a silent copy):

(27) a.   Which friends does Mary hope that John will like t ?
    b.   What did the Party Chairman send t to John?
    c.   Who did the Party Chairman send a book to t ?
    d.   To whom did the Party Chairman send a book t ?

These examples show us that the direct objects in (32a,b) are constituents, that the NP following the P *to* in (32c) is a constituent, and that the PP *to whom* is a constituent.

Non-constituents, i.e. strings of words that do not form an independent, unique phrase, bolded in (28), cannot be fronted:

(28) a.   *__What to__ did the Party Chairman send t John?
    b.   *__What to John__ did the Party Chairman send t ?

Strictly speaking the ungrammaticality of (28) does not give us information about constituency; only the successful cases of wh-movement do this. Wh-movement does not apply to VP: the various wh-phrases correspond to different grammatical categories: *who, what* are NPs (respectively animate and inanimate), *which* is a D, *why* an AdvP or PP ('for what reason'), *when* a temporal NP or PP, *where* a PP, *how* an AP or AdvP and *how (many)* a measure expression. But there is no wh-word which questions a VP. Hence, we cannot use wh-movement as a diagnostic for a VP constituent. It does not follow from this that there is no VP constituent.

A further permutation we can apply to sentences in order to isolate constituents is fronting. This operation 'highlights' phrasal constituents by placing them at the beginning of the sentence. The fronted phrase often functions as a **topic** which 'is commented on' by the rest of the sentence. So, from the neutral sentence (29a) we can derive (29b), where the direct object *the new car* is fronted:

(29) a.   Mary hopes that John will like the new car.
     b.   The new car, Mary hopes that John will like t.

Again, we see a trace in the position where the direct object would normally be in (29b). Fronting can apply to CP and VP, as in (30):

(30) a.   That John will like her friends, Mary hopes t.
     b.   (Mary hoped that John would like her friends) ... and [vp like her friends] he did t.

For (30b) to sound natural, it helps to give some context, as shown here. Sentence (30a) may sound a little stilted, but it certainly seems acceptable. The examples in (30) should be contrasted with (31) (where again non-constituents are bolded):

(31) a.   ***A present to**, the Party Chairman sent t John.
     b.   ***A present to John**, the Party Chairman sent t.

We still have no evidence that the sequences *a present to* or *a present to John* are constituents, but now we have some evidence that VP and CP are constituents.

A further permutation-based constituency test is clefting. Clefting is the permutation of the order of elements illustrated in (32):

(32) a.   The Party Chairman sent a book to John.   →
     b.   It was to John that the Party Chairman sent a book t.
     c.   It was John that the Party Chairman sent a book to t.

The sentence in (32a) is 'neutral'. In (32b), the sequence *to John* has been clefted; in (32c) just the NP has been clefted, 'stranding' the preposition *to*. The general schema for clefting is given in (33):

(33)   S → It was XP that S.

(33) is not a PS-rule. It represents a different kind of rule, a transformational rule, that we will introduce properly in Chapter 5. The S on the left of the arrow represents the neutral sentence, e.g. (32a); what is on the right of the arrow is the clefted version of that sentence, e.g. (32b). The S on the right of the arrow contains a gap (similar to the gaps in relative clauses which we observed in the fish sentences in Chapter 1). Here it is marked as 't' (standing for trace); this indicates where the XP would normally be in the non-clefted version of the sentence. We can think of 't' as a silent copy of the XP. It stands for a single constituent, so in (32b) we do not have two traces following *book*, one for P and one for NP, but just one, standing for PP.

For our purposes here, the most important thing about clefting as schematised in (33) is that XP has to be a constituent. In (32b), the clefted XP is the PP *to John*. The sentences in (34) are two further cases of clefting:

(34) a.   It was the Party Chairman that t sent a book to John.
      b.   It was a book that the Party Chairman sent t to John.

In (34a), the NP *the Party Chairman* is clefted, while in (34b) it is the NP *a book*. So the clefting test has isolated three constituents for us: *[PP to John]*, *[NP the Party Chairman]* and *[NP a book]*.

If we try to cleft non-constituents, bolded in (35), the result is ungrammatical:

(35) a.   *It was **the Party Chairman sent** that t a book to John.
      b.   *It was **a book to** that the Party Chairman sent t John.

In (35a) the sequence *the Party Chairman sent* is clefted, and in (35b) *a book to*. In both cases the result is ungrammatical. Since there could be independent reasons why clefting some constituents is not good, the failure of a constituency test does not really tell us anything. For example, clefting VP yields a rather odd result (although probably not as bad as (35)):

(36)   ??It was send a book to John that the Party Chairman did.

Despite the oddity of (36), we do not immediately conclude that VP is not a constituent in (32a) and, as we have seen, other tests can successfully pick out VP for us.

So, the success of the test tells us that the fronted sequence is a constituent, but the failure of the test, strictly speaking, doesn't tell us anything. Unlike the VP, however, no constituency test will isolate the strings *the Party Chairman sent* or *a book to* as in (35). These strings are equivalent to the putative VP in (25c) and the possible constituents discussed in relation to (26).

The fourth type of constituency test involves substitution of pro-forms. **Pronouns** (*I/me, he/him, she/her*, etc.) are noun-like elements that have little semantic content of their own but stand in for something else. This 'something else', known as the **antecedent**, determines what the pronoun refers to. So, in an example like (37), *John* can be naturally interpreted as the antecedent of *he* (although it doesn't have to be; *he* could refer to any contextually salient male individual):

(37)   John hopes that he will win.

So (37) is interpreted to mean 'John hopes that he, John, will win.' Since *John* is an NP, we should really call pronouns NPs too, since they stand for whole NPs rather than just nouns. We can see this from the two cases of pronoun substitution in (38b) and (38c):

(38) a.   [NP The man who wears glasses] hopes that he will win.
      b.   * The he who wears glasses hopes that he will win.
      c.   He hopes that he will win.

Treating *he* as a noun in (38b) leads to ungrammaticality, while treating *he* as occupying the same position as the whole relative clause gives the grammatical (38c). The ungrammaticality of (38b) doesn't necessarily imply that the position of *he* is not a constituent; in fact, the noun *man* clearly is a consitituent. It shows us that pronouns are NPs (and not Ns).

Other categories have pro-forms too. Most VPs can be replaced by *(do) so*, as in (39):

(39)   John has promised Mary a book, and Bill has done so too.

Here we see the VP *promised Mary a book* in the first conjunct, i.e. the verb along with both the direct and the indirect object, are replaced in the second conjunct by *done so*. As with pronoun (i.e. pro-NP) substitution in (38), *do so* stands for the whole VP:

(40) a.   * ... , and Bill has done so Mary too.
      b.   *... , and Bill has done so a book too.
      c.   *... , and Bill has done so Mary a book too.

In (40a), just the verb and the direct object (*promise a present*) have been substituted; in (40b), just the verb and the indirect object (*promise Mary*), and (40c) just the verb *promise*. Again, the fact that these examples are all ungrammatical doesn't necessarily imply that the substituted categories are not constituents (in fact, the verb on its own clearly is a consitituent); what it shows is that *do so* substitutes an entire VP (and not, for example, V).

In the light of the conclusion that *do so* substitutes for a whole VP, consider the following examples:

(41) a.   John put his car in the garage on Tuesday, and Peter did so too.
      b.   *John put his car in the garage on Tuesday, and Peter did so on the driveway on Wednesday.
      c.   *John put his car in the garage on Tuesday, and Peter did so his bike on Wednesday.
      d.   John put his car in the garage on Tuesday, and Peter did so on Wednesday.

In (41a), which is grammatical, *do so* in the second conjunct appears to be replacing the sequence *put his car in the garage on Tuesday*, i.e. the verb *put*, the direct object *his car*, the locative PP *in the garage* and the temporal PP *on Tuesday*. We therefore conclude that all of these elements are in the VP. This conclusion seems to be confirmed by the ungrammaticality of both (41b) and (41c): in (41b), the locative PP *on the drive* is not substituted and ungrammaticality results, while in (41c) the object NP *his bike* is not substituted, again leading to ungrammaticality.

But (41d) behaves differently. Here the temporal PP *on Wednesday* is not substituted by *do so* in the second conjunct, but the sentence is grammatical. The difference between the temporal PPs *on Tuesday/on Wednesday* in these examples and the direct object and the locative PPs is that the former are not obligatory with the verb *put*. The direct object and the locative are, though, as the ungrammaticality of sentences like (42b–d), where one or other (or both) of them is left out, shows in contrast with the grammatical (42a):

(42) a.   John put the car in the garage.
      b.   *John put the car.
      c.   *John put in the garage.
      d.   *John put.

The grammaticality of (42a) also shows us that the temporal PPs are not required for grammaticality. Such PPs are optional modifiers, or **adjuncts**, giving 'extra' information about the time the event took place, but their presence is not required in order for the sentence to be intuitively 'complete'. On the other hand, (42b–d) feel 'incomplete': required information about what is being put (or) where is not given. This is because the direct object and the locative PP are arguments of the verb *put*; they must appear in the VP when *put* is V. More technically, *put* categorially selects for a direct-object NP and a locative PP. But it does not select for an adjunct temporal PP.

What the ungrammaticality of (41b,c) tells us then is that selected arguments of V must form part of the VP with the verb, and hence must undergo *do so* replacement. Then (41d) can be taken to indicate that adjuncts are outside the VP, and so do not correspond to *do so* replacement. But what about (41a)? The fact that the substituted VP is interpreted as *put the car in the garage on Tuesday* indicates that the adjunct PP is part of the VP. So (41d) appears to be telling us that the adjunct PP is outside VP, and (41a) appears to be telling us it is inside VP. We conclude for now that adjuncts (of this kind, at least) are optional constituents of VP, while selected arguments are obligatory constituents of VP. This conclusion accounts for the pattern seen in (41) as well as the examples in (42) and is consistent with the idea that *do so* corresponds to VP. We will see a more sophisticated treatment of adjuncts in the next chapter.

The *do so* test and the fronting test allow us to find VPs. We can now apply these tests to our two structures for *John ate the cake* in (25), repeated here as (43):

(43) a.   [s [NP John] [VP ate the cake]]
      b.   [s [VP John ate] [NP the cake]]

Fronting gives the following results:

(44)   (I thought John would eat the cake and)
      a.   .. eat the cake he did t!
      b.   *... John eat did t the cake!

With a slight tweak to the tense of the verb to create a natural context for VP-fronting, (44a) is perfectly grammatical. Example (44b), on the other hand, is strongly ungrammatical (bordering on what is sometimes called 'word salad', a sequence of words so unintelligible that it is almost impossible to impose any kind of structure or meaning on it).

Do so substitution, seen in (45), gives rise to a similar contrast:

(45) a.   John ate the cake, and Mary did so too.
      b.   *John ate the cake, and did so the cake too.

Example (45b) is not word salad, but it is not acceptable. We can also notice that *Mary* has completely disappeared from this example. This is a reflection of a very general fact about substitution and ellipsis operations: substituted and elided material is subject to a **recoverability** condition, i.e. the operations of substitution and ellipsis (the latter of which we will look at in depth in Volume II) must be such that the semantic representation can find, i.e. recover, what has been sub-stituted or elided. In (45b), *Mary* is not recoverable. The contrast in (45) clearly supports the structure in (43a) over that in (43b). This is a good result because, as we noted above, it seems that the constituents line up with the functions of sub-ject and predicate (although our PS-rules cannot and do not state this).

As a final point on substitution, consider the following examples:

(46) a.   %The Party Chairman sent it John.
     b.   The Party Chairman sent it.

Example (46a) is ungrammatical for most English speakers, although there are varieties in the north-west of England, around Liverpool and Manchester, where it is accepted (the '%' is used to indicate a form which is acceptable in one vari-ety of a language but not another) of course, this kind of variation simply reflects the fact that the sociocultural E-language concept 'English' does not correspond exactly to aggregates of I-languages – people from the relevant area of England have slightly different I-languages from those from elsewhere, a fact reflected in their differing grammaticality judgements of examples like (46a). However, in these varieties *it* is interpreted as the direct object (*a/the book*); it cannot be interpreted as substituting for *a present to*. Similarly, (46b) is grammatical, but *it* can only be the direct object. An indirect object (i.e. *to John*) cannot be recovered here. Again, then, *a book to* and *a book to John* fail the constituency test.

Ellipsis is the next kind of constituency test. Ellipsis elides, or deletes, mate-rial, subject to the recoverability requirement we have already seen in relation to substitution. **VP-ellipsis** is quite natural in English, as in:

(47) a.   John can speak Mandarin and Mary can ~~speak Mandarin~~ too.
     b.   John will leave tonight and Mary will ~~leave tonight~~ too.
     c.   John has passed the exam and Mary has ~~passed the exam~~ too.
     d.   John is writing a book and Mary is ~~writing a book~~ too.

(48)   John ate a cake and Mary did ~~eat a cake~~ too.

This example illustrates an aspect of the English auxiliary system that will play a major role in our analysis of clauses from the next chapter on. The struck-out sequence in the second conjunct here consists of the verb and its direct object, and so we can quite reasonably analyse this as VP. This would be consistent with our other results for constituency tests for VP: fronting and *do so* substitution (see (44a) and (45a)). Example (48) differs from (47) in that there is no auxiliary in the first conjunct and the auxiliary *do* appears in the second one. There is a difference between the two conjuncts here: in the first one, the verb bears the tense marking: we have *ate*, not *eat*. In the second conjunct, the past-tense marking is carried by the auxiliary *do*, in the form of *did*, and so the struck-out verb form lacks tense marking (hence ~~eat~~, not ~~ate~~). We see from (47) and (48) that, generally speaking, auxiliaries do not have to be deleted under VP-ellipsis. This suggests that finite auxiliaries are not part of VP. VP-fronting confirms this:

(49) a.   (I expected John can speak Mandarin) and speak Mandarin he can t!
     b.   (I expected John will leave tonight) and leave tonight he will t!
     c.   (I expected John to pass the exam) and pass the exam he has t!
     d.   (I expected John was writing a book) and writing a book he is t!

This raises the question of where auxiliaries are situated. Our basic PS-rule (6i) has nothing to say about this and will need to be revised. We defer this question to Chapter 4.

The exact counterpart of (47), but with *did* also apparently deleted is grammatical too:

(50)   John ate the cake and Mary ~~did eat the cake/ate the cake~~ too.

(The struck-out forms indicate that it's unclear where the tense marking is inside the elided sequence: on *do* or on *ate*.) The sequence in (50) is ambiguous in that it can also mean 'John ate both the cake and Mary too'; this latter reading involves coordination inside the direct object of *ate* and no ellipsis. The reading that the strike-out in (50) indicates is the one where *Mary* is the subject, not the object, of *ate*. Alongside (50), we have ellipsis patterns comparable to those in (48), but where the auxiliary is also deleted:

(51) a.   John can speak Mandarin and Mary ~~can speak Mandarin~~ too.
     b.   John will leave tonight and Mary ~~will leave tonight~~ too.
     c.   John has passed the exam and Mary ~~has passed the exam~~ too.
     d.   John is writing a book and Mary ~~is writing a book~~ too.

These examples, along with (50), indicate that the auxiliary can form a constituent with VP. It may be then that there is a mystery constituent in the clause, indicated in (52):

(52)   [s [NP John] [?? [Aux has] [VP passed the exam]]]

The VP is elided in (47) and (48), and the mystery category ?? in (52). In (23a) we saw that infinitive *to* may occupy a mystery category in a similar position; there we noted that PS-rule (6i) needs modification, a point we will return to in the next chapter.

Consider once more our alternative structures for the simple sentence *John ate the cake* in (43a,b):

(43) a.   [s [NP John] [VP ate the cake]]
     b.   [s [VP John ate] [NP the cake]]

VP-ellipsis clearly favours (43a) here, just like *do so* substitution and VP-fronting, as we have seen. Applying VP-ellipsis to (43b) yields:

(53)   John ate the cake and ~~Mary eat~~ did the cake.

(53) is not exactly acceptable, but it is difficult to work out what the second conjunct means. Moreover, *Mary* is unrecoverable in (53). Hence we must take

this to be an ill-formed application of ellipsis. Again, then, we see that (43a) is the correct structure for *John ate the cake* and (43b) is not.

The second kind of 'VP-ellipsis', which appears to apply to our mystery category ?? in that it deletes the auxiliary as well as the VP, gives (54) from (43b):

(54)   John ate the cake and ~~Mary eat did~~ the cake.

Aside from being rather odd and redundant, here again *Mary* is unrecoverable. Once again, (43b) seems to give the wrong results, while (43a) makes correct predictions. We conclude that (43a) is the correct structure. Thus the traditional functional division of the clause into subject and predicate has a structural correlate.

Coordination can also function as a constituency test. By and large, only constituents of the same type can be coordinated. Thus we can observe the following (examples from Radford 2016:134):[1]

(55) a.   The chairman has resigned from the board and the company.
     b.   The chairman has resigned from the board and from the company.
     c.   The chairman has resigned from the board and gone abroad.
     d.   The chairman has resigned from the board and is living in Ruritania.
     e.   *The chairman has resigned from the board and company has replaced him.
     f.   The chairman has resigned from the board and the company has replaced him.

In (55a), we see coordination of the NPs *the board* and *the company*; in (55b) we have coordination of the PPs *from the board* and *from the company*; in (55c), we have VP-coordination of *resigned from the board* and *gone abroad*. Example (55d) confirms our suggestion above of a mystery constituent combining the auxiliary and the VP, since two occurrences of this constituent appear to be coordinated: *has resigned from the board* and *is living in Ruritania*. Example (55e) is unacceptable, and so we do not have evidence that the sequences *chairman resigned from the board* and *company has replaced him* are constituents; in fact each seems to consist of the N of the subject NP (*chairman, company*) and our mystery category. This confirms the suggested structure in (52) for S where the mystery category is a constituent of S and not of the subject. The structure for *The chairman has resigned from the board*, on analogy with (52), would be (56):

(56)   [s [NP [D The] [N chairman]] [?? [Aux has] [VP resigned from the board]]]

Here we clearly see that the sequence *chairman has resigned from the board* is not a constituent. This is consistent with the fact that the coordination test yields an ungrammatical result when we attempt to combine strings of this type as in (55e). Finally, (55f) shows us that S is a constituent.

The final kind of constituency test relates to fragments. These are most naturally found in answers to questions. Generally speaking, only phrasal constituents form grammatical fragments. So, for example, the following answers are ungrammatical (here again, I borrow, and slightly adapt, examples from Radford 2016:137–8):

[1] A. Radford (2016), *Analysing English Sentences*, Cambridge: Cambridge University Press.

(57)   A: What has the chairman resigned from?
    *B: The.

(58)   A: What has the chairman resigned from?
    *B: Board.

The respondent B in (57) could reasonably be accused of being obtusely uncom-municative in responding by indicating some unspecified but unique, existing thing or things known to the speaker (recall our discussion of the meaning of the definite article in Chapter 1). But in (58), B provides a real answer as far as the content is concerned. However, fragments are unable to be non-phrasal cat-egories such as single nouns, and, as we have seen, singular count nouns cannot constitute an NP on their own in English, so the fragment response in (58) is ungrammatical. The principle that fragment answers must be phrases will also account for the ungrammaticality of the response in (57), independently of its pragmatic failings.

The dialogue in (59), on the other hand, is straightforwardly grammatical:

(59) A: What has the chairman resigned from?
    B: The board/from the board.

The grammaticality of the response confirms that NP and PP are constituents. Similarly, (60) confirms once more that VP, minus the auxiliary, is a constituent:

(60) A: What has the chairman done?
    B: Resigned from the board.

The plot thickens around our mystery category given the ungrammaticality of the response in (61), however:

(61) A: What has the chairman done?
    B: *Has resigned from the board.

Recall that the failure of a constituency test does not show us that a given sequence is not a constituent; there may be other reasons certain constituents cannot pass a given constituency test. We have seen evidence in (50), (51) and (55e) that the mystery category, the sequence *Aux + VP*, is a constituent. Some independent factor must then be responsible for the failure of the fragment test in (61). If fragments can only be phrasal and the mystery category is not phrasal, that could be the solution; again, we return to this in the next chapter.

The various constituency tests isolate NP, PP, S, VP and the mystery cate-gory, as we have seen, although not all of them isolate every category. What about APs? APs come in two different syntactic and semantic contexts, attribu-tive (modifying a noun, as in *sweet cookies*) and predicative (constituting, usu-ally with the help of *be*, a predicate: *the cookies are sweet*). Here the simple adjective *sweet* forms an AP on its own (just as *John* and *he* form NPs on their own). Let us see how the different APs fare under our constituency tests, begin-ning with predicative APs:

(62)   Permutation:
            a.   ??It's sweet that the cookies are t.   (clefting)
            b.   How sweet are the cookies t?   (wh-movement)
            c.   ?(I expected those cookies to be sweet), and sweet, they really are!
                    (fronting)

(63)   Pro-form:
            John likes his cookies sweet → John likes his cookies (just) so.

(64)   Ellipsis:
            The cookies are sweet and the cake is s̶w̶e̶e̶t̶ too.

(65)   Coordination:
            The cookies are sweet and extremely fattening.

(66)   Fragment:
            A: How are the cookies?
            B: Sweet/very sweet/*very.

From (62–66) we can conclude that *sweet* is an AP constituent in a predicative sentence like *The cookies are sweet*. The permutation tests are little tricky: (62a) is marginally grammatical (some speakers many find that examples like this sound vaguely 'Irish'; this is because many varieties of English spoken in Ireland do allow this kind of cleft – again we see that E-English does not correspond to a homogeneous set of I-languages). Example (62c) is perhaps a little forced but seems grammatical (it appears that AP-fronting needs a special discourse context similar to VP-fronting: compare (35), (44a) and (49)). The AP pro-form is *so* (note again the similarity with VP), but seems more natural where there is a substantive verb introducing the predicate rather than auxiliary *be*, as (63) shows. The other tests work straightforwardly.
    Now compare attributive APs:

(67)   Permutation:
            a.   *It's sweet that John ate [the t cookies].   (clefting)
            b.   *How sweet did John eat [the t cookies]?   (wh-movement)
            c.   *Sweet, John ate [the t cookies].   (fronting)

(68)   Pro-form:
            John likes his sweet cookies → *John likes his so cookies.

(69)   Ellipsis:
            *John ate the sweet cookies and the s̶w̶e̶e̶t̶ cake.

(70)   Coordination:
            John ate the sweet and extremely fattening cookies.

(71)   Fragment:
            A: What kind of cookies did John eat?
            B: Sweet ones/*sweet.

Here the only test that works is coordination. In (67), we can interpret the AP as predicative, with the examples deriving from *John ate the cookies sweet*, but

this, as we have seen, is a different syntactic context. For this reason, I bracketed the NP to indicate that *sweet* here corresponds to the prenominal position
inside NP. Understood this way, these examples are clearly ungrammatical.
Similarly, pro-form *so* and ellipsis are impossible in the NP-internal position.
In (69), the sequence *John ate the sweet cookies and the cake* is of course grammatical, but *sweet* cannot be recovered as a modifier for *cake* and so the ellipsis
indicated is ungrammatical. In (71), *sweet* seems to need a nominal pro-form
ones for grammaticality. Nevertheless, the fact that coordination yields a grammatical result supports the idea that adnominal APs are constituents.

Finally, let's compare the two possible structures for (26b), repeated here:

(26b)   They gave [NP Mary] [AP sweet] cookies.

(72) a.   They gave [Mary sweet] [cookies].
       b.   They gave [Mary] [sweet cookies].

Here are the results of the tests applied to *Mary sweet* in (72a):

(73)   Permutation:
            a.   *It's Mary sweet that they gave t cookies. (clefting)
            b.   *What/how/who did they give t cookies? (wh-movement)
            c.   *Mary sweet, they gave t cookies. (fronting)

(74)   Pro-form:
            John gave Mary sweet cookies → *John gave her so cookies.

(75)   Ellipsis:
            *John gave Mary sweet cookies and Bill gave ~~her sweet~~ cake.

(76)   Coordination:
            ?John gave Mary sweet and Bill extremely fattening cookies.

(77)   Fragment:
            A: Who did John give what kind of cookies?
            B: *Mary sweet.

The only test which does not yield an ungrammatical result is coordination.
However, the (slightly marginal) structure is a special kind of coordinate
structure known as 'right node raising', involving permuting *cookies* to the
right and deleting a copy of this element. So the structure of (76) is actually
something like:

(78)   ?John gave Mary sweet ~~cookies~~ and Bill extremely fattening cookies.

What this shows is that *cookies* is a constituent (a noun), but nothing about
the sequence *Mary sweet*. So no tests reveal *Mary sweet* to be a constituent as
in (72a). Combined with the absence of any semantic or functional motivation for grouping these words together, in that *sweet* does not modify *Mary*,
we may conclude that the structure in (72a) is mistaken.

Now let us apply our tests to *sweet cookies* in (72b):

(79)   Permutation:
          a.   It's sweet cookies that they gave Mary t. (clefting)
          b.   What kind of cookies did they give Mary t? (wh-movement)
          c.   Sweet cookies, they gave Mary t. (fronting)

(80)   Pro-form:
          John gave Mary sweet cookies → *John gave her them.

(81)   Ellipsis:
          *John gave Mary sweet cookies and Bill gave Mary ~~sweet cookies~~ too.

(82)   Coordination:
          John gave Mary sweet cookies and Bill gave Mary extremely fattening cakes.

(83)   Fragment:
          A: What did John give Mary?
          B: Sweet cookies.

Here all the tests work straightforwardly except ellipsis. English does not allow ellipsis of argument NPs. We can see this from the following contrast:

(84) a.   John brought his friend but Bill didn't ~~bring his friend~~.
     b.   *John brought his friend but Bill didn't bring ~~his friend~~.

VP, but not NP, elides in English. The opposite is true in Japanese:

(85) a.   *Kai-ga piza-o   tabeta, Lina-mo ~~piza-o tabe~~   sita.   [Japanese]
           Kai-NOM pizza-ACC eat.PST, Lina-also pizza. ACC eat do.PST
     b.   Taroo-wa zibun-no tomodati-o turetekita, demo Hanako-wa ~~zibun-no~~
           ~~tomodati-o~~
           Taroo.TOP self.GEN friend.ACC bring.PST, but Hanako.TOP self.GEN
           friend.ACC
           turetekona katta.
           bring not.PST
           'Taroo brought his friend, but Hanako did not bring her friend.'

Here we see ungrammatical VP-ellipsis in (85a), alongside grammatical NP-ellipsis on (85b). For reasons that are not at all well understood, languages vary as to which categories they allow to elide; we will return to this important observation in Volumes II and III. Obviously, the ellipsis possibilities a given language has will affect the results of ellipsis as a constituency test.

  Since all the other tests work for the structure in (72b), and none of them work for (72a), we take (72b) to be the correct structure for the sequence in question. This is consistent with the semantic, functional observation that *sweet* modifies *cookies*, but not *Mary*.

  Finally, constituency tests can be used to demonstrate that a string of words is structurally ambiguous, i.e. that the same string of words corresponds to two distinct structural descriptions with two distinct meanings. An example is the following sentence (attributed to Groucho Marx):

(86)   I shot an elephant in my pyjamas.

This sentence has two meanings, depending on who was wearing the pyjamas. The natural reading is that I was wearing my pyjamas (perhaps because the elephant broke into my house one night). The other reading is that the elephant was wearing the pyjamas (this was the one Groucho intended as he went on 'I've no idea why he was wearing them').

The two interpretations of the sentence correspond to the following structural descriptions:

(87) a.   I shot [NP an elephant [PP in my pyjamas]].
     b.   I shot [NP an elephant] [PP in my pyjamas].

In (87a), the PP *in my pyjamas* is inside the object NP and so modifies *elephant*; this is Groucho's intended interpretation: the elephant was wearing his pyjamas. In (87b), that PP is outside the object NP and is interpreted as modifying the subject, so this is the perhaps more 'normal' reading where I was wearing my pyjamas.

Let us now apply the constituency tests to the sequence *an elephant in my pyjamas* ((i)-examples below) and *an elephant* ((ii)-examples below). I have written 'Groucho' or 'normal' after each unambiguous example, 'Groucho' meaning the elephant was wearing the pyjamas (structure (87a)) and 'normal' meaning I was wearing the pyjamas (structure (87b)). If the example is ambiguous, this is indicated; if the example is ungrammatical, no indication of interpretation is given.

(88)   Permutation:
       a.   i.   It was an elephant in my pyjamas I shot. (Groucho)
             ii.   It was an elephant I shot in my pyjamas. (normal/ambiguous)
       b.   i.   What did I shoot?   (Groucho/vague)
             ii.   What did I shoot in my pyjamas?   (normal)
       c.   i.   An elephant in my pyjamas, I shot.   (Groucho)
             ii.   An elephant, I shot in my pyjamas.   (normal)

(89)   Pro-form:
       i.   I shot it.   (Groucho/vague)
       ii.   I shot it in my pyjamas.   (normal)

(90)   (VP-)ellipsis:
       i.   I shot an elephant in my pyjamas and John did ~~shoot an elephant in my pyjamas~~ too.   (Groucho)
       ii.   I shot an elephant in my pyjamas and John did ~~shoot an elephant~~ in my pyjamas too.   (John)

(91)   Coordination:
       i.   I shot an elephant in my pyjamas and a tiger in my favourite teeshirt. (ambiguous)
       ii.   I shot an elephant and a tiger in my pyjamas. (ambiguous)

(92)   Fragment:
            A: What did you shoot?
            B: i.   An elephant in my pyjamas. (Groucho)
                  ii.   An elephant.   (normal/vague)

The permutation tests, especially clefting in (88a) and fronting in (88c), clearly
distinguish the two structures in (87) and each reading is consistent: where *an
elephant in my pyjamas* is a constituent, we have Groucho's interpretation, where
it is not, we have the 'normal' one. Example (88b,i) is slightly equivocal, in that
in my pyjamas may be completely unspecified, hence the designation 'vague'.
However, if forced to choose between the two readings in (87) for (88b,i), the
Groucho one is clearly preferred. Similar considerations apply to (89i): *in my
pyjamas* may be left unspecified. But (89ii) allows only the 'normal' reading.
VP-ellipsis gives an interesting result in (90ii), as the interpretation is that John
was wearing my pyjamas. This is consistent with the structure in (87b), where
pyjamas modifies the subject. The fragment test in (92) gives a completely
unambiguous result in (92i), the Groucho reading, but, again, the possibility of a
vague reading in (92ii). Leaving aside the coordination result for a moment, all
of these tests, with one or two provisos, disambiguate the structural ambiguity
of (86) and reveal that the ambiguity is attributable to the different structural
descriptions, associated in turn with different semantic interpretations, in (87).

The coordination examples in (91) are both ambiguous, however. This is due
to the ambiguity of coordination more generally. The bracketings given in (93)
illustrate the ambiguities:

(93) i.   I shot [an elephant [in my pyjamas]] and [a tiger [in my favourite tee-
            shirt]].   (Groucho)
            I shot [an elephant] [in my pyjamas] and [a tiger] [in my favourite tee-
            shirt].   (normal)
      ii.   I shot [[an elephant and a tiger] [in my pyjamas]].   (Groucho)
            I shot [an elephant and a tiger] [in my pyjamas].   (normal)

The first example in (93i) coordinates two direct objects each with the internal
structure seen in (87a), and so unambiguously yields the Groucho interpretation.
The second example coordinates a constituent consisting of the sequence *NP
PP*, where PP is not a constituent of NP and so does not modify NP. This constituent is probably a VP, where the verb in the second conjunct has been 'gapped'
(a form of ellipsis affecting just V, not VP, as in *I spoke to Mary about John
and to Bill about Pete*). In the first example of (93ii), both the elephant and the
tiger were wearing my rather capacious pyjamas; clearly a case of the Groucho
reading which is rather more absurd than even he intended. The second example in (93ii) is a straightforward case of the normal reading. So the ambiguities
in (91) result from ambiguities regarding exactly which constituents are being
coordinated, disambiguated by the bracketings in (93). Finally, the bracketing in
(94) gives a further example of the ambiguities of coordination:

(94)   I shot [an elephant] and [a tiger [in my pyjamas]].

Example (94) is clearly interpreted to mean that the tiger, but not the elephant, was wearing my pyjamas. This reading arises from the fact that *in my pyjamas* modifies *tiger* here, since it is a constituent of the same NP. Once again, we see that constituency tests can probe for structural ambiguity and reveal that ambiguity to be a consequence of the different structural descriptions, each unambiguously associated with different semantic interpretations.

In this section we have introduced, explained and applied the principal kinds of constituency tests. Two important points should always be borne in mind in connection with these tests. First, only a positive result is a real result: if a test for constituent X fails, it does not show that X is not a constituent; in fact, it does not show anything. Second, one aspect of syntactic variation across languages involves the range of permutation operations, pro-forms, ellipses, coordinations and even fragments a given language allows. So what may work as a good test in one language (e.g. VP-ellipsis in English) may not work in another language, as we have just seen in relation to VP-ellipsis in Japanese.

3.5 Summary and Conclusion

In this chapter we have seen how PS-rules generate the well-formed structural descriptions in a grammar. This formal, technical notion of well-formedness (and its contrary, ill-formedness, i.e. putative structural descriptions not generated by PS-rules) aligns fairly closely with the intuitions concerning acceptability of native speakers of the I-language the grammar is a theory of. The PS-rules are therefore an important part of our account of native-speaker competence. Some basic PS-rules were introduced and illustrated in Section 3.2.

In Section 3.3, we showed how even quite small sets of PS-rules can interact so as to generate structural descriptions of unlimited length and depth. This is the recursive nature of systems of PS-rules, a feature of enormous theoretical importance, since it accounts for the unlimited expressive power of language. Recursive PS-rule systems directly capture the fact that natural language makes infinite use of finite means. Since this is an aspect of human cognition (seen not only in language but also in numbers), PS-rules formally capture an important aspect of cognition.

The structural descriptions generated by PS-rules consist of particular arrangements of categories and constituents that we can represent as tree diagrams or labelled bracketings (we have seen numerous examples of both in this chapter). The particular choices of structural descriptions can be supported by constituency tests of various kinds, which we introduced and illustrated in Section 3.4. The constituency tests are, to a degree which remains to be fully determined, in part language particular; the ones we have seen work quite well for English, but they may not give such clear results when applied to other languages. For this reason, and also because they can only verify a postulated structural description, failure of a constituency test to isolate constituent X does not prove that X is not a constituent. Constituency tests may also reveal the presence of categories we did not expect to find, such as the mystery category in (52) and (55d).

As we have pointed out several times, PS-rules simultaneously specify three kinds of formal information: relations of linear precedence among constituents, relations of hierarchical dominance/constituency among constituents and the category labels of the constituents. Being purely formal devices, however, they do not on their own specify semantic or functional relations among constituents, such as 'subject', 'predicate', 'modifier', etc. For this, we need to add something to our theory, a matter we come back to in Section 5.2. But we also need to limit the formal power of the rules themselves. This will be the goal of the next chapter.

Exercises

1. Phrase-Structure rules
    Take the following set of PS-rules:

      i.   S → NP VP
      ii.   VP → V (NP) (PP)
      iii.   NP → (D) N (PP)
      iv.   PP → P NP

    Give five structurally distinct, grammatical English sentences that these rules generate, showing their structure as a tree diagram.

2. Give the tree diagrams for the following sentences:

      a.   Goona hoped that Vurdy would eat the curry.
      b.   Harry thought that Ron said that Hermione knew the answer.
      c.   Pep wanted to know how much money Paul would want.
      d.   Andy wondered whether Lou would write a song.
      e.   Ron wondered whether to talk to Hermione.

3. Using the constituency tests discussed in this chapter (permutation, pro-forms, ellipsis, coordination, fragments), justify the constituent structure you have assigned to one of the sentences in (1) and (2).

4. The following sentences are structurally ambiguous. Explain the ambiguity, assign distinct structural representations (i.e. draw a tree or give labelled brackets) corresponding to each reading of the sentence, and show how constituency tests support the structures you propose in each case.

      a.   Mary ate the cake on the shelf.
      b.   Olly dreamt that his team won last night.
      c.   The chickens are ready to eat.

For Further Discussion

At the beginning of his 1957 book *Syntactic Structures* (The Hague: Mouton), Noam Chomsky writes that '[m]ost of our linguistic experience, both as speakers and hearers, is with new sentences; once we have mastered a language, the class of sentences with which we can operate fluently and without difficulty or hesitation is so vast that for all practical purposes (and, obviously, for all theoretical purposes), we may regard it as infinite' (p. 7). How do PS-rules of the kind we have seen in this chapter connect to this observation?

Further Reading

All of the readings given here introduce the notions of category, constituency and constituency tests, with some variations in emphasis and details. Sportiche et al. (2014) are particularly thorough and Freidin goes into interesting detail on coordination.

Carnie, A. 2010. *Constituent Structure*. Oxford: Oxford University Press, Chapter 2.

Carnie, A. 2013. *Syntax: A Generative Introduction*. Oxford: Blackwell, Chapters 3 and 4.

Freidin, R. 2012. *Syntax: Basic Concepts and Applications*. Cambridge: Cambridge University Press, Chapter 3.

Larson, R. 2010. *Grammar as Science*. Cambridge, MA: MIT Press, Unit 7.

Sportiche, D., H. Koopman & E. Stabler. (2014). *An Introduction to Syntactic Analysis and Theory*. Oxford: Wiley, Chapter 3.

Tallerman, M. 1998. *Understanding Syntax*. London: Routledge, Chapter 5.

4   X′-theory

4.1   Introduction

In the previous chapter we saw how PS-rules provide structural descriptions of sentences, in the form of labelled bracketings or tree diagrams, in terms of the key notions of categories and constituents. PS-rules specify the grammatical structures (the well-formed structural descriptions) of a given grammar, corresponding as far as possible to the I-language grammar of competent native speakers. PS-rules, or systems of PS-rules, can be recursive, in that they apply to their own output; they thereby specify an infinite set of well-formed structural descriptions. We saw several illustrations of this is in the previous chapter and in Chapter 1 with the fish examples. Constituency tests of various kinds show, on the basis of native-speaker well-formedness judgements, which structural descriptions are correct. Thus these tests can support the postulation of a given set of particular PS-rules. In this chapter we will revise and simplify the system of PS-rules.

4.2   Possible and Impossible PS-Rules

In (1), we see some PS-rules of English. We have already seen some of these, e.g. (1a) in the previous chapter:

(1) a.   NP → (D) N (PP)
    b.   AP → (Mod) A (PP)
    c.   PP → (Mod) P (NP)
    d.   VP → (AdvP) V (NP)

In (2a–d), we see the respective structural descriptions that rules (1a–d) generate, presented as labelled bracketings. Each one corresponds to the full expansion of each rule, i.e. with optional material realised:

(2) a.   [$_{NP}$ [$_D$ the] [$_N$ picture] [$_{PP}$ [$_P$ of] [$_{NP}$ [$_N$ John]]]]
    b.   [$_{AP}$ [$_{Mod}$ very] [$_A$ angry] [$_{PP}$ [$_P$ with] [$_{NP}$ [$_N$ John]]]]
    c.   [$_{PP}$ [$_{Mod}$ just] [$_P$ beyond] [$_{NP}$ [$_D$ the] [$_N$ frontier]]]
    d.   [$_{VP}$ [$_{AdvP}$ really] [$_V$ enjoy] [$_{NP}$ [$_D$ the] [$_N$ movie]]]

The examples in (2) show us that the PS-rules in (1) generate a series of well-formed structural descriptions and as such are PS-rules in good standing. In each case there is a lexical category (N, V, A or P) on the right of the arrow corresponding to the phrasal category on the left of the arrow.

Now compare the rules in (3):

(3) i.   NP → V AP
   ii.   PP → N V
   iii.   AP → V NP

None of these rules has a lexical category on the right of the arrow corresponding to the phrasal category on the left. These rules are certainly not rules of English: there is no NP constituent which consists of a verb and an AP, no PP which contains the sequence N V and no AP consisting of V and NP. The strings found to the right of the arrows do exist: *look nice* is a case of V AP; *Clover slept* is the string N V and any transitive verb followed by its object is a case of V NP order (*eat a mouse*, *like cake*, *visit London*, etc.). But *look nice* is not an NP, as we can see if we apply the basic distributional test for NPs given in Chapter 2. That test consisted in seeing whether a putative NP could appear in subject position, i.e. in the dash position in (4):

(4)   ___ can be a pain in the neck.

(5) shows us that the result of inserting *look nice* in that position is ungrammatical:

(5)   *Look nice can be a pain in the neck.

Similarly, we saw in Chapter 2 that N V sequences like *Clover slept* are really NP VP sequences, which make up an S. They cannot form a PP. This is shown by the fact that PP-modifiers like *straight* and *right* can't precede them:

(6)   *straight/right Clover slept

Furthermore, V NP sequences like *eat a mouse*, etc., cannot appear in the AP-frame we identified in Chapter 2:

(7)   *The students are very eat a mouse/like cake/visit London, ...

We can safely conclude that, while the PS-rules in (2) certainly do generate well-formed structural descriptions for English, those in (3) do not. Languages differ somewhat from one another regarding their PS-rules, but we might reasonably ask whether any language would counter structures of the kind generated by the rules in (3). Since each PS-rule specifies a relation of immediate dominance/constituency, the rules in (3) generate trees of the kind shown in (8):

(8)   i.

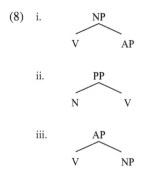

      ii.

      PP
      ⌃
   N   V

      iii.

      AP
      ⌃
   V   NP

Structures of this kind have never been postulated, and it seems highly unlikely
that they ever will be. If it is true that these structures are part of the grammar of
no natural language, then our theory of UG must rule them out. That means that
the PS-rules in (3) should be ruled out of our theory. The theory of PS-rules, as
we presented it in the previous chapter, does not do this. Hence we must develop
a way of doing this.

4.3   Introducing X'-theory

What is the difference between the 'good', attested, PS-rules in (1)
and the 'crazy', unattested (as far as we know) PS-rules in (3)? Let us look again
at both sets, side by side:

(1) a.   NP → (D) N (PP)
     b.   AP → (Mod) A (PP)
     c.   PP → (Mod) P (NP)
     d.   VP → (AdvP) V (NP)

(3) i.   NP → V AP
     ii.   PP → N V
     iii.   AP → V NP

The main difference between the rules in (1) and the rules in (3), as we observed
in the previous section, is that those in (1) have 'different versions' of the same
category on each side of the arrow, while that is not true of those in (3). In fact,
the rules in (1) have phrasal categories on the left of the arrow and word-level
versions of the same categories on the right of it. Not only that, but everything
else in the expansion of the respective categories is optional. So the rules in (1)
could be written in a more schematic form as:

(9) a.   NP → ... N ...
     b.   AP →... A ...
     c.   PP →... P...
     d.   VP →... V ...

We have seen examples of the minimal expansions of each of these categories:

(10) a.   [NP [N Clover]]
   b.   [AP [A sweet]]
   c.   [PP [P on]]
   d.   [VP [V slept]]

So one generalisation about the well-formed PS-rules in (1) is that they all consist of a phrasal category to the left of the arrow and at least a single-word version of that category to the right. Call the single-word version of the phrasal category the **head** of the phrase, or just the head. So, the generalisation is that whatever else appears to the right of the arrow, the head of the phrase that appears to the left must appear there. To put it another way, every phrase must have a head. The technical term for 'having a head' is **endocentric** (as opposed to **exocentric**, not having a head). So every phrase generated by the well-formed PS-rules has a head. This is the endocentricity requirement: virtually all phrasal categories are headed.

Now we can see what is wrong with the PS-rules in (3): they all generate exocentric categories. None of the rules in (3) meets the endocentricity requirement, while all of those in (1) do. We can generalise the endocentricity requirement by generalising over the partial rules in (9) as follows:

(11)   XP → ... X ...

Here 'X' is a categorial variable ranging over the syntactic categories (just as in algebra x is a variable ranging over numbers). Since all the good PS-rules in (1) conform to (11) and none of the crazy ones in (3) do, let us make (11) a general requirement on PS-rules. So all PS-rules must conform to the template in (11). This significantly limits the number and the form of PS-rules. So we have now successfully eliminated the PS-rules in (3).

Looking again at the well-formed PS-rules in (1), we can make a further generalisation. In addition to requiring a head of the same category as the category on the left of the arrow, all the rules allow optional material both to the left and to the right of the head. In the case of AP, PP and VP, the material to the left of the head is always modificational and, as such, optional. In the case of NP, it is D(eterminer), which we will take for now to also be a kind of modifier although we know that Ds are sometimes obligatory (e.g. singular count nouns cannot stand alone in subject or object position: recall *Boy fish* from Section 1.4). Turning to the material following heads in (1), we see that N and A are followed by PP, while V and P are followed by NP. In (2), we exemplified these as follows:

(12) a.   The picture of John
   b.   very angry with John
   c.   just beyond the frontier
   d.   really enjoy the movie

In (12c) and (12d) the NPs are clearly objects of P and V respectively. We can maintain the same for N and A in (12a,b), noting that these objects are obligatorily prepositional, i.e. they must be introduced by a Preposition (*of*, *with*).

So, the well-formed PS-rules obey the endocentricity requirement in (11), have modifiers to the left of the head and **complements** to the right. In other words all the good rules conform to the template in (13):

(13)   XP: (Modifier) X (complement)

The material preceding X is called the **Specifier** of X; this term generalises over truly optional modifiers like *right*, *very*, etc., and determiners: the notion is that what is common to all these pre-head elements is that they specify something about the head. So the Determiner 'specifies' something about the Noun (through quantification, for example); the modifier 'specifies' something about the A, P, etc.

The material following X is called the complement of X. Complements may be obligatory; this depends on the lexical properties of X. This is easiest to see with verbs, as verbs have the richest range of complements. As we briefly saw with *put* in the previous chapter, verbs **categorially select**, or **c-select**, for their complements. Here are some further examples of verbal c-selection requirements:

(14) a.   watch(V) ___ NP   So: VP → V NP
     b.   rely(V) ___ PP   So: VP → V PP
     c.   put(V) ___ NP PP   So: VP → V NP PP
     d.   say(V) ___ S′   So: VP → V S′

(Strictly speaking, verbs and other categories c-select the head of their complement, but the endocentricity requirement has the effect that c-selection introduces phrasal categories corresponding to the selected head.) On the left in (14a–d), we see examples of the **lexical entries** of verbs. The lexicon is the mental dictionary (stored in the long-term memory of every competent native speaker of an I-language) containing idiosyncratic information about all the words in the I-language (i.e. all the words a given speaker knows). We will say more about selection and the lexicon in Chapter 8 and in Volume II; for now, the simplified lexical entries given in (14) suffice.

The lexical entry on the left of (14a) says that *watch* is a verb that c-selects an NP; the '__NP' notation means the verb must appear in the position immediately before NP. On the right in (14a), we have the PS-rule which expands VP so as to create the structure required by the c-selection property of *watch*. This rule generates NP as the complement of V. Clearly, *watch* here represents the very large class of basic transitive verbs, verbs which take just a direct object. Having a lexical entry like this (with further information about the phonological and semantic properties of the word) stored in long-term memory is a part of what it means for a native speaker to 'know' the word.

The lexical entry in (14b) states that *rely* c-selects a PP, which in fact must be headed by *on*: *rely on/*with/*for/*up John*. The PS-rule generating the corresponding expansion of VP, needed to accommodate this requirement, generates a PP in the complement of V. The lexical entry in (14c) is the one for *put*, which we briefly saw in Chapter 3. Here VP needs both an NP and a PP position, since *put* c-selects both; see the discussion around (42) in Chapter 3. Finally, in (14d) we have the lexical entry for *say*, which specifies that this verb c-selects S': *say [$_{S'}$ that the world is round]*. The corresponding expansion of VP is given on the right. Putting all the PS-rules on the right of (14) together, we come to something fairly close to the expansion of VP given in (24iii) of Chapter 3.

In (15), we see the first version of the full **'X'-schema' for PS-rules** (pronounced 'X-bar'):

(15) a.   XP → Specifier X'
     b.   X' → X complement

(Recall that X is a categorial variable whose possible values are one of N, V, A, P.) The rules in (15) are slightly more complicated than (13), in that they introduce an extra level of structure; this is the X'-level which gives this version of the theory of phrase structure its name.

The tree structure generated by the rules in (15) is (16):

(16)

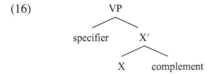

In (16) we can readily see how the X'-level creates different levels of syntactic 'closeness' for the complement and the Specifier in relation to the head. This relative 'closeness' is structurally represented. The complement is closer to the head, since it is obligatory and its category depends on the lexical c-selection properties of the head, as illustrated for various verbs in (14). The Specifier is usually (but not always, as we have seen) optional and modifies or 'determines' the head in various ways. The structure in (16) represents the greater relative closeness, both syntactic and semantic, of the complement to the head.

The terms 'Specifier' and 'complement', although more abstract than 'subject', 'object', etc., are equally relational. We have repeatedly stated that PS-rules do not (directly) give relational information. These relational terms should be replaced with categories. With the apparent exception of S', all the complements in (14) are phrasal; in X'-theory terms, they are all XPs. To distinguish them categorially from the head X that c-selects them, let us call them YP (where Y is just another, distinct categorial variable). We will return to the status of S' below. The Specifier elements, with the exception of D, are all phrasal modifiers. For uniformity, let us also then treat D as phrasal, DP. Then Specifiers are always phrasal. To distinguish them from the X'-category they specify and from the YP complement to X, call them ZP (Z is yet another distinct categorial variable). So the correct version of the X'-schema for PS-rules is (17):

(17) a.   XP → ZP X'
     b.   X' → X YP

The tree diagram representing the structural description (or the template for structural descriptions, where X, Y and Z are all categorial variables) generated by (17) is given in (18):

(18)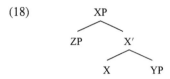

Y and Z are further categorial variables, substitutable with different values from X. So YP and ZP are each expanded as in (17) and so have the internal structure seen in (18). Clearly, then, the X′-system is fully recursive.

We have posited a new kind of constituent in (17) and (18): the intermediate level category X′. So far, we have only given a functional justification for X′, saying that it allows us to distinguish the relative closeness of complements to 'their' heads, as opposed to Specifiers. But we must be able to prove its presence using constituency tests of the kind introduced in Section 3.4. The coordination test clearly isolates X′, in that X′-level constituents can be coordinated:

(19) a.   the [pictures of John] and [books about Mary]
     b.   just [beyond the frontier] and [down the road]
     c.   very [angry with John] and [worried about Mary]
     d.   really [enjoy the movie] and [dislike the book]

In (19a), *the* modifies the head of both conjuncts: *books about Mary* can be interpreted as definite despite the fact that the string *books about Mary* can stand alone as a plural indefinite NP (with a silent determiner). Similarly, in (19b–d) Mod can apply to both conjuncts in each case.

The permutation tests do not give good results, however:

(20) a.   *It's pictures of John that we saw the t.   (clefting)
     b.   *Which pictures of John did you see the t?   (wh-movement)
     c.   *Pictures of John, we saw the t.   (fronting)

The pro-form test does give a good result, using *one* as the pro-form, as the following examples illustrate:

(21) a.   John read a book of poems and Mary read one too.
     b.   *John read a book of poems and Mary read one of stories.
     c.   John read a book with a red cover and Mary read one too.
     d.   John read a book with a red cover and Mary read one with a blue cover.

In (21a), *one* appears to stand for the whole NP *the book of poems*. The unacceptability of (21b) shows that *one* must stand for the complement of *book*, the PP *of stories*. In (21c), *one* once again appears to stand for the whole NP *the book with a red cover*. But in (21d) we see that *with a blue cover* is not obligatorily part of the constituent *one* stands for. Here we see a pattern similar to the one we saw with the examples in (41) in Chapter 3: the *with*-phrase, which is not a complement of *book* but an optional modifier, does not have to be substituted by the pro-form *one*. On the other hand, the *of*-phrases in (21a,b) are complements of *book* (they are not obligatory, but few complements to nouns are fully obligatory) and, as the unacceptability of (21b) shows, must be part of the constituent *one* stands for. Since *the* occupies the Specifier of N' (abbreviated SpecN'), and the complement must be part of what *one* stands for along with the head, we conclude that *one* is an N'-proform. We will come back to the question of the *with*-modifiers in Section 4.5 below; clearly they cannot be in the complement of N. So the structure of the NP *one with a blue cover* in (21d) is as in (22):

(22)

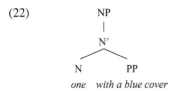

With certain Specifiers, N'-ellipsis is also possible:

(23) a.   John likes these shirts but I like those ~~shirts~~.
    b.   John read these books of poetry and I read those ~~books of poetry~~.
    c.   *John read these books of poetry and I read those ~~books~~ of poetry.
    d.   John read these books with red covers and I read those ~~books~~ with blue covers.
    e.   John read two books and I read three ~~books~~.
    f.   *John read every book but I read no ~~book~~.

Other determiners do not allow N'-ellipsis, either requiring the pro-form *one*, or not allowing ellipsis at all. We do not need to go into the details of this here; it suffices to note, once again, that the conditions under which ellipsis is possible are hard to define.

Finally, N'-fragments are not allowed:

(24) A: What did you read?
    B: *Book of poems.

We conclude that the coordination, pro-form and ellipsis tests reveal that N' is a constituent.

Concerning the other X' categories, neither P' nor A' can be permuted, like N':

(25) a.   *On the nose, she hit him right t.   (Radford 2016:126)[1]
    b.   *Proud of him, she certainly seems to be very t.   (Radford 2016:127)

P' can be substituted by the pro-form *there*:

(26)   She hit him right there.

---

[1] See Chapter 2, Further Reading.

A′ can, at least marginally, be substituted by the pro-form *so* (taking the comparative marker *more* to be in SpecA′) in predicative position but not in attributive position:

(27) a.   John is nice, but Mary is more so.
      b.   *John is a nice man, but Bill is a more so man.

PPs and APs can elide in predicative position (we did not look at these examples of PP-ellipsis in the discussion of ellipsis in Chapter 3), but P′ and A′ cannot:

(28) a.   John is intelligent/in London, and Bill is ~~intelligent/in London~~ too.
      b.   *John is very intelligent/right in London, and Bill is very ~~intelligent~~/right ~~in London~~ too.

So coordination and pro-forms provide some evidence for P′ and A′. I will leave the question of evidence for V′ aside, since we will entertain in later chapters a very different view of what is in SpecV′ from that suggested in (1d) and (2d) above.

  X′-theory presents a category-neutral view of hierarchical relations and linear precedence; the central idea is that these are the same for all categories. As such, idiosyncratic categorial information is removed from the PS-rules and supplied independently by **categorial features**: thus, the way in which we give a value to the categorial variable is by assigning a feature to it. However, the endocentricity of all X′-structures has one important consequence: if we specify the head X of a category as, say, N, then X′ must be N′ and XP must be NP. This is the notion of **projection** of categorial features. This idea leads to the following terminological conventions for X′-structures:

(29)

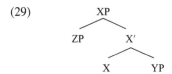

In a representation like this one, XP is called the **maximal projection** (of X), X′ is called the intermediate projection (of X), X is the head (of both X′ and XP) and, as we have seen, ZP is the Specifier of X′ (abbreviated SpecX′) and YP is the complement of the head X. The dominance and constituency relations are clear: XP dominates everything in XP and immediately dominates ZP and X′, while X′ immediately dominates X and YP.

  As we have seen, the nature of the complement depends on the c-selection properties of the head. We saw examples of this with various verbs in (14). Certain heads (common nouns, intransitive verbs, simple adjectives and some prepositions) may not c-select a complement at all:

(30) a.   Clover [VP slept].
      b.   [NP the cat]

c.   [_AP_ fat]
d.   John walked [_PP_ out].

Here, the relevant lexical entries specify that X c-selects nothing. For example, compare the lexical entry for *sleep* with those in (14):

(31)   sleep(V)__

Given (31), we must allow for a unary-branching expansion of V′. The same holds for N′, A′ and P′ in (30). Nonetheless, as a default we will assume that the hierarchical structure is complete. A proper name like *Goona*, for example, has the full non-branching structure shown in (31):

(32)

Of course, no information is lost if the full specification of this structure is left out, but X′-theory is assumed to operate in a consistent way. We will return to this issue in Chapter 8 of Volume II.

In this section we have seen the basics of X′-theory. This approach reduces the PS-rules to the rule schemata in (17), giving rise to the structural description (or template for structural descriptions) in (18). In this way, crazy rules like those in (3) are eliminated, since they cannot be reduced to (17). In (17), there is a further intermediate level of structure, the X′-level. We saw evidence from constituency tests for N′, A′ and P′ in favour of this level, leaving V′ aside for now. Finally, we introduced the relevant category-neutral terminology along with the idea of projection of categorial features. In contrast to more traditional PS-rules of the kind introduced in Chapter 3, the rules in (17) do not give category information: they do not provide constant categorial labels for nodes other than the categorial variables X, Y... Like the traditional PS-rules, however, the X′ rules do provide information about hierarchical relations of dominance and constituency and linear relations of precedence.

4.4   X′-theory and Functional Categories: The Structure of the Clause

In the previous section, we saw the basics of X′-theory in relation to the lexical categories N, V, A and P. Here we will extend the approach to functional categories, concluding that all categories are generated according to the schema in (17), i.e. resulting in structures like (18) (with the possibility of YP and ZP being absent).

Let us begin with auxiliaries. How do they fit the X′-schema? One possibility would be to treat the combination of the main verb and auxiliary as a complex verb form inside VP, along the lines shown in (33):

(33)   [$_{V'}$ [$_V$ Aux V] NP]

Constituency tests show us that this is wrong. We saw in Chapter 3 that VP-fronting, substitution of the VP pro-form *do so*, VP-ellipsis and coordination all show that VP is a constituent separate from the auxiliary:

(34) a.   (We expected John to talk to Mary),
            ... and [$_{VP}$ talk to Mary], he will/can/should/would t.
     b.   You said John should [$_{VP}$ talk to Mary] and he has already [$_{VP}$ done so].
     c.   I have [$_{VP}$ talked to Mary] and John has ~~talked to Mary~~ too.
     d.   The chairman has [$_{VP}$ resigned from the board] and [$_{VP}$ gone abroad].

This evidence rules out a structure like (33). We also saw in Chapter 3 that the exact counterpart of (34c), but with *has* also apparently deleted, is grammatical too:

(35)   I have talked to Mary and John ~~has talked to Mary~~ too.

The sequence in (35) is ambiguous, in that it can also mean 'I have talked both to Mary and to John'; this latter reading involves coordination inside the indirect object and no ellipsis. The reading that the strike-out in (35) indicates is the one where *John* is the subject, not the indirect object, of *talked*. We also saw that alongside (34d), we also have coordination patterns where the auxiliary is coordinated along with the verb and its complements:

(36)   The chairman has resigned from the board and is living in Ruritania.

So we see that constituency tests tell us that the sequence containing the verb and its complements is separate from the auxiliary, and that the auxiliary can combine with the verb and its complements to form a constituent. In Chapter 3, we referred to the latter as the mystery constituent, treating the former as VP:

(37)   [$_S$ [$_{NP}$ John] [$_{??}$ [$_{Aux}$ has] [$_{VP}$ passed the exam]]]

(37) represents one possibility. Another possibility is that Aux is in SpecV′ and what is labelled VP in (37) is actually V′. In other words, (38) could be the correct representation:

(38)   [$_S$ [$_{NP}$ John] [$_{VP}$ [$_{Aux}$ has] [$_{V'}$ passed the exam]]]

There are four reasons to favour (37) over (38). First, the verb+complement sequence (VP in (37), V′ in (38)) acts more like an XP than an X′ in relation to constituency tests. Second, complex sequences of auxiliaries can appear which do not act like a single constituent, but in which each auxiliary acts like a complement of the preceding one. Third, the auxiliaries carry sentential information regarding negation and interrogatives; SpecV′ does not seem the right place for carriers of such information. Fourth, we will see that when we bring the apparently exocentric category S into line with the X′-template there is a natural head position that we can place auxiliaries in. Let us look at these reasons one by one.

First, as we saw above several constituency tests for X′ fail: permutation, ellipsis (except N′-ellipsis under demonstratives and numerals) and the fragment test. But the putative V′ in (38) passes them all (permutation is restricted to fronting, for reasons given in Chapter 3):

(39) a.   (I expected John to pass the exam), and [passed the exam] he has!
    b.   John passed the exam and Mary did ~~pass the exam~~ too.
    c.   A: What did John do?
           B: Pass the exam.

The other XPs pass the permutation, ellipsis (with the exception of NP) and fragment tests and none of the X′s do. This makes the putative V′ in (38) look very different to the other categories. On the other hand, if we treat this sequence as VP, as in (37), it falls into line with the other XPs. Since X′-theory treats all lexical categories as participating in the same structural configurations, (37) thus appears to be a more desirable option than (38).

The second argument relates to sequences of auxiliaries. English allows up to four auxiliaries in a row, rigidly ordered as *Modal > Perfect have > Progressive be > Passive be*, as in:

(40)   (When you arrived), John must have been being interviewed.

If auxiliaries are Specifiers of V′, then (40) must have the structure in (41):

(41)   [s [NP John] [VP [Aux? must have been being] [v′ interviewed]]]

Constituency tests, particularly ellipsis, show us, however, that the sequence 'Aux?' in (41) comprises several separate constituents, along with V′ (some speakers, especially Americans, find (42d) ungrammatical, but I don't; this is further evidence that E-English does not correspond to a homogeneous set of I-languages and does not affect the argument being made here):

(42)   John must have been being interviewed right then, and …
    a.   Bill must have been ~~being interviewed~~ too.
    b.   Bill must have ~~been being interviewed~~ too.
    c.   Bill must ~~have been being interviewed~~ too.
    d.   Bill ~~must have been being interviewed~~ too.

Any sequence of auxiliaries and the main verb can be elided, but not a passive main verb on its own (recall that this doesn't show that the passive main verb is not a constituent). So we must have a structure like (43) for the auxiliary+main verb sequence where each bracketed constituent can be elided:

(43)   [must [have [been [being interviewed]]]]

We could label (43) as in (44), in line with (38):

(44)   [_{VP} must [_{V'} have [_{V'} been [_{V'} being interviewed]]]]

But now V' looks very different from other X' categories, in that it can have three Specifiers (or probably four, since *being* could be a fourth SpecV' although the ellipsis test doesn't show this). Furthermore, X'-ellipsis is hardly found with the other lexical categories. Instead, then, we could treat each V' in (44) as an AuxP of some kind. This is consistent with (37), but not with (38), so again (37) is favoured.

The third argument concerns negation and question-formation (in main clauses). The rule for negation of finite clauses in English is 'insert *not* after the first auxiliary'. We see this rule in action in (45), where *not* is contracted to *n't* and attached to the auxiliary (in some cases causing a phonological change to the auxiliary):

(45) a.   John can't speak Mandarin.
     b.   John won't leave tonight.
     c.   John hasn't passed the exam.
     d.   John isn't writing a book.

If there is no auxiliary in the positive sentence, the 'dummy' auxiliary *do* must appear in the negative:

(46)   John doesn't speak Mandarin.

Negation is semantically a sentence-level operation, denying the **proposition** asserted by the sentence. The structure in (38) obliges us to place *not* in SpecV', which seems an odd place for an element whose meaning affects the whole clause. At the very minimum, this complicates the relation between syntax and semantics. We will see below that such a complication is unnecessary.

As we saw in Chapter 2, auxiliaries undergo 'subject-aux inversion' in main-clause questions:

(47) a.   Cambridge will flood as a consequence of global warming.
     b.   Will Cambridge flood as a consequence of global warming?

Subject-auxiliary inversion clearly affects the meaning of the whole sentence, changing it from a declarative to an interrogative. As with negation, this seems an odd thing to attribute to a category that normally occupies SpecV' and leads to an unnecessarily complex relation between syntax and semantics. Furthermore, we have to find a way to account for the permutation relating SpecV' and the initial position in the sentence in order to account for the purely formal relation between (47a) and (47b), while we will see in Chapter 5 that there is a simpler alternative in terms of (37). Once again, (37) is favoured over (38).

Our fourth reason to prefer (37) over (38) is that it helps us bring S into line with X'-theory. Let us look again at the structure in (37):

(37)   [s [NP John] [?? [Aux has] [VP passed the exam]]]

When we first discussed the mystery category '??' here in the previous chapter, we pointed out that it entails a complication of the basic PS-rule for S:

(48)   S → NP VP

We could simply add Aux to (48), as follows:

(49)   S → NP Aux VP

However, rule (49) does not fit the X'-schema, and we have evidence from coordination and ellipsis that Aux and VP form a constituent distinct from NP here. At the very minimum, then, we need the two rules in (50):

(50)   i.   S → NP ??
       ii.   ?? → Aux VP

The rules in (50) will generate the structure in (37). So, the question we must now answer is: what category is '??'?

     X'-theory now suggests a simple answer: Aux is a head, '??' is the intermediate projection of Aux, Aux', and S is really the maximal projection of Aux, AuxP. In this way, Aux and its projections conform to the general X'-theory template; S ceases to be an exocentric exception to X'-theory; we know what '??' is (Aux'); the structure is consistent with the results of the various constituency tests we have been applying and consistent with the fact that negation and question-formation are sentence-level operations applying to Aux, since Aux is the head of the sentence.

     The tree diagram (51) gives the full structural description of a simple sentence as AuxP, generated by the rules in (50):

(51)

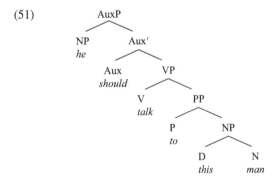

Here we see that the subject NP is in SpecAux' and VP is the complement of Aux. Everything is fully in line with the X'-template.

     What we have seen so far answers the question about the nature of the mystery category and brings S into line with X'-theory where an auxiliary is present. But what about sentences without an auxiliary, i.e. simple examples like the following?

(52) a.   John left.
    b.   Mary smokes.
    c.   Fish fish fish.

Although there is no auxiliary in examples like (52), there is still a tense: (52a) is marked for past tense, (52b) is, at least indirectly, marked for present tense by the third-person singular agreement and, as we argued in Chapter 1, the verb *fish* in (52c) has a silent present-tense marker. Auxiliaries often mark tense too, notably English future *will* and *shall*, while *have* marks perfect, which is at least partly a tense. So let us rechristen AuxP as TenseP, or TP. This is arguably a less parochially English label than AuxP, as very many languages have tense marking but auxiliaries are arguably somewhat rarer. Very few languages have an auxiliary system as rich as English, allowing, as we saw in (42), up to four auxiliaries in a row.

So we replace (51) with (53):

(53)

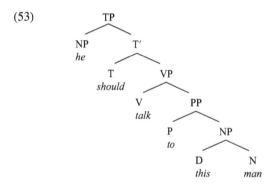

Here the subject is in SpecT′, the head of the clause is T and VP is the complement of T in T′.

We can make some sense of the English phenomenon of '***do*-support**' in terms of the structure in (52). The basic rule is that if no auxiliary is independently present in the main clause, *do* appears where VP is elided, where the sentence is negated or where subject-auxiliary inversion takes place:

(54) a.   Sarah finished her paper, and Mary did ~~finish her paper~~ too.
    b.   Sarah didn't finish her paper.
    c.   Did Sarah finish her paper?

The appearance of *do* where the verb is elided implies that tense and agreement must always be expressed. If there is no verb or auxiliary independently available, *do* is inserted. Similarly, we can think that the presence of negation in (54b) and the intervening subject in (54c) mean that the operation combining T with V, which clearly takes place in examples like (52a,b) (and covertly in (52c)), is somehow prevented from applying, and so the meaningless auxiliary *do* is inserted, in order to mark tense and agreement. The auxiliary *do* should be distinguished from the homophonous main verb *do*, as in *do the tango*: the latter *do* also requires *do*-support in the relevant contexts, as (54) shows:

(55) a. Mary did the tango.
  b. Mary didn't do the tango.
  c. *Mary didn't the tango.
  d. Did Mary do the tango?
  e. *Did Mary the tango?

Generalising from AuxP to TenseP also gives us a way to analyse infinitival *to*, a question we left open in Section 3.3. There we saw that there were two possible analyses for the infinitival complement sentence in *Goona arranged for [Vurdy to arrive on time]*, repeated here:

(56) a. [s [NP Vurdy] [? to] [VP arrive on time]]
  b. [s [NP Vurdy] [VP to arrive on time]]

Two of the four arguments we gave for treating VP in finite clauses as a constituent separate from Aux/T apply to the infinitives with *to*. Constituency tests such as fronting, ellipsis and fragments give very similar results to those seen in (39) for finite clauses, for example (although (55a) is not quite as natural as the other examples):

(57) a. ?(Goona arranged for Vurdy to arrive on time) and [arrive on time] he managed to!
  b. Goona wanted to arrive on time and Vurdy wanted to ~~arrive on time~~ too.
  c. A: What did Goona want Vurdy to do?
    B: Arrive on time.

Furthermore, infinitival *to* can be followed by a sequence of auxiliaries which shows the same order as in finite clauses. The only difference with finite clauses is that modals cannot appear:

(58) We arranged for Bill to (*must) have been being interviewed, when you arrived.

Since modals are intrinsically finite in Modern English, they are in complementary distribution with *to*, which is intrinsically non-finite. Modals and *to* are always followed by an uninflected verb or auxiliary; similarly, *do* is in examples like (54a,b). The arguments related to negation and inversion given above do not apply to *to*: the contracted negation *n't* is restricted to finite clauses and inversion can only apply in main clauses, while infinitives are always embedded. But we can conclude from (57) and (58) that the mystery category in (56a) is T and that *to* is the marker of non-finite T.

So we can bring S fully into line with X′-theory as TP. The next question concerns S′. Can this apparently exocentric category be reduced to the X′-template? Here we will see how this can be done, but we will leave one major question open until the next chapter. Let us look again at the representation of a sentence containing an embedded complement clause introduced by the complementizer *that* (here S has been replaced by TP, Aux by T, and T′s have been added, along with specification [Pres] in the main-clause T):

(59)

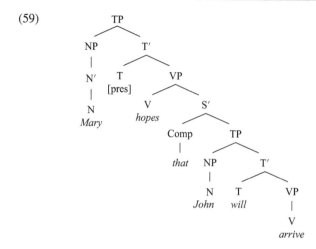

In Chapter 3, we introduced the following rule expanding S':

(60)   S' → Comp S

If we treat complementisers as heads, then we restate (60) as:

(61)   CP → C(omp) TP

Here, CP stands for 'Complementiser Phrase', i.e. the maximal projection of C(omp). So we render S' endocentric by treating complementisers as heads and by treating TP as the structural complement of C. This seems justified in that different elements occupying C select for different kinds of TP: *that* requires a finite TP, *for* requires a non-finite TP and *whether* allows either (*John wondered whether to leave/whether he should leave*).

The step from (60) to (61) does not actually accord with the X'-template, however. Strictly, to bring CP in line with the template we should have the two rules in (62):

(62) i.   CP → ZP C'
      ii.   C' → C TP

This raises the question of what corresponds to ZP in (62i), i.e. what can function as SpecC'. I will leave this question open until Chapter 5.

Another question is whether we need CP in main clauses. Up to now we have treated S'/CP as the category for subordinate clauses and S/TP as that for main clauses. This is justified to the extent that the material following *that* in a finite subordinate clause corresponds to a stand-alone main clause. But this does not, in itself, preclude the possibility of a silent C introducing main clauses. Furthermore the rules in (62) would clearly generate this structure. Some languages, e.g. some varieties of Welsh and Gascon, seem to have overt Cs introducing declarative main clauses, and many languages have interrogative particles similar to English *if* and *whether* introducing main-clause questions, supporting the idea that main clauses are CPs, i.e. introduced by the rules in (62). In Chapter 7, when we look at the syntax of languages other than English, we will see that German supports the presence of a main-clause CP.

4.5   Adjuncts in X′-theory

We saw in Chapter 3 that the pro-form test enables us to see whether a phrase is an argument or an adjunct. Here are our examples from Chapter 3 (see (41) of Chapter 3):

(63) a.   John put his car in the garage on Tuesday, and Peter did so too.
     b.   *John put his car in the garage on Tuesday, and Peter did so on the drive on Wednesday.
     c.   *John put his car in the garage on Tuesday, and Peter did so his bike on Wednesday.
     d.   John put his car in the garage on Tuesday, and Peter did so on Wednesday.

We saw that (63d) can be taken to indicate that adjuncts are outside the VP and so are not substituted under *do so* replacement, but the fact that the substituted VP in (63a) is interpreted as *put his car in the garage on Tuesday* indicates that the adjunct PP is part of the VP. We concluded that adjuncts are optional constituents of VP, while selected arguments are obligatory constituents of VP.

In terms of X′-theory, selected arguments are complements of X inside X′, so the NP *his car* and the PP *in the garage* in (63) are in V′. This, combined with the two-layer structure of XPs given by the X′-template, allows us to make a structural distinction between arguments and adjuncts. We can treat adjuncts as categories adjoined to V′ in a structure like (64):

(64)

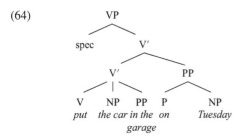

The sequence *V – object NP – locative PP* forms the V′. It consists of *put*, a V head of V′ and VP, and the c-selected arguments of *put*; NP and (locative) PP. The optional modifier, the adjunct temporal PP *on Tuesday*, is adjoined to V′ as sister of one occurrence of V′ and daughter of another occurrence of V′. If we now construe *do so* substitution as applying to V′, it can freely substitute either the upper or the lower V′ in (64), giving the two possibilities in (63a) and (63d), and giving rise to the interpretation of the elided larger V′ in (63a) as containing the PP *on Tuesday*.

Similar considerations apply in the case of the examples in (21), repeated here:

(21) a.   John read a book of poems and Mary read one too.
      b.   *John read a book of poems and Mary read one of stories.
      c.   John read a book with a red cover and Mary read one too.
      d.   John read a book with a red cover and Mary read the one with a blue cover.

Since selected arguments are complements of X inside X′, the PPs *of poems*
and *of stories* in (21a,b) are in N′, as complements of the noun *book*. Since *one*
substitutes for N′, it must substitute the complement to N, hence the ungrammaticality of (21b). On the other hand, the two *with*-PPs in (21c,d) are optional
N′-adjuncts in a structure like (65):

(65)

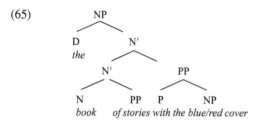

In cases of N′-substitution the adjunct PPs are optionally substituted, while the
complement PPs are obligatorily substituted.

Putting this approach to adjuncts together with the rest of the X′-template, we
have the following set of category-neutral PS-rules:

(66) a.   XP → ZP X′
      b.   X′ → X′ WP
      c.   X′ → X YP

These rules define the following relations:

(67) a.   Complement = sister of X, daughter of X′
      b.   Adjunct = sister of X′, daughter of X′
      c.   Specifier = sister of X′, daughter of XP

We can generalise the notion of adjunction in (67b) to 'sister of X^n' and 'daughter of X^n', where X^n may be any bar-level. This allows adjunction to maximal
projections (XPs) and heads (Xs). We will largely leave these possibilities aside
here and return to the nature of adjunction in Volume II.

The universalist assumption is that, by default, all phrasal categories in all languages will have the internal structure generated by the rules in (64) and so can
be described in terms of (65), along, of course, with the central notions of head
(X) and maximal projection, XP. This represents a very strong claim about UG
and about the possible structures we expect to find in the languages of the world.

4.6   Conclusion

In this chapter we have seen how we can posit a single X′-template
which subsumes the PS-rules of English which we saw in Chapter 3 and explains

why only rules of that kind and not 'crazy' rules like those in (3) are possible. The template, complete with the possibility of X′-adjunction, is given in (68):

(68)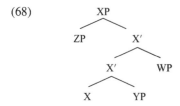

Here ZP is the Specifier (SpecX′), WP is an adjunct adjoined to X′ and YP is the selected complement of X.

X′-theory also captures the endocentricity of phrases, always consisting of a head, and possibly taking other phrases as its complement and Specifier; exocentric categories are predicted not to exist. Furthermore, we saw evidence from constituency tests for the intermediate levels of phrase structure at X′ (i.e. N′, P′, A′, etc.). In this connection, the apparently exocentric categories S and S′ were replaced with TP and CP, examples of how functional categories obey the X′-template. A natural further assumption would be that the other 'satellite' functional categories we saw in Chapter 1 (Mood, Agr, Num and D) also conform to X′-theory. This point will be further developed in Volume II.

We have left one important question open, though: we have not said what can fill SpecC′, i.e. what ZP in (62i) can be. This question will be answered when we look at wh-movement, the topic of the next chapter.

Exercises

1. Give the tree diagrams for the following NPs, and comment on how they instantiate, or fail to instantiate, the X′-schema:

    a. him
    b. the composer of *Yesterday*
    c. two pints of beer
    d. my cat
    e. his professor of phonetics
    f. John's cat

2. Give the tree diagrams for the following APs and PPs, and comment on how they instantiate, or fail to instantiate, the X′-schema:

    a. in Paris
    b. just over the fence
    c. out from under the bed
    d. just there
    e. very worried about the result
    f. really amused that Boris hates Michel

3.   Give the tree diagrams for the following clauses, and comment on how they instantiate, or fail to instantiate, the X′-schema:

    a.   Andy visited.
    b.   Andy has insulted Lou.
    c.   We had guessed that Andy would insult Lou.
    d.   We had thought that Andy would admit that she had insulted Lou.
    e.   I have very much enjoyed this lecture.
    f.   Lou asked if he should ignore Andy.
    g.   Lou asked whether to ignore Andy.
    h.   Lou could have ignored Andy.
    i.   Lou decided on the plane.

For Further Discussion

Discuss the ways in which X′-theory improves on the format of Phrase-Structure rules we saw in the previous chapter. Are there are any disadvantages of X′-theory in relation to the earlier format?

Further Reading

Carnie, A. 2013. *Syntax: A Generative Introduction*. Oxford: Blackwell, Chapters 6–8.

Freidin, R. 2012. *Syntax: Basic Concepts and Applications*. Cambridge: Cambridge University Press, Chapter 5.

Fromkin, V., R. Rodman & N. Hyamset. 2000. *Linguistics: An Introduction to Linguistic Theory*. Oxford: Blackwell, Chapter 3.

Haegeman, L. 1995. *Introduction to Government and Binding Theory*. Oxford: Blackwell, Chapter 3.

Haegeman, L. & J. Guéron. 1999. *English Grammar: A Generative Perspective*. Oxford: Blackwell, Sections 1.2.4 and 1.2.5.

Larson, R. 2010. *Grammar as Science*. Cambridge, MA: MIT Press, Units 14–18.

Sportiche, D., H. Koopman & E. Stabler. 2014. *An Introduction to Syntactic Analysis and Theory*. Oxford: Wiley, Chapters 4–6.

5 Movement

5.1 Introduction and Recap

In the previous chapter we saw how X′-theory can give us a sim-plified and more abstract format for PS-rules and, correspondingly, for the struc-tures they generate. The basic template for categories that X′-theory specifies is given in (1):

(1)
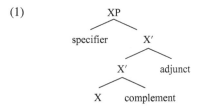

Here, as we saw, the complement is the sister of X and daughter of X′, the adjunct is the sister of X′ and the daughter of X′ (we mentioned that XP- and head-adjunction may also be possible) and the Specifier is sister of X′ and daughter of XP. Specifier, adjunct and complement are all relational notions, defined in terms of two positions in the tree. The truly primitive notions are the structural ones X, X′ and XP. These relations are in turn defined in terms of the categorical value of X (remember that X is a variable ranging over categories) and the notion of projection from X to X′ to XP.

More generally, what we have seen up to now is that PS-rules generate well-formed structural descriptions (whether formulated in terms of X′-theory or not, although in the last chapter we saw good reasons to prefer X′-theory over the more 'traditional' kind of PS-rules). The structural descriptions are represented as tree diagrams or labelled bracketings, those generated by X′-theory being more abstract, in particular in that they generate a category-neutral template which is in principle the same for all lexical and functional categories. In either format, the PS-rules can create recursive, and therefore potentially infinite, structures.

All of this gives us a good basis for the theory of constituent structure, but there are two questions which we need to address, one quite specific and one much more general. The specific question is one we have held over from our discussion in the previous chapter of how X′-theory applies to functional cate-gories: what goes in the Specifier of CP?

The general question relates to the kinds of rules PS-rules are, whether restricted to X′-theory or not. An obvious way to think about PS-rules is as 'building rules': as we apply them, we build up the constituent structure. As we saw in Chapter 3, we can relate each PS-rule to a specific 'treelet', a little piece of a tree diagram; look again at (13) of Chapter 3 and the preceding discussion. The same can be said of X′-theory. We can relate the X′ PS-rules given in (66) of Chapter 4 and repeated here as (2) to the tree in (3):

(2) a.   XP → ZP X′
    b.   X′ → X′ WP
    c.   X′ → X YP

(3)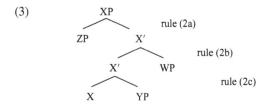

PS-rules generate structures: to put it in less technical terms they 'build trees'.

The very general question we can ask at this point, having seen how PS-rules and X′-theory work, is whether we need any other kind of rule in our theory. Here we will propose that there is a further kind of syntactic rule of a somewhat different nature from PS-rules. These are known as transformations. Transformations map phrase markers into other phrase markers. In other words, they convert one tree into another tree. There are several kinds of transformations, including deletion rules, **movement rules** and others. The goal of this chapter is to introduce movement rules, showing how they interact with and complement PS-rules. We will concentrate on one particular kind of movement rule: wh-movement.

5.2   Types of Movement Rules

Movement rules differ from PS-rules in that they do not create structures; instead they manipulate them in various ways. The principal way in which movement rules manipulate trees involves transforming a tree in which a given constituent occupies one position into one in which it occupies another, where the positions can be seen and defined in relation to a tree diagram or labelled bracketing. We see this in the different positions of the auxiliary in (4):

(4) a.   Cambridge will flood as a consequence of global warming.
    b.   Will Cambridge flood as a consequence of global warming?

The auxiliary *will* is in one position in the declarative (4a) and in another in the interrogative (4b). Informally, we say that *will* 'moves' from one place in the structure to another.

We have already seen several examples of movement rules in our earlier discussions, only earlier we did not draw attention to the technical nature of these processes. There are in fact three main kinds of movement rules: **head-movement, NP-movement** and **wh-movement**. Here we briefly describe all three before moving on to a more detailed discussion of wh-movement.

Head-movement is seen in English subject-auxiliary inversion in questions. In Chapter 2, we observed how subject-auxiliary inversion forms direct yes/no questions from declaratives in English in examples like (4). We observed that the declarative sentence (4a) has the order *Subject – Auxiliary – Verb …* while the interrogative (4b) shows the 'inverted' order of subject and auxiliary: *Auxiliary – Subject – Verb …* The rule that relates the two sentences takes the T-position occupied by *will* in (4a) and moves it to the C-position. Since the subject, *Cambridge*, occupies the SpecT' position and linearly intervenes between C and T, this has the effect of inverting the order of *will* (in T, moved to C) and *Cambridge*. The rule relates the tree in (5a) to that in (5b) (for simplicity I have left out the adjunct *as a consequence of global warming*, which is probably a PP adjoined to T'; I have also left out V' as there is very little in VP aside from the main verb *flood*):

(5) a.

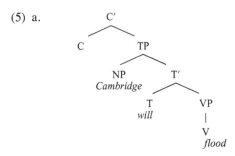

   b.

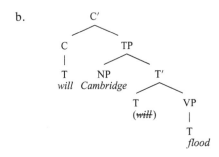

We see from (5) that subject-auxiliary inversion in English is a case of movement of T to C. Thus the structure in (5a) is mapped into that in (5b). No other changes are made to the trees here, as can easily be observed. What is left behind in T is a **copy**, which we will also refer to as a **trace**, of the auxiliary in its original position; this copy is not pronounced, as the strikeout is intended to indicate. Movement, then, can be usefully thought of as a kind of copy/paste operation familiar from word-processing applications: a given element is copied to a new position and pasted in there. From the fact that the original copy of *will* in the T position is not heard, we can add that there is a general **copy-deletion rule** applying to moved elements in their original position (we will look at this operation in more detail in Section 8.6). Since T is a head, this is a case of head-movement. Head-movement does what it says: it takes a head, copies it to a new position and deletes the content of the original head (but not the actual position). The basic tree is unchanged by the movement operation, aside from the substitution of T into a position dominated by C. So English subject-auxiliary inversion is a case of T-to-C movement, itself a case of the general operation of head-movement. There is much more to say about head-movement, and we will come back to it in Chapter 7 and at greater length in Volume II. But for now we have the basics, and an illustration of how movement operates.

The second kind of movement, NP-movement, is found in passives in English. We saw an example of a passive in the discussion of ellipsis and English auxiliaries in Chapter 4:

(6)   (When you arrived), John must have been being interviewed.

If we take away the complex auxiliary sequence, we can construct the following active-passive pair:

(7) a.   Oprah interviewed John.   (active)
     b.   John was interviewed (by Oprah).   (passive)

These two sentences are very close to synonymous; in particular, the who's-doing-what-to-whom relations (known as **argument structure**) are the same: both sentences describe a situation in which Oprah is the interviewer and John is the interviewee. Furthermore, *interview* is a transitive verb; in terms of the c-selection frames given in (14) in Chapter 4 it acts like *watch*, so it has a lexical entry like (8):

(8)   interview (V) ___ NP

This c-selection requirement is clearly satisfied in (7a), where *John* is the NP. We also saw in Chapter 4 that this c-selection frame is associated with the PS-rule which generates NP as the complement of V. In turn, this position corresponds to the direct-object function for NP, so in (7a) *John* is the direct object of *interview*. The position of complement of V and corresponding direct-object function is typically associated, in English and in many other languages, with the semantic, or **thematic**, **role** of **Patient** or **Undergoer** of the action described by the verb. In other words, *John* is the interviewee, as we already observed. In (7a), *Oprah* is the subject; NPs in this position are typically associated, in English and in many other languages, with the thematic role of **Agent**: *Oprah* is the interviewer.

Now, if we compare the passive sentence in (7b) with the active one in (7a), we can make two observations. First, *John* has the subject function in (7b): we can see this from the word order (it precedes both the auxiliary and the main verb) and from subject-verb agreement, in that if we replace *John* with a plural NP (*the boys*) then the auxiliary changes to its plural-agreement form: *The boys were interviewed (by Oprah)*. There are other ways to see that *John* is the subject of (7b), but these will do.

We have already made the second observation: the who's-doing-what-to-whom/argument structure relations are the same as in (7a).

So active–passive pairs change grammatical function: the NP which is the direct object of the active is the subject of the passive (while the NP which is the subject of the active goes into the *by*-phrase of the passive and can even disappear altogether: (7b) is grammatical if we leave out *by Oprah*). In our brief discussion of subjects and predicates in Chapter 3, we observed that phrase structure does not represent grammatical functions: it merely deals with categories, hierarchies and linear order. However, we can define the functions of subject and direct object in X′-theoretical terms as follows:

(9) a.   The subject is the NP in the Specifier of TP.
    b.   The direct object is the NP in the complement of V.

Strictly speaking, this reduces traditional grammatical relations to X′-theoretic relations. In turn, as we saw at the beginning of this chapter, these can be reduced to structural positions.

It then follows that saying that *John* is the object in the active (7a) and the subject in the passive (7b) implies that the same NP, with the same thematic role of interviewee, is in the complement of V in (7a) and in the Specifier of TP in (7b). We can account for this by saying that this NP moves from one position to the other; this is one aspect of the relation between active and passive sentences. The relationship can be captured by the trees in (10):

(10) a.

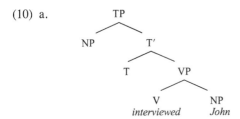

b.

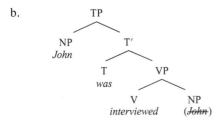

(The trees in (10) leave aside the active subject NP *Oprah*; accounting for the relationship between the subject in the active sentence and the *by*-phrase in the passive sentence is a tricky business which would take us too far afield here.) Looking at the representation of the direct-object NP *John* in (10), we can see that it is moved, by the same copy/paste + deletion operation as that applied to T in (5), from the VP-internal direct-object position to the Spec,T′ subject position. As with the head-movement operation in (5), a silent copy, or trace, is left behind in the original position (indicated by strikeout). Because what is moved here is an NP we call this NP-movement. In (10), again as in (5), the tree is unchanged; just the position of one NP is changed. The object NP here is substituted into the subject NP position in SpecT′.

As with head-movement, there is much more to say about NP-movement, and we will come back to it at great length in Volume II. But, again, for now we have the basics, along with a further illustration of how movement operates.

For the rest of this chapter, though, we will focus on the third type of movement, wh-movement.

5.3   Wh-Movement: The Basics

Wh-movement appears in **wh-questions**, both direct and indirect, and in a range of other constructions, including relative clauses (which we mentioned in our discussion of the fish sentences in Chapter 1). Wh-questions, sometimes called partial or constituent questions, ask about a given constituent of the clause. (11) is a simple example of a direct wh-question:

(11)   What did you catch (~~what~~)?

Here the **wh-phrase** *what*, an NP, moves from the direct-object position (indicated here by the copy in parentheses) to the initial position of the sentence to form a direct question. The question is interpreted as 'asking about' the nature of the direct object, so a natural answer could be 'fish', for example. Wh-questions contrast with yes/no-questions of the kind seen in (4b), as the latter simply ask whether a given situation (e.g. Cambridge flooding as a consequence of global warming) holds or not.

Wh-questions are so-called because, in English, the words and phrases that introduce them, i.e. which stand in initial position of the interrogative clause, nearly all begin with the letters 'wh': *when, who, which, what, where, why, how,* etc. Wh-movement is the most important and interesting type of movement for various reasons, some of which we will see directly.

In order to get a reasonably full picture of wh-movement, there are several questions to be addressed. These include the following (note in passing that these are all themselves wh-questions):

(12) a.   Which XPs can move?
      b.   Where do they move from?
      c.   Where do they move to?

    d.   Why do they move?

    e.   How far do they move?

Looking first at question (12a), we can see from the following examples that quite a range of categories can move (although, as (12a) implies, these are all phrasal categories, XPs, so wh-movement is clearly distinct from head-movement):

(13) a.   Which man will David see t ?

      b.   Who should John talk to t ?

      c.   To whom can John talk t ?

      d.   How disappointed is Fred t ?

      e.   What does Don believe t ?

In all of these examples and from now on, I abbreviate the copy in the starting position as 't' for trace; this is purely for convenience; strictly speaking, there is a whole phrasal copy in the relevant positions. In (13a), as in (11), we see wh-movement of the object NP. The difference with (11) is that here we have the wh-determiner *which* followed by the Noun *man*, while in (11) we have the pronominal form *what* which substitutes the whole NP. In (13b), the indirect object NP is moved; here we have the animate wh-pronoun *who*. The NP *who* is moved from inside the indirect-object PP, headed by *to*. Since *to* is unaffected by the movement, this kind of example is known as **Preposition stranding**. Preposition stranding is very natural in English, as (13b) shows. It is, however, quite rare in the languages of the world; the only other languages which clearly allow it are the Scandinavian languages. In (13c), we see movement of the whole indirect object PP. This is known as **pied-piping** (the terminology alludes to the Pied Piper of Hamelin, who having led the town's rats to a watery death and not been paid, led the town's children to a similar fate in revenge). Here the Preposition, which is not itself questioned in (13c), is 'pied-piped' along with the questioned NP. In languages which do not allow Preposition stranding (which, as just observed, is most languages), pied-piping of the Preposition is the only way to question the indirect object. In English, on the other hand, pied-piping of this kind, although grammatical, sounds rather 'stilted', at least in the spoken language. The sense of artificiality is added to by the use of the archaic accusative form of the wh-word: *whom*. This form is all but moribund in most varieties of colloquial English and is associated with formal, literary registers.[1]

---

[1] However, it is arguably more natural in (13c) than the corresponding example with *who*:

    (i)   ??To who can John talk t?

Compare also the Preposition-stranding example (13b) with *whom*:

    (ii)   ?Whom did you talk to t?

Strictly speaking, *whom* should also appear in direct-object function in (13a):

    (iii)   ?Whom will David see t?

In (13d) we see wh-movement of a predicate AP, questioned by *how*. In (13e) we have, potentially, questioning of a CP by *what*; the answer here could be a CP such as *That the world is flat*. So we see, in answer to question (12a), that wh-movement, with the right wh-word, can apply to NPs, PPs, APs and CPs, whereas TP and VP do not undergo wh-movement.

Let us turn now to question (12b), where do wh-phrases move from? In examples like (11) and (13) the starting position of wh-movement seems reasonably clear from the interpretation of the question, but can we demonstrate this syntactically? A related question is whether wh-movement is always obligatory: do wh-phrases always move? There are two constructions in English which give us answers to both questions, as they show the wh-phrases in their unmoved (*in-situ*) position. The first of these are so-called **echo questions**. These are questions which – either because an interlocutor simply fails to properly hear a previous sentence, or because they are astonished by what has been said – show the wh-phrase in its original position, as in:

(14) a.   Bill bought WHAT?!
     b.   You talked to WHO?!

Here the capitals and other punctuation are intended to indicate that the wh-phrase is heavily accented. Most important for our present purposes, though, these examples clearly show the wh-phrases in their unmoved positions.

The second construction is **multiple questions**. These are questions featuring more than one wh-phrase, and hence questioning more than one constituent. In English, only one wh-phrase can move per clause, and so any others must remain *in situ*. Some examples are:

(15) a.   Which prizes did we award t to which students this year?
     b.   Which girls did you say t danced with which boys at the party?

In these examples one wh-phrase moves to the beginning of the sentence, while the other one stays *in situ*: we can see that in both of these examples the *in-situ* wh-phrase is inside a PP. If we make the moved wh-phrase into a non-wh-phrase, then the other one must move, and we have the usual choice of Preposition stranding or pied-piping:

(16) a.   Which students did we award the Schlumpfenberger Prize to t this year?
     b.   To which students did we award the Schlumpfenberger Prize t this year?
     c.   Which boys did you say Mary danced with t at the party?
     d.   With which boys did you say Mary danced t at the party?

Native-speaker judgements vary on these marginal examples. My own judgement is that (i) sounds very strange, as it involves a clash of colloquial (preposition-stranding) and formal registers, while both (ii) and (iii) sound rather archaic and/or very formal. Native-speaker readers should judge for themselves (don't take the question marks in front of these examples too seriously). Here again, we see that the cultural E-language concept 'English' masks a range of I-language diversity.

Clearly, the simplest assumption about *in-situ* wh-phrases in both echo questions and multiple questions is that they simply do not move; in that case, these examples confirm our semantically based intuitions about the original position of wh-phrases in wh-movement examples in general.

   These points are further confirmed by evidence that the position and function of the wh-phrase are occupied in wh-movement examples, even if the wh-phrase has apparently moved away from that position. We can see this in two ways. First, if we insert a wh-phrase in the beginning of a sentence with no corresponding functional or positional 'gap' in the sentence, the result is ungrammatical:

(17) a.   *Who does Grandma like Fido?
      b.   *Which student did we award the prize to Bloggs?
      c.   *How many people did you say Mary had been to Chicago?

Clearly, the examples in (17) contrast minimally with those in (18):

(18) a.   Who does Grandma like t ?
      b.   Which student did we award the prize to t ?
      c.   How many people did you say t had been to Chicago?

The contrasts between (17) and (18) can be straightforwardly accounted for if we take seriously the copy/paste + deletion idea about movement. In each of the examples in (18), the wh-phrase is moved from the position indicated by the trace; hence it fills the position occupied by the trace and, derivatively therefore, has the function associated with the trace's position: direct object in (a), indirect object in (b) and subject in (c). The examples in (17) are ungrammatical because either the wh-phrase or the constituent in the respective trace positions has no syntactic home; there is no position or function available for it in the structure. They are ungrammatical for the same reason as (19):

(19) a.   *Grandma likes Fido Bill.
      b.   *We awarded the prize to Bloggs Smith.
      c.   *You said Mary more people than me had been to Chicago.

A second way to make the same point is to take, for example, an intransitive Verb of a kind that really cannot take a direct object however hard we try, e.g. *arrive*:

(20) a.   The train/Mary arrived.
      b.   *John arrived the train/Mary.

This example cannot allow what is sometimes called the causative reading of otherwise intransitive verbs, in that it cannot mean 'John made the train/Mary arrive.' Compare *break* in (21):

(21) a.   The vase broke.
   . b.   John broke the vase.

If we now add a wh-phrase to (20a), ungrammaticality results as we see in (22a). Compare (22b), based on (21a):

(22) a.   *What did John arrive t ?
     b.   What did John break t ?

Again, in (22a) the wh-phrase, or more precisely its copy/trace, has no syntactic 'home' in the structure, no position and therefore no function. Therefore the result is ungrammatical (and semantically nonsensical).

So the answer to question (12b) is that wh-phrases move from independently needed structural positions associated with particular grammatical functions: direct object, indirect object, subject and predicate positions for example. Hence, going back to our original example (11), we can give the pre-wh-movement structure in (23):

(23)

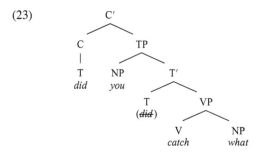

Here we see *what* in the direct-object position, which we can motivate from the semantic interpretation, echo questions, multiple questions and examples equivalent to (19) and (20b). Since (11) is a direct question, we also have subject-auxiliary inversion (i.e. head-movement of T to C, as we saw in the previous section) here, this time moving T containing the 'dummy' auxiliary *do* to C.

Now we can turn to question (12c): where do wh-phrases move to? In the light of the structure in (11) and the general X'-template introduced in Chapter 4, the answer to this question is now quite clear. Let us look just at the top part of the structure in (23) and compare it with the X'-template in (1):

(24)

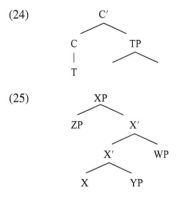

(25)

Mapping the general template in (25) onto the structure in (24), we can see that C′ contains the head C (the target of head-movement of T, in fact) and the complement TP. There is no adjunct WP adjoined to T′ here; recall that adjuncts are always optional. What is missing in (24) is ZP Specifier of C′. Given the linear order of the wh-phrases and the inverted auxiliary in all our examples of wh-movement so far, the obvious conclusion is that the wh-phrase is in SpecC′. So the structure for (11) after wh-movement has applied is (26):

(26)

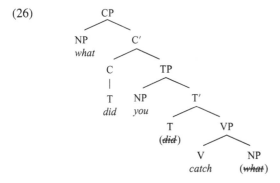

Wh-movement copies the wh-phrase *what*, pastes it into SpecC′ (without disturbing the X′ template), and the copy in the starting position is left silent.

Turning next to question (12d): why do wh-phrases move? This is a much more difficult question, and I won't try to give a full answer here. However, we can make an interesting and perhaps rather telling observation if we look again at our basic clausal template of CP, TP and VP:

(27)

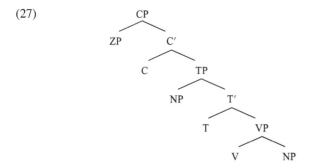

Here we see the three phrasal categories CP, TP and VP. Loosely speaking, each one seems to play a characteristic syntactic-semantic role in building up a full-fledged clause.

The three clausal domains are, first, the VP, which specifies basic argument relations, i.e. who does what to whom. In (27), the subject NP is outside VP; this may be because subjects have a special status in relation to the VP because of the importance of the subject-predicate relation, or it may be that subjects originate inside VP and are moved to SpecT' by a variant of the NP-movement operation introduced in Section 5.2. For now we will leave this point open.

The second clausal domain is TP: this is the domain of the functional elements, foremost among them Tense, but also Agreement, Mood and other 'satellite' functional categories associated with the clause which we saw in Chapter 1. In this connection, it is worth briefly reconsidering complex auxiliary sequences in English such as (6):

(6)   (When you arrived), John must have been being interviewed.

In Chapter 4, we considered and rejected a structure like (28) for the auxiliary sequence in (6):

(28)   [$_{VP}$ must [$_{V'}$ have [$_{V'}$ been [$_{V'}$ being interviewed]]]]

We suggested instead that each V' of (28) should be treated as 'an AuxP of some kind'. Since the first auxiliary is always the finite one (in a finite clause), we can treat this one as Tense itself. The others encode aspectual (perfect *have*, progressive *be*) and voice (passive *be*) information. So, we could tentatively replace (28) with (29):

(29)   [$_{TP}$ must [$_{PerfP}$ have [$_{ProgP}$ been [$_{VoiceP}$ being [$_{VP}$ interviewed]]]]]

Each auxiliary occupies the head of its functional category and takes the next one to its right as its complement, with Voice taking VP as its complement. The subject occupies SpecT'; for now we leave open the question of what, if anything, occupies the other Specifier positions (remember that Specifier positions don't have to be filled, as in simple NPs like *John*). Heads expressing Mood, Tense, Aspect and Voice are often realised by inflections in other languages (and indeed there are inflections in the English auxiliary sequence, e.g. the progressive *-ing*). So what we might loosely call the 'extended TP' is the domain where notions such as Tense, Aspect and Mood are realised. Depending on the language, these may be realised by auxiliaries, inflections, both together, or not at all. English relies mainly, but not exclusively, on auxiliaries.

The third domain is the one relevant for wh-movement. We could take CP, as the highest category in the clause, to be the one that relates the otherwise complete clause (TP complete with subject and satellites, the VP saying what the subject is doing to whom) to the 'outside'. What's outside the clause will vary depending on whether the clause is a main clause or not. If the clause is a main clause, there is no further, higher, syntactic structure. The clause is a root clause (the CP node is the root of the tree). But root clauses have a function in a wider discourse context; in particular, it is relevant for the discourse whether the clause is a declarative, stating something, an interrogative, asking something, an imperative, ordering someone to do something, etc. In other words, the root clause must express discourse-relevant information regarding clause type. There is much more to say about this matter, but for now it suffices to observe that declaratives and interrogatives are two of the most basic clause types.

We have already observed that root interrogative Cs, expressing direct questions, have special syntactic properties in English. In yes/no questions, we observe subject-auxiliary inversion, i.e. T-to-C movement, the example of head-movement introduced in Section 5.2. There we saw that a yes/no question like *Will Cambridge flood?* has the structure in (5b), repeated here (we should also add the CP node to (5b) for completeness, but for now we'll continue to assume that there's nothing in SpecC′ in yes/no questions):

(5b)

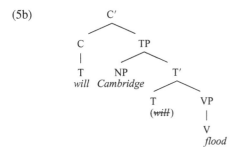

With this word order, i.e. with subject-auxiliary inversion, the sentence is interpreted as a yes/no question. So we could add a special clause-type feature to C, to indicate this. Let us call the feature Q (for Question) and write C_Q to designate an interrogative C, a particular subcategory of C. So now we can say that C_Q attracts T, i.e. it has the syntactic effect of triggering subject-auxiliary inversion and the discourse-semantic effect of saying 'I'm asking you a yes/no question' (however, exactly that is to be analysed by the semantic component of the grammar, but we leave this aside since it is not a matter for syntax).

Wh-questions are obviously a type of question, so we can further type C with the feature Wh; $C_{Q, Wh}$ is another subcategory of C. We can say this type of C has the syntactic effect of triggering wh-movement of some XP into SpecC′. Since in main clauses wh-questions also involve subject-auxiliary inversion, we could say that Q is also present on C. So the full structure of a simple wh-question like (11) is (30):

(30)

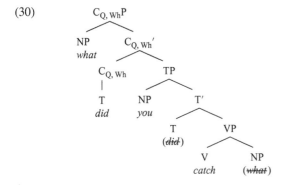

Following the X′-theoretic notion of projection, we can take it that the Q and wh-features of this kind of C are marked on C′ and CP. Hence, in the discourse, CP is a wh-question, with its particular discourse semantics (which, again, we leave aside here as extra-syntactic). The syntactic property of $C_{Q, Wh}$ in a main clause is that it triggers both subject-auxiliary inversion and wh-movement. In this way, we can answer question (12d) above: the clause-typing wh-feature of C triggers wh-movement to SpecC′.

Finally, we come to question (12e): how far can wh-phrases move? This is a very important and difficult question that will, in various ways, occupy a great deal of Volume II. I will postpone addressing this question for now, although we'll make a start on it in the next two sections, after looking at some further aspects of wh-movement.

5.4   Subject Questions, Indirect Questions and Long-Distance Wh-Movement

We saw in the previous section that wh-movement can affect NPs in various functions, including direct and indirect objects. The relevant examples from (13) are repeated here:

(13) a.   Which man will David see t ?
     b.   Who should John talk to t ?
     c.   To whom can John talk t ?

It is possible to apply wh-movement to subjects. However, complications arise in this case. In (31b), we see an example of a wh-question formed on the subject:

(31) a.   Mary saw John.
     b.   Who saw John?

Here it looks as though the wh-phrase is *in situ*, since the example appears to correspond point-for-point with the declarative in (31a). However, it is clear that this is not an echo question; that would presumably be (32):

(32)   WHO saw John?!

Furthermore, (31b) clearly has the discourse semantics of a wh-question; it just seems to be syntactically different. We could therefore assign a structure like (33) to (31b) (I have left the Q-feature off C for reasons that will become apparent immediately below):

(33)

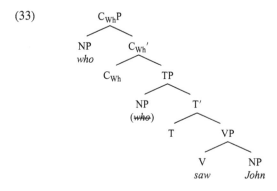

Here, the subject wh-phrase has moved from SpecT′ to SpecC′ in the standard copy/paste + deletion manner, and this movement is presumably triggered by the wh-feature on T, as in the examples we saw in the previous section. This example of wh-movement does not change the linear order of the words in the sentence, though; it is **string-vacuous movement**. That is why (31a) and (31b) appear to line up (while, if (33) is the correct analysis of (31b), they actually don't). There is nothing in the notion of movement rule that states that movement operations, copy/paste + deletion, have to change the linear order of elements; the fact is that they usually do, and all the examples we have seen so far have involved such a change. But, as long as we don't require this, then there is no bar to positing the structure in (33) for (31b).

The problem, of course, is the absence of subject-auxiliary inversion, signalled in the absence of other auxiliaries by *do*-support, in (31b). In fact, if we apply subject-auxiliary inversion to (31b), the result is strongly ungrammatical, as long as *do* is left unstressed:

(34)   *Who did see John?

If *do* is stressed, the sentence becomes grammatical, as (35a) shows. But stressed *do*, strongly asserting the statement or question being made, is always possible in finite clauses, as (35b) shows:

(35) a.   Who DID see John?!
     b.   Mary DID see John!

Since, as (35b) shows, stressed *do* can appear in T, we can assume that the stressed *do* in (35a) is also in T. In that case, what seems to give rise to the ungrammaticality of (34) is subject-auxiliary inversion.

We can connect (34) to another strange feature of subject wh-movement. As we saw with the multiple wh-question in (15b) in the previous section, movement of wh-subjects from a subordinate clause to a main clause is grammatical:

(36) a.   Who did you say [t likes John] ?
     b.   Which student do you think [t will win the prize] ?

Here the brackets show the subordinate clause, ambiguously indicating either CP or TP. In these examples the complementiser *that* is absent; this is consistent with the general optionality of this complementiser introducing the clausal complements to verbs like *say* and *think* in English. However, if we take the option of inserting *that* in (36), the examples become ungrammatical:

(37) a.   *Who did you say [$_{CP}$ that [$_{TP}$ t likes John]] ?
     b.   *Which student do you think [$_{CP}$ that [$_{TP}$ t will win the prize]] ?

We only see this contrast with subject wh-movement. If we wh-move the object in examples like this, *that* is fully optional, just as in subordinate clauses where no wh-movement takes place:

(38) a.   Who did you say [CP (that) [TP John likes t]] ?
     b.   Which prize do you think [CP (that) [TP Bloggs will win t]] ?

We could generalise over (34) and (37) as follows:

(39)   C-trace generalisation: A filled C is not allowed when adjacent to the trace
        of a wh-moved subject.

The relevant parts of (34) and (37) which violate the constraint in (39) are
shown in (40):

(40) a.   * ... [C do] [TP t ... (34)
     b.   * ... [C that] [TP t ... (37)

The generalisation in (39) is our first example of a condition limiting the
application of wh-movement. We will see many more, starting in the next
section.
   So let's say that some constraint like (39) applies to subject wh-movement
in English. This is admittedly a very odd constraint: it looks very parochial and
particular, not at all the kind of generalisation we'd like to have as part of the
theory of Universal Grammar. But we can see that there is a motivation for it:
in main clauses, we can maintain the analysis in (33) for string-vacuous subject
wh-movement and, in embedded clauses, we can understand why the otherwise
optional complementiser is banned in examples like (37). We can also observe
further cases, assuming, as we mentioned in Chapter 2 that *if* and *for* are complementisers. The complementiser *if* shows up in indirect questions, as we will
see in more detail directly, and is not optional. Moreover, wh-movement out of
indirect questions is never very good. Nonetheless, we can see a contrast in the
following examples:

(41) a.   *Who did you ask [CP if/whether [TP t likes John]] ?
     b.   ?Who did you ask [CP if/whether [TP John likes t]] ?

Similarly with *for*: many speakers of English allow optional *for* with certain
infinitive-taking verbs, e.g. (in my English at least) *prefer*:

(42)   I would prefer (for) John to win the prize.

We see the same disappearing optionality with subject wh-movement, but not
with object wh-movement, as we saw with *that* in (36) and (37):

(43) a.   Who would you prefer [t to win the prize] ?
     b.   *Who would you prefer [CP for [TP t to win the prize]] ?
     c.   Which prize would you prefer [CP (for) [TP John to win t]] ?

Strange though it is, (39) seems to account for a range of facts.
   Optional complementisers like *that* and *for* can, under the right circum-
stances, be omitted (by definition). But we said in the previous section that
the Q-feature associated with C appears in both yes/no and wh-questions and

types the clause for discourse semantics. Its syntactic effect is to trigger subject-auxiliary inversion, T-to-C movement. But subject-auxiliary inversion is impossible in (34), where we have subject wh-movement. What does this mean for the Q-feature? Clearly, since (31b) is interpreted as a question, we want to say that C still has a Q-feature, but (39) prevents it from triggering subject-auxiliary inversion where there is an adjacent subject trace, i.e. where there is subject wh-movement. We will see directly that there are further examples where C has a Q-feature but does not trigger subject-auxiliary inversion.

This brings us to the topic of wh-movement in indirect questions. As in direct questions, we see a range of possibilities for wh-movement:

(44) I wonder …
    a.   which man John will see t ?
    b.   who John should talk to t ?
    c.   to whom John can talk t ?
    d.   how angry Alex is t ?
    e.   what John believes t ?

In each of these examples, we have wh-movement to the SpecC′ of the selected CP complement of *wonder*, a verb which selects for an indirect question (more precisely C_Q; see below). These examples exactly parallel those in (13): in (44a) we have wh-movement of an object NP, in (44b) wh-movement of an indirect object NP with Preposition stranding, in (44c) wh-movement of an indirect object PP with pied-piping of the Preposition, in (44d) wh-movement of an AP and in (44e) wh-movement, potentially, of a CP. The embedded questions here are all exactly like their direct-question counterparts in (13), with the single exception that there is no subject-auxiliary inversion.

Subject-auxiliary inversion is unacceptable in examples like (44) (for most English speakers):

(45) *I wonder …
    a.   … which man will John see t ?
    b.   … who should John talk to t ?
    c.   … to whom can John talk t ?

In fact, the embedded C must be empty in all these examples: no complementiser (*that*, *if* or *whether*) can appear:

(46) *I wonder …
    a.   … which man that John will see t ?
    b.   … who if John should talk to t ?
    c.   … to whom whether John can talk t ?

We mentioned in the previous section that CP types the clause and we saw there how this works for yes/no questions and wh-questions in main (root) clauses. In subordinate clauses, CP bears clause-typing features that are c-selected by the main verb of the superordinate clause. So, for example, the verb *wonder* selects C_Q, since its complement must be an interrogative of some kind (yes/no or wh-), while *think* does not allow the head of its CP complement to be C_Q:

(47) a.   I wonder if/*that the world is flat.
        b.   I think *if/that the world is flat.

Unlike the C_Q of main clauses, however, the C_Q in embedded clauses cannot trigger subject-auxiliary inversion (i.e. T-to-C movement), although it can be realised by *if* or *whether*. Where C also has the wh-feature, it cannot be realised by any complementiser, as (46) shows; this is parallel to what we observed above with subject wh-movement in main clauses.

   In indirect wh-subject questions, the situation is parallel to main clauses. As in all other indirect questions, C must be empty. No subject-auxiliary inversion or complementisers are possible. So all indirect wh-questions have a silent $C_{Q, wh}$:

(48) a.   I wonder who t saw John ?
        b.   *I wonder who did t see John ?
        c.   *I wonder who that/if t saw John ?

These restrictions on how C_Q and $C_{Q, Wh}$ are realised in main and embedded clauses are quite complicated and idiosyncratic. In other languages, things can be different. For example, certain non-standard varieties of Dutch allow the equivalent of *that* in indirect wh-questions. After a verb like 'wonder', then, we find clauses like the following:

(49)   ...wie   dat   het   gedaan   heeft.
             ...who   that   it   done   has
             '... who did it'   [non-standard Dutch]

Here *wie* ('who') occupies SpecC' and *dat* ('that') is in C. So this example is exactly equivalent to the ungrammatical English sentence in (46a). Even in earlier stages of English, we can find something similar. The first line of Chaucer's *General Prologue* to the *Canterbury Tales*, written in the Middle English of the late fourteenth century, begins with the wh-word *whan* ('when') and is immediately followed by *that* and then the subject:

(50)   **Whan that** Aprill with his shoures soote ...
             When that April with its showers sweet ...

Although not a wh-question (but an adjunct clause functioning as a time adverbial), we see the wh-phrase directly followed by *that*, which is not allowed in Modern English. So the restrictions on the realisation of C_Q and $C_{Q, wh}$ are complex and idiosyncratic in Modern English. The one thing which is constant, however, is that where we have $C_{Q, Wh}$, a wh-phrase always moves to SpecC'.

   Let us now begin to address question (12e) from the previous section: how far can a wh-phrase move? We have already seen some examples of wh-movement from embedded clauses to the root SpecC', primarily involving movement of the subject

of the embedded clause (see (35), for example). In fact, we can find examples of all
the other kinds of wh-movement from an embedded clause to a main clause:

(51) a.   Which man did you say [(that) John will see t] ?
      b.   Who did you say [(that) John will talk to t] ?
      c.   To whom did you say [(that) John will talk t] ?
      d.   How angry did you say [(that) Alex is t] ?
      e.   What did you say [(that) John believes t] ?

In (51a), object NP wh-moves from the subordinate clause; in (51b), indirect
object NP moves from the subordinate clause, stranding the Preposition; in
(51c), the indirect object PP moved from subordinate clause, pied-piping the
Preposition; in (51d), the predicate AP moves from the subordinate clause and in
(51e) the wh-CP moves from the subordinate clause. In all of these cases, where
the verb of the main clause is *say*, the complementiser *that* is optional.

    We saw in Chapter 3 that PS-rules can generate indefinitely long sequences
of subordinate clauses, each one embedded in the one superordinate to it. Hence
examples such as (20) from Chapter 3, repeated here, are possible:

(52)   Mary hopes that John expects that Pete thinks that Dave said that …

Since wh-movement can move material from a subordinate clause to the root
SpecC′, we expect this to be possible from any subordinate clause, however
deeply embedded. At first sight, this certainly appears to be true, as the following examples show:

(53) a.   Who did you say [(that) Mary believes [(that) John saw t]] ?
      b.   Who did you say [(that) Mary believes [(that) Fred knows [(that) John saw t]]] ?
      c.   Who did you say [(that) Mary believes [(that) Fred knows [(that) I asserted
            [(that) John saw t]]]] ?

There doesn't appear to be any limit to how deeply embedded the subordinate clause from which wh-movement takes place can be. So we see that
wh-movement can produce constructions with an **unbounded dependency**.
The dependency between the trace/copy of the wh-phrase in the starting position and the SpecC′ which the wh-phrase moves to appears to be unbounded:
wh-movement can be as 'long-distance' as we like. The same appears to be true
for wh-movement in indirect questions. If we change the main-clause verb to
wonder in (53), then we have wh-movement to the first embedded SpecC′, the
one c-selected by *wonder*. Here, too, wh-movement appears to be unbounded:

(54) a.   I wonder [who Mary believes [(that) John saw t]] ?
      b.   I wonder [who Mary believes [(that) Fred knows [(that) John saw t]]] ?
      c.   I wonder [who Mary believes [(that) Fred knows [(that) I asserted [(that)
            John saw t]]] ?

The fact that wh-movement is unbounded does not imply it is unconstrained:
we have already seen a constraint on wh-movement of subjects, the C-trace

generalisation of (38). In the next section, we will see that there is a whole class of important restrictions on wh-movement.

In this section we have seen some more complex aspects of wh-movement: the special properties of subject wh-movement, including the strange C-trace generalisation in (39); the behaviour of wh-movement and wh-Cs in embedded clauses and, most importantly, the apparently unbounded nature of wh-movement. In the next two sections we will focus on some consequences of this last observation.

5.5   The Nature of Movement Rules

The unbounded nature of wh-movement is important. It gives us a reason for distinguishing PS-rules from movement rules. Wh-movement is an operation which places a wh-phrase in a higher SpecC′ by copy/paste, leaving a copy/trace in its original position. Seemingly, the target SpecC′ can be arbitrarily structurally distant from the original position of the wh-phrase. On the other hand, as we have seen, PS-rules (including those generating the X′-template) are local: they define little bits of the tree at a time. For example, a rule like (55a) generates the 'treelet' in (55b):

(55) a.   V′ → V CP

  b.   V′

              V   CP

Could we generate wh-movement dependencies just using PS-rules? We could certainly introduce the wh-feature into the rule in (55a), and distinguish $C_{Wh}P$ from a declarative CP. Specifying verbs such as *wonder* as c-selecting C_{Wh} (which may be a special case of C_Q, as our earlier discussion implied) will allow *wonder*, but not *think*, for example, to be V in (55a). We can also specify root C as optionally C_{Wh}. We can then add further PS-rules like (56):

(56) a. $C_{Wh}P → WhP\ C'_{Wh}$
    b. $C'_{Wh} → C_{Wh}\ TP$

Rule (56a) will guarantee that exactly one wh-phrase appears in the Specifier of C_{Wh} and rule (56b) introduces TP as the complement to C_{Wh}, seemingly in the standard way (see (62ii) of Chapter 4). But now we run into a problem. The rules in (56) tell us what the properties of a CP which attracts a wh-phrase are, but we need to also specify that the TP must contain a trace/copy of the WhP in (56a). If we do not do this, we cannot rule out ungrammatical examples like (17), repeated here:

(17) a.   *Who does Grandma like Fido?
    b.   *Which student did we award the prize to Bloggs?
    c.   *How many people did you say Mary had been to Chicago?

We could specify TP in (56b) as Wh, meaning that it dominates a trace/copy of a wh-phrase. Then we could say that the examples in (17) do not have a $T_{wh}P$, so TP doesn't dominate a trace/copy of a wh-phrase and ungrammaticality results. We would have to extend this to every node dominating a trace/copy of a wh-phrase in an example with long-distance movement. So in (57) every XP-node (except the subject NP-nodes dominating *you*, *Mary* and *John*) would have a wh-feature:

(57)   [CP-wh Who did [TP-wh you [VP-wh say [CP-wh that [TP-wh Mary [VP-wh believes [CP-wh that [TP-wh John [VP-wh saw t]]] ?

But the wh-features everywhere except on the root C and CP are not the same as the 'true' clause-typing wh-features we have seen until now. We can see this particularly clearly in the embedded CPs. These are not indirect questions, but they have to be marked 'wh' to show that they contain a trace/copy. So we need to find a way to distinguish the 'trace/copy-marking' wh-feature from the clause-typing one. The clause-typing feature clearly has a lexical motivation (some verbs c-select indirect questions and some don't) and a discourse-semantic motivation, as we saw above. The 'trace/copy-marking' feature is there simply to say that there is a trace/copy somewhere 'lower down' in the structure. If traces/copies are not independently existing lexical or functional categories, then indicating them in a PS-rule is no more than a way to encode the movement dependency. Moreover, this approach goes against the general locality of PS-rules, in that it states there is a trace/copy somewhere lower in the structure, but this trace/copy could be arbitrarily deeply embedded, given the unbounded nature of wh-movement. So marking movement dependencies in PS-rules makes the PS-rules significantly more complex by effectively introducing whole classes of new categories to mark traces/copies, and effectively makes PS-rules non-local. Furthermore, the complexity increases greatly if we try to introduce a similar method for marking head- or NP-movement dependencies.

So, rather than complicating the PS-rules very significantly as sketched above, although this can be and has been done, we will stick to the idea that we there are two relatively simple rule types. On the one hand there are PS-rules of the kind introduced in Chapters 3 and 4 (including the X'-template), which *build* structure, i.e they generate phrase markers in a strictly local, incremental fashion. On the other hand, there are movement, or transformational rules, which map phrase markers into other phrase markers, preserving the X'-template. Movement consists of the copy/paste + deletion operations, as we have seen. The former rules are highly local, the latter, at least wh-movement, appear to be unbounded. The former rules do not create traces/copies; the latter do.

To summarise what we have seen concerning movement so far, we have seen three types of movement: head-movement, NP-movement and wh-movement. Head-movement is illustrated by subject-auxiliary inversion, as in (5b), repeated here with CP and the Q-feature added:

(5b)

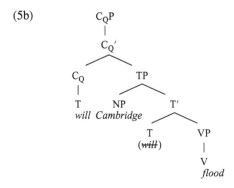

By definition, head-movement moves a head. The target is also a head. The move-ment operation copies the head T and pastes it into the 'target head'. The copy left behind remains in the structure but is not phonologically realised (from a phono-logical perspective, it is deleted; from a structural perspective it is not, however).

The second type of movement is NP-movement. The example we saw was movement of the object NP from the complement position of V to the subject position, SpecT', in passives. We saw the derived structure of a passive in (10b), repeated here:

(10b)

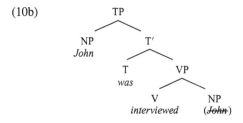

NP-movement moves NPs, as the name implies. Passives are a typical, but not the only, case. Here the object is copied and pasted into the subject position, and the copy in object position is phonologically deleted. NP-movement always targets the subject position, SpecT'.

Third, there is wh-movement, which moves a wh-phrase to the Specifier of C_{Wh}. Wh-phrases can be NPs, APs, PPs or CPs, but not VPs or TPs (or other clausal functional categories such as PerfP, ProgP or VoiceP; see (28)). A basic case of object wh-movement is (30), repeated here:

(30)

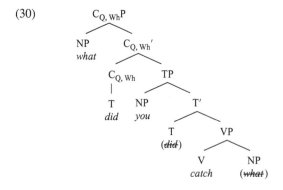

Here the wh-phrase is copied and pasted into $SpecC_{Q, wh}'$, and the copy is phonologically silenced. Wh-movement always targets a $SpecC_{wh}'$. We have been taking C_{wh} to imply C_Q, since wh-questions are a kind of question; we will return to this point below.

All three cases of movement have certain things in common: they copy/paste a constituent into a distinct position created by the X'-rules of phrase structure. Technically, what we have informally been calling copy/paste is known as **substitution**. So all the movement rules we have seen so far are **substitution transformations**. (There are also **adjunction transformations**, which create adjoined positions of the kind generated by PS-rules like (2b), but we will leave these aside for now.) All of the movement rules leave a copy in the original position and this copy is deleted phonologically; in other words, it is present in the syntax (we have mostly abbreviated it as 't' for trace) but lacking phonological content, i.e. silent. We can also note that each movement rule places the new copy (i.e. the 'moved' category) in a position which is, in an obvious sense, higher up in the tree than the original position: C is higher than the original position of T in (5b), the subject position SpecT' is higher than the object position in (10b) and SpecC' is higher than the object position in (30). So movement appears to always move constituents 'upward' in the tree; this is an important generalisation which we will make more precise in later chapters.

The three operations differ both in what is moved and in the target of the movement. Head-movement moves heads, and in fact moves the head to another, higher head position; again, this can be easily seen in (5b). NP-movement moves NPs into subject position; in fact it moves NPs from one grammatical-function position (object) to another (subject). This is why operations like passive are often described in purely grammatical-function terms ('passives turn objects into subjects'). As usual, we take the grammatical-function terminology as a useful shorthand for the correct, phrase-structural description. Finally, wh-movement moves a wh-XP into $SpecC_{Wh}'$.

In the above description, we can note an interesting match between the starting position and the target position of movement: head-movement moves heads from one head position to another; NP-movement moves NPs from one grammatical-function position to another and wh-movement moves wh-XPs from one wh-position to another (recall that *in-situ* wh-phrases in echo questions and multiple questions show us that any NP position can host a wh-phrase).

Putting the last two observations together, we can give a general characterisation of movement rules as follows:

(58)   Movement substitutes an element of type X into a higher position of type X, where X ranges over heads, wh-phrases and grammatical-function NPs.

Although somewhat rough and ready, and certainly causing us to wonder why heads, grammatical-function NPs and wh-phrases might fall together in this way, (58) contains the germ of a very important set of generalisations, which we investigate in full in Volume II.

Finally, we have observed that wh-movement is unbounded. The other types of movement do not seem to be unbounded. Moving a head from an embedded clause into a main clause gives a strongly ungrammatical result:

(59)   *Will you can say [that Cambridge (will) flood] ?

Compare the fully grammatical (60), with 'local' T-to-C movement in the main clause:

(60)   Can you (can) say [that Cambridge will flood] ?

Similarly, NP-movement from a finite embedded clause into a main clause is very bad, as the contrast between (61a–c) and (61d) shows:

(61) a.   It was believed that Oprah interviewed John.
     b.   It was believed that John was interviewed (by Oprah).
     c.   John was believed to have been interviewed (by Oprah).
     d.   *John is believed [that Oprah interviewed (John)].

Sentence (61c) shows that movement from a non-finite complement clause is acceptable.
    Compare (62a), where the verb in the embedded clause is passivized and *John* moves to the 'local' subject position and (62b), where, again, *John* is moved out of a finite clause:

(62) a.   We believe [that John was interviewed (John)].
     b.   *John was believed [that (John) was interviewed].

Wh-movement seems to differ markedly from the other types of movement in this respect. This brings us back to question (12e), which we have still not fully answered: how far can wh-movement go? In the next section, we will introduce an important class of limitations on long-distance wh-movement.

5.6   Limiting Wh-Movement

        We have seen that wh-movement can apply to most categories, but not to VP or TP (or other clausal functional categories such as PerfP etc., see (28)). We have also seen that wh-movement can move wh-phrases across multiple clause boundaries, as in (53), repeated here:

(53) a.   Who did you say [(that) Mary believes [(that) John saw t]] ?
     b.   Who did you say [(that) Mary believes [(that) Fred knows [(that) John saw t]]] ?
     c.   Who did you say [(that) Mary believes [(that) Fred knows [(that) I asserted [(that) John saw t]]] ?

So a natural question now arises: is movement of wh-XPs unrestricted in general? In fact, we already know that the answer to this question is negative, in that subject wh-phrases have to obey the C-trace generalisation in (39). But we

could still ask about non-subject wh-phrases. Here we will see that the answer is
definitely negative, and that the limits to wh-movement are quite significant and
very interesting from a theoretical perspective.

Let us begin by looking at NPs which contain a possessor NP, such as *my
guitar* or *John's cat*. The structure of these NPs is shown in (63) (here the subscript numerals 1 and 2 are there just to keep the two NPs distinct; they have no
theoretical significance):

(63)

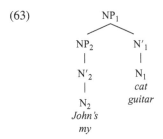

Here we see that the possessor NP, NP_2, occupies the Specifier of the possessee
NP, NP_1. Everything is completely in conformity with X'-theory. Since the possessor is an NP, it can be a wh-phrase, giving *whose cat*, for example, with the
same structure as (63):

(64)

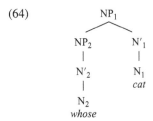

NP_2 looks like a wh-phrase in good standing. But if we try to apply wh-movement
to it we run into ungrammaticality:

(65)   * [NP2 Whose] did you feed [NP1 t cat] ?

NP_2 is unable to move alone. Instead, the whole of NP_1 must be pied-piped:

(66)   [NP1 Whose cat] did you feed t ?

In (66), we have a straightforward case of object wh-movement, so of course
there is no difficulty here. But the ungrammaticality of (65) shows us that
wh-movement cannot apply directly to the possessor NP_2.

The contrast between (65) and (66) reflects an important limitation on
wh-movement, known as the **Left Branch Constraint (LBC)**:

(67)   Wh-movement can't apply to the left branch of an XP, or to part of a left branch.

Since, in (64), NP_2 *whose* is on the left branch (i.e. the Specifier) of NP_1, the LBC
prevents it from moving alone. This accounts for the ungrammaticality of (65).
Pied-piping NP_1 as in (66) is unproblematic, since the entire object is not on a

left branch; being the complement of V, it is on the right branch inside V'. So the LBC doesn't affect object movement. (In order to allow for movement of wh-subjects as in (31b) we have to exempt TP from (67).)

The LBC extends beyond possessors to APs. Consider an example like (68), which we have seen several times:

(68)   [AP How angry] is Alex t ?

Here we have the wh-AP *how angry*, which we can analyse as containing the Specifier *how* and the A' (and A) *angry*. The LBC predicts that Specifiers, being on a left branch cannot undergo wh-movement alone. This prediction is correct for *how angry*, as (69) shows:

(69)   *How is Alex [AP t angry] ?

Here again, the whole AP must pied-pipe, as in (68).

The LBC is one of several constraints on wh-movement called **island constraints**. The terminology is based on the idea that islands are difficult to move off, so the syntactic contexts which block wh-movement are islands for wh-movement. Hence the left branch, or Specifier, of NP and AP are islands. There are several other island constraints. Here I will briefly illustrate two; in Volume II we will look at island constraints and how to account for them in detail.

One further island constraint concerns **wh-islands**. This constraint bans wh-movement out of indirect questions, or any context introduced by a separate wh-word. So, we start from an indirect question introduced by *ask*, e.g. (70a). Then, we replace the direct object *John* with another wh-phrase, e.g. *which movies*. Then we wh-move *which movies* to the main-clause SpecC'. This gives rise to the ungrammatical (70b):

(70) a.   Mary asked Bill who t saw John?
     b.   *Which movies did Mary ask Bill who (~~who~~) saw (~~which movies~~)?

There is a clear contrast in grammaticality between (70a) and (70b); this is because wh-movement of *which movies* in (70b) violates the wh-island constraint. Example (70b) can also be compared with (71), where there is comparable long-distance wh-movement, but in this case there is no wh-island:

(71)   Which movies did Mary say John saw (~~which movies~~)?

Another island constraint is the **Complex NP Constraint** (CNPC). This constraint bans wh-movement from complex NPs meaning, at least to a first approximation, an NP containing a full CP. Hence wh-movement is banned in examples like the following:

(72) a.   *Which hobbit did you read [NP a story [CP that a wizard met t]] ?
     b.   *Which hobbit did you read [NP a story [CP which was about t]] ?

In (72a), there is a CP inside the NP in the complement of *story* (cf. *I read a story that a hobbit found a ring*). In (72b), the CP inside the NP is a relative clause; there is a gap in the subject position corresponding to *story* here (this indicates that relative clauses involve movement, a matter we haven't gone into here, with string-vacuous movement of *which* from SpecT′ to SpecC′ here; see the discussion of subject wh-questions in Section 5.4). Compare (72b) with the 'reduced-relative' NP in (73), where there is no CP inside the NP:

(73)   Which hobbit did you read [NP a story about t] ?

In addition to the LBC, the CNPC and the wh-island constraint, there are several other island constraints. But this is not the place for a thorough discussion, still less an analysis, of the phenomenon. Here we can simply observe that, despite appearing to be unbounded, the operation of wh-movement is not unlimited: it is subject to island constraints. Subject wh-movement is also subject to the C-trace generalisation in (39).

So we see that wh-movement combines two contrasting properties: it appears to be unbounded and yet is subject to island constraints. Here we have concentrated on wh-movement in interrogatives, although it is also found in other constructions, notably relative clauses, as in (74):

(74) a.   the hobbit which you read a story about t
     b.   the hobbit [which Mary believes [(that) Fred knows [(that) I asserted [(that) John saw t at the bottom of the garden]]]]
     c.   *the hobbit which you read [NP a story [CP that a wizard met t]]

Example (74a) illustrates a basic relative clause, with the wh-relative pronoun *which* and an associated trace/copy as marked. We can take it that *which* is in the SpecC′ of the CP which modifies *hobbit*. Example (74b) shows that relative-clause formation is unbounded, and (74c) that it is subject to the CNPC. So *which*-movement, forming the relative clause here, is clearly a further case of wh-movement. Presumably this case of wh-movement is not associated with C_Q, as it does not form an interrogative; we may want to define C_{rel} for relative clauses, or perhaps generalize the notion of C_{wh} beyond interrogatives. These are among many issues we have not explored here.

English also allows relative clauses where there is no apparent wh-relative pronoun. These can be marked with the complementizer *that*, which, as usual, is optional. Where *that* is optional it appears that there is no overt marker of the relative clause:

(75) a.   the hobbit (that) you read a story about t
     b.   the hobbit [(that) Mary believes [(that) Fred knows [(that) I asserted [(that) John saw t at the bottom of the garden]]]]
     c.   *the hobbit (that) you read [NP a story [CP that a wizard met t]]

The evidence from the presence of a trace/copy, the unbounded dependency in (75b) and the CNPC violation in (75c) shows us that there is wh-movement here despite the absence of an overt wh-relative pronoun. One possibility is that the wh-relative marker is deleted here. We cannot go into these questions fully here, however.

5.7   Conclusion

In this chapter we have seen that movement rules are necessary, alongside the PS-rules which generate the X′-template. We saw in Section 5.6 that although it is technically possible to complicate PS-rules in such a way that they can generate the structures that result from movement, the complications involved change the nature of PS-rules, in particular in that they lose their fundamentally local character.

We saw that there are three types of movement: head-movement, NP-movement and wh-movement. These three types of movement have a number of properties in common: they all involve substitution of a category into a position generated by the PS-rules (hence they manipulate, rather than generate, structure), they all copy the 'moved' element, leaving the copy in the starting position to be deleted by the phonology, and they all involve a 'like-for-like' substitution, captured by the rough generalisation in (58), repeated here:

(58)   Movement substitutes an element of type X into a higher position of type X, where X ranges over heads, wh-phrases and grammatical-function NPs.

Wh-movement seems to differ from the other types of movement in that it involves an (apparent) unbounded dependency, although we saw that it is nonetheless subject to the LBC and other island constraints, as well as the C-trace generalisation in (38).

The following structures illustrate each kind of movement that we have introduced in this chapter:

(76) a.   Head-movement:

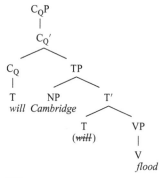

  b.   NP-movement:

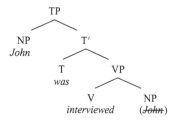

c.   Wh-movement:

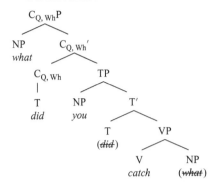

The general characterisation of movement given here combines with the PS-rules generating the X'-template, given in (2) and repeated here, to give us the mechanisms which generate and manipulate structure:

(2) a.   XP → ZP X'
     b.   X' → X' WP
     c.   X' → X YP

We now have quite a good picture of the basics of the theory of syntax. However, many questions have been left open here. One of the most important ones concerns the 'upward' nature of movement, also captured by our generalisation in (58). In the next chapter, we will look at a different set of rules which account for certain kinds of meaning dependencies among elements; this will give us a way of making the 'upwards' aspect of movement both more precise and integrating it into the theory properly.

Exercises

1.   Provide the trees for the following sentences. Indicate the gap (t) left by wh-movement in each case:

     a.   Which car did Mary buy?
     b.   What did Mary buy?
     c.   With which knife did Mary cut the bread?
     d.   Which knife did Mary [v' [v' cut the bread] [pp with t]]?
     e.   Which books did Mary say [cp (that) she will buy t]?
     f.   Who did Mary say [cp (that) [TP t sold her the books]?
     g.   Which knife did Mary say that she cut the bread with?
     h.   How did Mary say that she will solve this problem?
     i.   I remembered [who Ed said [t had visited Wanda]].
     j.   Ed asked [cp who [TP t knew [cp who [TP Greg had visited t]]]].
     k.   I will ask [cp which books [TP PRO to buy t]].

2.   Provide the trees for the following sentences, both the grammatical and the ungrammatical ones. Indicate the gap (*t*) left by wh-movement in each case:

    a.   I fed [NP [NP my [N' neighbour's]] [N' cat]].
    b.   Which neighbour's cat did you feed t ?
    c.   I wonder [CP [NP which neighbour's cat] [TP he fed t]].
    d.   [CP [NP Which neighbour's cat] [C did] [TP you say [CP (that) [TP you fed t]]]] ?
    e.   *[CP [NP Which neighbour's] did you feed [NP t cat] ?
    f.   *Which did you say you fed [NP [NP t neighbour's] cat] ?

What constraint do (e) and (f) violate?

3.   The following examples feature another island constraint:

    a.   *Who did [pictures of t] annoy John?
    b.   *Who did they say that [TP [TP PRO to talk to t] [T is] [AP forbidden]]?
    c.   *Who was [TP [CP that John spoke to t] t_was a shock?

Can you formulate this constraint (*hint*: try to generalize the Left Branch Constraint).

For Further Discussion

4.   Here is a very interesting construction, usually known as '*tough*-movement' or the '*easy-to-please* construction':

    a.   It is [AP tough [CP for [me/John/NASA to build space-ships]].
    b.   Spaceships are [AP tough [CP for [NASA to build t]].
    c.   It is [AP easy [PRO to cook pasta]].
    d.   Pasta is [AP easy [PRO to cook t]].

In (b) and (d), it seems natural to suggest that *spaceships/pasta* have moved to the main-clause subject position. Is this a further case of WH-movement? How could we determine whether it is or not?

Further Reading

Adger, D. 2003. *Core Syntax*. Oxford: Oxford University Press, Chapters 9 and 10.
Carnie, A. 2011. *Modern Syntax: A Coursebook*. Cambridge: Cambridge University Press, Chapter 4.
Carnie, A. 2013. *Syntax: A Generative Introduction*. Oxford: Blackwell, Chapters 9–11.

Larson, R. 2010. *Grammar as Science*. Cambridge, MA: MIT Press, Units 24–27.

Freidin, R. 2012. *Syntax: Basic Concepts and Applications*. Cambridge: Cambridge University Press, Chapter 8.

Radford, A. 2016. *Analysing English Sentences*. Cambridge: Cambridge University Press, Chapter 6.

Roberts, I. 1997. *Comparative Syntax* London: Arnold, Chapter 4.

Sportiche, D., H. Koopman & E. Stabler. (2014). *An Introduction to Syntactic Analysis and Theory*. Oxford: Wiley, Chapters 10 and 14.

Tallerman, M. 1998. *Understanding Syntax*. London: Routledge, Chapter 8.

6   Binding

6.1   Introduction and Recap

In the previous chapter we made the distinction between the rules which generate structure, PS-rules, including those which generate the X′-template, and movement rules, which map phrase markers into phrase markers. In this section I will introduce a third type of rule, **interpretative rules**, which specify the relationships between constituents in a hierarchical structure generated by PS-rules. These rules do not generate structure, so they are clearly distinct from PS-rules. Furthermore, they do not appear to involve movement. As the name suggests, though, they are relevant for the semantic interpretation of relations between constituents, including, as we will see, the relations between moved elements and their copies. The particular kind of dependency we will be concerned with involves **binding** of various types; the exact nature of binding will be elucidated as we proceed. We will see that the account of binding relations we arrive at provides important support for the hierarchical organisation of constituents of the kind we have been developing up to now.

6.2   Pronouns and Anaphors

We introduced pronouns in the context of substitution operations as tests for constituency in Chapter 3. There we observed that pronouns (e.g. *I/me, he/him, she/her, we/us, you, they/them*) are noun-like elements that have little semantic content of their own. Their semantic content is limited to **Person**, **Number**, **Gender** and **Case**. Concerning Person, *I/me* and *we/us* are **first person**, in that they refer to the speaker (or author) of a sentence and, in the plural, some unspecified other(s); *you* is second person, referring to the addressee(s), and the other pronouns are third person, in that they refer to neither speaker nor addressee. Number refers to the singular vs plural opposition; note that the Engish second-person pronoun *you* is ambiguous in Number. Gender, in English, relates to 'natural' rather than 'grammatical' gender: animate males are masculine, normally referred to with *he/him* and animate females are feminine, referred to as *she/her*; all inanimate objects are referred to as *it*. We saw in Chapter 1 that some languages, such as Italian, have grammatical gender, categorising all Nouns as masculine or feminine on what appear to be arbitrary grounds in many cases. Case refers to the nominative vs accusative distinction between *I* and *me*, *he* and *him*, etc. We saw in Chapter 2 that nominative is the typical case for subjects and accusative for objects. There are also the genitive forms of pronouns: *my, your, his, her, its, our* and *their*. The features of pronouns are features which are found elsewhere in the grammatical system: in verbal agreement and in the functional categories associated with nominals (e.g. Number, as we mentioned in Chapter 1).

The featural make-up of pronouns makes them semantically rather 'light'. They generally do not pick out referents on their own, unlike typical NPs such as *John, the boy* or *the man who lives next door*. Instead, they stand in for something else. This 'something else' is the antecedent, and this determines what the pronoun refers to. So, in an example like (1), *John* can be naturally interpreted as the antecedent of *he*:

(1)   John hopes that he will win.

In that case, (1) is interpreted to mean 'John hopes that he, John, will win.' Alternatively, *he* in (1) could refer to any contextually salient male individual distinct from John. In the latter case, we say that the pronoun has a non-linguistic antecedent, while in the interpretation where *he* stands for *John*, the pronoun has a linguistic antecedent.

As we will see, binding theory makes an important distinction between pronouns and **anaphors.** This distinction is not made in traditional grammar, where anaphors are described as a particular type of pronoun: **reflexive pronouns** such as *herself, himself, myself, yourself, yourselves*, etc., and **reciprocal pronouns** such as *each other*. On the other hand, binding theory groups reflexives and reciprocals together as a class of anaphors distinct from normal, simple pronouns such as *I/me, he/him, she/her, we/us, you, they/them*. The reasons for making this distinction will become clear below.

Both pronouns and anaphors are distinct from non-pronominal NPs, notably **R(eferring)-expressions**, NPs with the intrinsic semantics not dependent on the interpretation of some other NP in the linguistic expression in which they occur, e.g. *John, Mary, the idiot, the pet shop owner*, etc.

The goal of binding theory is to account for the distributions and interpretations of each class of NP. A simple way to do this is to adopt the **coindexing** convention: whenever two NPs have the same index, one is dependent on the other for its interpretation. The indices are subscript letters of the alphabet starting from 'i': $i, j, k \ldots$ This is linked to the idea that every distinct individual in our mental representation of the world has an integer which identifies it: $John_{23}$, *the man next door, the pet shop* boy_{666}, etc. However, this last point has little bearing on what follows. Adopting the coindexing convention, we can repeat (1) as (2):

(2) $John_i$ hopes that he_i will win.

Unlike (1), (2) is unambiguous: the coindexing of *John* and *he* means that *John* is the antecedent of *he*, i.e. (2) only has the first of the two interpretations of (1) discussed above.

So binding theory should be able to explain why the following sentences, with the interpretations indicated by the indices, are ungrammatical:

(3) a.   *Herself thinks that it's going to rain.
    b.   *A good friend of Mary$_i$'s has declared herself$_i$ bankrupt.
    c.   *John$_i$ likes him$_i$.
    d.   *He$_i$ likes John$_i$.

Furthermore, it should explain why the following examples are grammatical, again with the interpretations indicated by the indices:

(4) a.   John$_i$ said that the person who had upset him$_i$ should be fired.
    b.   Mary$_i$ has declared herself$_i$ bankrupt.
    c.   His$_i$ mother thinks John$_i$ is a genius.

Here we will see how binding theory deals with these examples in terms of the three classes of NP. We will look first at anaphors, then at pronouns and finally at R-expressions.

6.3   Anaphors

So let's begin with anaphors, concentrating mainly on reflexives. Consider first (5):

(5)   Goona betrayed herself.

Here, for (5) to be grammatical, we must interpret *Goona* as the antecedent of *herself*. We should therefore write (5) as (6), following the coindexing convention:

(6)   Goona$_i$ betrayed herself$_i$.

Compare now the ungrammatical (7):

(7)   *Herself left.

Comparing the grammatical (6), where *Goona* must be the antecedent of *herself*, with the ungrammatical (7), where *herself* has no antecedent, we can conclude that *herself* needs an antecedent.

Now consider (8):

(8)   * Herself$_i$ betrayed Goona$_i$.

Here, given the coindexing, *herself* has an antecedent, namely *Goona*. The sentence is nonetheless clearly ungrammatical. How can we account for this?

The structure of both (6) and (8) is (9):

(9)

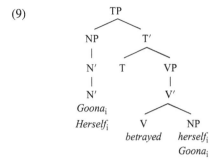

We will now review several hypotheses concerning what might be the best analysis of the required structural relation between the antecedent of the reflexive and
the reflexive. Here is the first hypothesis:

(10)   Hypothesis One: The antecedent of an anaphor must be a subject.

Hypothesis One will correctly distinguish the grammatical (6) from the ungrammatical (8). In (6), the antecedent of the reflexive, *Goona*, is a subject and in (8)
it is not.

However, in English non-subjects can be the antecedents of reflexives, as in:

(11)   I asked John$_i$ about himself$_i$.

This example is grammatical, but *John* is not a subject, although it can still be
the antecedent for *himself*. So this disconfirms Hypothesis One. Compare also:

(12)   *I asked himself about John.

Here *I* is the subject, but it still cannot be the antecedent for *himself*. This is
because the antecedence relation requires agreement in number, gender and person. First-person *I* therefore cannot bind third-person *himself* (contrast *I$_i$ asked
myself$_i$ about John* where *myself* and *I* agree for first person and so *I* can be the
antecedent of *myself*). We will see further examples of the agreement condition
on antecedence below. Hence subjecthood, on its own, is neither necessary nor
sufficient for being a well-formed antecedent for a reflexive.

To a good approximation, the structure of (11) and (12) is as in (13):

(13)

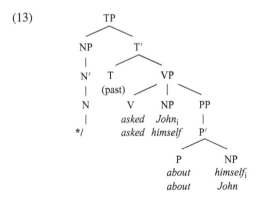

These examples lead to the postulation of Hypothesis Two, as follows:

(14)   Hypothesis Two: The antecedent of an anaphor must precede it.

Hypothesis Two accounts for the grammaticality of (6) and (11), where the antecedent precedes the anaphor, and for the ungrammaticality of (8) and (12), where anaphor precedes the antecedent. In fact, precedence may be a necessary condition for a well-formed antecedent antecedent–anaphor relation, but it is not a sufficient one, as there are examples where the antecedent precedes the anaphor which are nonetheless ungrammatical, such as the following:

(15) a.   *John$_i$'s friends talked about himself$_i$.
     b.   *Friends of John$_i$'s talked about himself$_i$

Here we must pay careful attention to the indices. The coindexation in (15a) indicates that *John* is the intended antecedent of *himself*, and this is impossible. We can assign a grammatical interpretation to the string in (15a) if we interpret *John's friends* as the antecedent of the plural anaphor *themselves*; here we see the requirement that the antecedent and anaphor must agree for number in action. But this would correspond to the coindexing in (16):

(16)   [John's friends]$_i$ talked about themselves$_i$.

Here the index *i* is associated with the whole NP *John's friends* (incidentally, this shows that indices are associated with NPs, not with Nouns). Similar reasoning applies to (15b): with the indexing given, *John* cannot be the antecedent of *himself*. *John's friends* can be, if *himself* is changed to *themselves* as just mentioned, but in that case the index is associated to that whole NP, and not to *John*.

   Keeping these points in mind, we can get a very important clue to what is going on if we look at the structure of (15a) (here, as in our discussion of possessive NPs in Section 5.3, the numerical subscripts on the NPs serve merely to keep them distinct; they are not to be taken as indices):

(17)

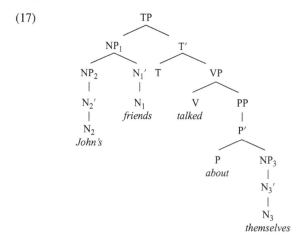

Here, if NP$_1$, *John's friends*, is the antecedent of *themselves*, the relation is structurally well-formed, as we pointed out above. On the other, NP$_2$, *John's*, cannot be the antecedent. What seems to make the difference here is the relation between the antecedent and the anaphor in terms of hierarchical structure. We could therefore tentatively formulate Hypothesis Three, as follows:

(18)   Hypothesis Three (to be revised): An antecedent must be *structurally higher* than the anaphor which it binds.

Since NP$_1$ is evidently structurally higher (higher up in the tree) in (17) than the anaphor NP$_3$, it is able to be its antecedent. NP$_2$, *John's*, on the other hand, is seemingly not in the requisite structural relation with the anaphor for this to be possible. Clearly, we need to make this intuitive notion of 'structural height' more precise.

The formal indicator of relative structural height is the relation of **constituent-command**, or **c-command**. This structural relation plays a central role in binding theory and, as we will see in Volume II, many other dependencies. The definition of c-command is given in (19):

(19)   A node X c-commands another node Y if and only if:
     i.   X does not dominate Y;
     ii. Y does not dominate X;
     iii. The first branching node dominating X dominates Y.

Let us revisit some of the structures we looked at earlier and apply this definition to the various antecedent–anaphor pairs. First, (9):

(9)
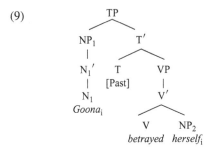

Taking the subject NP to be X and the object NP to be Y in terms of the definition of c-command in (19), we can apply the definition. First, it is easy to see that the subject NP doesn't dominate the object NP and NP$_2$ doesn't dominate NP$_1$ (remember the definition of dominance in Chapter 2, (26)). So the first two conditions in (19) are satisfied. Coming to the third, the first branching node dominating the subject NP is TP, and TP, as the root node here, dominates everything. Therefore TP dominates the object NP and so the third clause of the definition in (19) is met: the subject NP c-commands the object NP. If c-command is the condition for antecedence, then the subject NP *Goona* can be the antecedent of the object NP *herself*.

Now let's ask if the object NP c-commands the subject NP. As before the first two clauses of the definition in (19) are met, in that neither NP dominates the other. Turning to (19iii), though, we see that the first branching node dominating the object NP is V', and this node does not dominate the subject NP. Therefore the object NP does not c-command the subject NP in (9), hence in the ungrammatical (8), *Goona* cannot be the antecedent of *herself*.

Next, the structure in (13) (annotated with numerical subscripts):

(13)

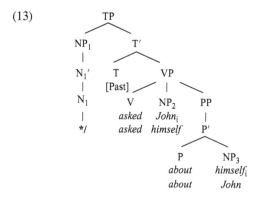

Here the question is whether NP₂ c-commands NP₃. Since it is easy to see neither NP dominates the other, the question again is whether the first branching node dominating NP₂, VP, dominates NP₃. The answer is clearly yes, and so NP₂ c-commands NP₃ and is able to be the antecedent for NP₃. Conversely, since the first branching node dominating NP₃ is P' and P' does not dominate NP₂, NP₃ cannot be the antecedent for NP₂; this accounts for the ungrammaticality of (12).

Finally, let us consider (17) in the light of c-command as defined in (19):

(17)

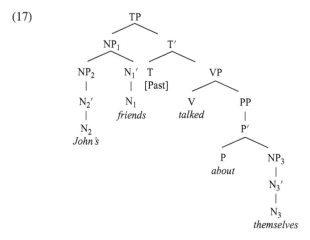

Here, since the first branching node dominating NP₁ is TP, which as the root node dominates everything, NP₁ c-commands NP₃. This is why *John's friends* can be the antecedent of *themselves* in (16). On the other hand, the first branching node dominating NP₂ is NP₁, which does not dominate NP₃. Therefore *John's* cannot be the antecedent of *themselves*.

So we can restate Hypothesis Three as follows:

(20)   Hypothesis Three (revised): An anaphor must be c-commanded by its antecedent.

Formulated in this way, with c-command defined as in (19), Hypothesis Three correctly captures all the grammatical and ungrammatical sentences we have looked at so far.

However, c-command, although of central importance, is just one component of binding theory. There is a further aspect, connected to how far away the anaphor is from its antecedent. We can see this from the following example:

(21)   *John_i said [_CP that himself_i left].

The structure of (21) is (22):

(22)
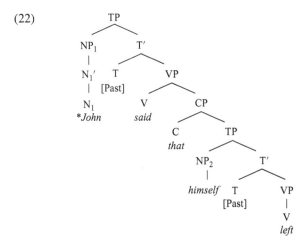

Here we can easily see that NP_1 c-commands NP_2, since, once again, the first branching node dominating NP_1 is TP, the root node, which dominates everything. With only Hypothesis Three, then, *John* should be able to be the antecedent for *himself*.

We can correctly rule out (22) and retain all our earlier results if we restate Hypothesis Three as follows:

(23)   Hypothesis Four: An anaphor must be c-commanded by a clause-mate antecedent.

We can define 'clause-mate' as 'dominated by the same CPs'. To put it more formally (and precisely):

(24)   X and Y are clause-mates if and only if there is no CP which dominates Y and does not dominate X.

By this definition, we see that *John* and *himself* are not clause-mates in (22) since the lower CP dominates *himself* without dominating *John*. In (22), then, *himself* is not c-commanded by a clause-mate antecedent and so Hypothesis Four rules out the antecedent-anaphor relation here. All the earlier examples we considered were monoclausal and the clause-mate condition was satisfied every time.

But compare now the following examples:

(25) a.   *John, thought [_CP_ that himself, was a genius].
     b.   John, believes [_XP_ himself, to be a genius].

We can account for the ungrammaticality of (25a) exactly as for (21): *John* and *himself* are not clause-mates by the definition in (24) and therefore *John* cannot be the antecedent of *himself*, given Hypothesis Four. But where does this leave (25b)? At a minimum, we have to say that, although XP looks like a clause in that it contains a subject and a predicate (at least from a semantic perspective), it does not qualify as a clause for the definition of clause-mates in (24). This would be the case if XP is not a CP. So instead, we take it to be TP, where infinitival *to* is in T. This is supported by the fact that verbs like *believe* cannot take C$_{Wh}$ complements, as we noted in Chapter 5. So we have contrasts of the following kind with verbs like *wonder*:

(26) a.   John wondered [_CP_ whether to leave].
     b.   *John believed [whether the world to be flat].

If there is no CP in the infinitival complement to *believe*, then there is no possibility of C$_{Wh}$.

So let us assign the structure in (27) to (25b):

(27)

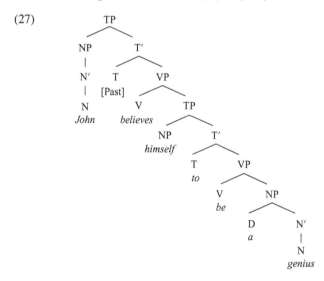

Since there are either no CPs dominating *John* and *himself* here, or there is just a root CP which is not shown here, there is no CP which dominates *himself* but does not dominate *John*. Therefore, *John* and *himself* are clause-mates. Therefore *John* can be the antecedent of *himself*. The contrast in (25) is now accounted for.

But now what can we make of the ungrammaticality of (28)?

(28)   *John$_i$ believes [$_{TP}$ Mary to like himself$_i$].

The structure of (28) is (29):

(29)

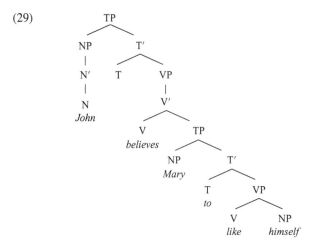

Unless we posit a CP in some strange place inside the embedded TP, *John* and *himself* will be clause-mates by the definition in (24). It also seems clear that *John* c-commands *himself*, since *John* is the main-clause subject in main-clause SpecT', and so the first branching node dominating *John* is the root TP, which dominates everything. It seems we need a further condition in addition to clause-mates and c-command.

Hypothesis Five can account for (28) while leaving all the earlier results intact:

(30)   Hypothesis Five: An anaphor must be c-commanded by a clause-mate antecedent such that no other NP intervenes between the antecedent and anaphor.

We can also define **intervention** in terms of c-command (a more general version of this notion of intervention, still defined in terms of c-command, will play a major role in Volume II):

(31)   Any NP which c-commands the anaphor and is c-commanded by the antecedent is an intervener.

Applying Hypothesis Five to (28), we see that the subject of the infinitival TP, *Mary*, c-commands the anaphor *himself* and is c-commanded by the antecedent *John*. *Mary* therefore intervenes between the antecedent and the anaphor, and so the relation cannot hold. In contrast, there is no such intervener in (25b/27) and so here the antecedent–anaphor relation is well-formed, as it was under Hypothesis Four.

However, the notion of intervener in (31) is too strong, in that it rules out certain well-formed antecedent–anaphor relations, as in (32) for example:

(32)   John, told Mary about himself.

The structure of (32) is (33):

(33)

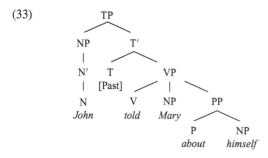

Here, *Mary* c-commands the anaphor and is c-commanded by the antecedent, just as in (28). So the antecedent–anaphor relation should fail to hold here too. But in this case it is allowed.

To allow for (33) while retaining our account of (28), we can reformulate Hypothesis Five as follows:

(34)   Hypothesis Five (revised): An anaphor must be c-commanded by a clause-mate antecedent such that no subject intervenes between the antecedent and anaphor.

The definition of intervention in (31) remains unchanged, but now Hypothesis Five only applies to subjects intervening between the antecedent and the anaphor. This means that the antecedent–anaphor relation is still blocked in (28), while (33) is allowed, since although *Mary* is still defined as a intervener by (31), it is an indirect object and not a subject.

We have now almost arrived at the final characterisation of the structural domain for well-formed antecedent–anaphor relations. There are two requirements: (i) the anaphor and antecedent must be clause-mates and (ii) no subject can intervene between the anaphor and antecedent. Furthermore, the antecedent must c-command the anaphor. We can replace the notion of clause-mate, defined as in (24), with the simpler notion of 'domain containing a finite T'. Here the key point is that while certain infinitives may be defective in that they are TP rather than CP, as in the complement of *believe* discussed above, finite clauses are never defective; they are always full TPs with an associated CP (this is true for finite root clauses although we have frequently not included the root CP in the structures we have given). Hence two NPs will fail to be clause-mates if they are not contained in the same minimal finite TP, although they may be clause-mates when contained in distinct non-finite minimal TPs.

We are now in a position to present the sixth and final hypothesis on antecedent–anaphor relations:

(35)   Hypothesis Six: An anaphor must be c-commanded by an antecedent which is contained in the same binding domain (BD).

We define binding domain (BD) as follows:

(36)   The BD for an anaphor A is the smallest XP containing A and either:
            (a)   a subject (distinct from A) or
            (b)   a finite T.

The crucial cases illustrating how this definition of BD works are the biclausal ones in (25) and (28), so let us go through those once more:

(25) a.   *John$_i$ thought [$_{CP}$ that himself$_i$ was a genius].
     b.   John$_i$ believes [$_{XP}$ himself$_i$ to be a genius].

(28)   *John$_i$ believes [$_{TP}$ Mary to like himself$_i$].

The BD for *himself* in (25a) is the embedded TP as this is the smallest XP containing a finite T (note that this TP does not contain a subject distinct from the anaphor). The antecedent *John* is outside this BD and hence Hypothesis Six is not satisfied and the relation does not hold. The sentence is therefore ungrammatical.

The BD for *himself* in (25b) is the root TP, as this is the smallest category containing both a subject distinct from the anaphor and a finite T. The embedded TP is non-finite and the subject is the anaphor itself, and therefore not distinct from the anaphor. Since that BD contains the antecedent *John*, the relation is well-formed and the sentence is grammatical. This account has the advantage over the clause-mate-based definition relying on the notion of clause-mate in (24), since we are no longer required to consider that XP is not CP.

The BD for *himself* in (28) is the embedded TP. Although non-finite, this is the smallest XP containing a subject, *Mary*, distinct from the anaphor. The antecedent *John* is outside this BD, and hence Hypothesis Six is not satisfied and the relation does not hold. The sentence is therefore ungrammatical.

Hypothesis Six therefore accounts for all the examples we have seen in this section. We can now add a general definition of binding, which will be relevant in the rest of this chapter, and as a consequence further simplify Hypothesis Six. The definition of binding is (37):

(37)   X binds Y if and only if X c-commands Y and X is coindexed with Y.

As long as antecedents are coindexed with their anaphors, all the cases of well-formed antecedent–anaphor relations we have seen involve the antecedent binding the anaphor by this definition. We can now restate Hypothesis Six in simpler form as follows:

(38)   An anaphor must be bound in its binding domain.

The statement in (38) captures all the facts we have seen in this section, both the well-formed and ill-formed antecedent–anaphor relations.

In the next sections, we will see that the definition of binding generalises to pronouns and R-expressions. We will also see that the notion of binding domain is relevant for capturing important aspects of the distribution and interpretation of pronouns, which is our next topic.

6.4   Pronouns

Remember that the definition of pronouns we are working with here excludes reflexives (*himself*, etc.) and reciprocals (e.g. *each other*); those are anaphors and the subject of the preceding section.

The first observation we can make about pronouns is that they do not require a linguistic antecedent (something we already noted in our discussion of (1)). Hence both examples in (39) grammatical:

(39) a.   He grew some vegetables.
     b.   Vurdy said he grew some vegetables.

In (39a) the pronoun *he* clearly has no linguistic antecedent. Nonetheless, the sentence is grammatical. In this respect pronouns contrast with anaphors; compare the ungrammaticality of (7). The pronoun here refers to some contextually salient male individual.

The following examples illustrate important aspects of the distribution of pronouns:

(40) a.   Vurdy$_i$'s mother loves him$_i$.
     b.   Goona$_i$ believes Vurdy to like her$_i$.

In (40a), we see that the antecedent of the pronoun doesn't have to c-command the pronoun; again this contrasts with the behaviour of anaphors seen in (15). In (40b), we see that the antecedent of the pronoun can be outside the pronoun's binding domain, unlike what we saw with anaphors in examples like (28). Here we are extending the idea of binding domain to pronouns. Binding domains were defined in (37) explicitly for anaphors; here we generalise that definition so that it applies to pronouns:

(41)   The BD for NP$_i$ is the smallest XP containing NP$_i$ and either:
     a.   a subject (distinct from NP$_i$) or
     b.   a finite T.

This definition applies to any (indexed) NP; therefore it can still apply to anaphors in exactly the way we saw at the end of the previous section, but now it can also apply to pronouns (and in principle to other NPs). To repeat, then, (40b) shows that a pronoun, unlike an anaphor, can be bound from outside its BD.

In fact, while anaphors must be in a local domain with their antecedents, as we saw, pronouns must not be too close to their antecedents, as the following examples show:

(42) a.   Vurdy$_i$ hates him$_{*i/j}$.
     b.   Vurdy$_i$ believes [him$_{*i/j}$ to be the best].
     c.   Vurdy$_i$ told Goona about him$_{*i/j}$.

Here we have starred certain subscripts in order to indicate the ungrammatical interpretations of the pronouns. So, in (42a) *him* cannot take *John* as its antecedent, although it is able to have some other non-linguistic antecedent. Similarly, in (42b) and in (42c); in each case the sentence as such is grammatical, but it does not allow the interpretation where the antecedent of *John* is *him*. Once again, there is a minimal contrast with anaphors: compare (6) with (42a), (25b) with (42b) and (32) with (42c).

The condition on binding of pronouns is in fact a negative one. There is no specification as to where pronouns appear, but rather a constraint which states where they *cannot* be interpreted as bound to an antecedent. This constraint can be stated as follows:

(43)   A pronoun cannot be bound in its binding domain.

The definition of binding domain is the generalised one in (41). The definition of binding is (37), repeated here:

(37)   X binds Y if and only if X c-commands Y and X is co-indexed with Y.

So no pronoun can have a coindexed, c-commanding antecedent in its binding domain. Otherwise, the distribution and interpretation of pronouns is quite free: they can have non-c-commanding local antecedents (as in (40a)), antecedents outside their BD (as in (39b) and (40b)) and they can fail to have linguistic antecedents (as in (39a)).

We can add one further definition and then restate (43):

(44)   If X is not bound, then X is **free**.

Now we restate (43) as a positive condition:

(45)   A pronoun must be free in its binding domain.

It is obvious that (43) and (45) are equivalent.

We can now move to briefly consider R-expressions.

6.5   R-expressions

In Section 6.2 we defined R-expressions as NPs with the intrinsic semantic capacity to pick out a referent, a specific individual from the domain of discourse (Goona, Vurdy, John, Mary, the Swedish Chef, the pet shop boy, etc.). Exactly how NPs refer, and what the relation of reference is, are important and difficult questions in semantic theory. For our purposes, it is sufficient to observe that R-expressions have an intrinsic referential capacity that pronouns and anaphors lack; at the very minimum, there is an obvious sense in which an NP like *John* or *that man* does not require a relation with an antecedent of some kind in order for its reference to be determined.

In terms of the notion of freedom introduced at the end of the previous section ('free' simply means 'not bound', with binding defined as in (37)), we might therefore expect that R-expressions are able to be free. This is, perhaps unsurprisingly, true. But the condition on R-expressions is stronger: R-expressions must always be free. What this means is that R-expressions can never have a c-commanding, coindexed antecedent. There is no locality condition associated with this constraint; the notion of BD plays no role. If an R-expression is bound by a pronoun, even at a distance, ungrammaticality results, as examples like the following show:

(46) a.   *He$_i$ thought [$_{CP}$ that [the idiot]$_i$ must be right]].
     b.   *He$_i$ said that John thinks that Mary believes that Nigel$_i$ is invited.

In (47a), the BD for the *the idiot* is the embedded TP, as this is the minimal XP containing that NP and a finite T, but binding by *he* in the main clause is nonetheless not allowed. If we replace *the idiot* with a coindexed pronoun, the example becomes grammatical; if we replace it with an anaphor it remains ungrammatical. These outcomes are predicted by (45) and (38) respectively. Here we can see the utility of the generalised definition of BD in (41). In (46b) *Nigel* is three clauses away from *he*; nonetheless *he* cannot bind *Nigel*. This clearly illustrates that R-expressions are subject to an absolute freedom requirement.

If R-expressions must be free in the technical sense of not bound, this means that they can have antecedents; the requirement is that such antecedents must not c-command the R-expression. So we find well-formed examples such as the following:

(47) a.   [His$_i$ mother] loves John$_i$.
     b.   [The fact that he$_i$ failed the exam] bothered Vurdy$_i$.
     c.   [The hobbit he$_i$ befriended] trusted Gandalf$_i$.

In all of these cases, the pronoun is embedded inside a subject constituent which it cannot c-command out of (it is a good exercise to draw the tree diagrams for these examples and work out the c-command relations). Hence, although there is coindexation, and therefore coreference, the R-expressions *John*, *Vurdy* and *Gandalf* are not bound by the pronouns in the sense defined in (37). Therefore the relation is allowed and the sentences are grammatical with the interpretations indicated by the coindexation.

6.6   The Binding Principles

We can now bring together what we have concluded regarding the conditions on anaphors, pronouns and R-expressions. These are unified as the three **binding principles** given in (48):

(48)   Principle A: an anaphor must be bound in its binding domain.
        Principle B: a pronoun must be free in its binding domain.
        Principle C: an R-expression must be free.

The definitions of binding, free and binding domain are repeated below:

(37)   X binds Y if and only if X c-commands Y and X is co-indexed with Y.

(44)   If X is not bound, then X is free.

(41)   The binding domain for NP_i is the smallest XP containing NP_i and either:
   a.   a subject (distinct from NP_i) or
   b.   a finite T.

The binding principles account for a wide range of facts concerning the distribution and interpretation of NPs. We can get a glimpse of this by reconsidering the grammatical and ungrammatical examples we introduced in (3) and (4) above:

(3) a.   *Herself thinks that it's going to rain.
     b.   *A good friend of $Mary_i$'s has declared $herself_i$ bankrupt.
     c.   *$John_i$ likes him_i.
     d.   *He_i likes $John_i$.

(4) a. $John_i$ said that the person who had upset him_i should be fired.
     b. $Mary_i$ has declared $herself_i$ bankrupt.
     c. His_i mother thinks $John_i$ is a genius.

Let us go through these examples one by one.

Example (3a) is ungrammatical because the anaphor *herself* has no (linguistic) antecedent, but Principle A in (48) requires anaphors to be bound, i.e. to have a c-commanding, coindexed antecedent. Example (3b) is ungrammatical because the anaphor *herself* is not c-commanded by its antecedent *Mary* (the first branching node dominating *Mary* is the P′ headed by *of*; clearly this node does not dominate *herself*). Example (3c) is ungrammatical because the pronoun *him* is bound in its binding domain (the root TP) by *John*, but Principle B in (48) requires pronouns to be free, i.e. not bound, in their binding domain. Finally, example (3d) is ungrammatical because the R-expression *John* is bound by *he*, but Principle C in (48) requires R-expressions to be free.

Turning now to the grammatical examples in (4), (4a) is grammatical because the pronoun *him* is bound by *John*, an antecedent outside the pronoun's binding domain (which is the TP of the relative clause *(who) had upset him*, the smallest XP containing a finite T and a subject distinct from *John*, the latter presumably the trace/copy of the moved relative pronoun *who*). This example is therefore in conformity with Principle B in (48). Example (4b) is grammatical because the anaphor *herself* is bound by the antecedent *Mary* in the same binding domain, the root TP (the smallest XP containing a finite T and a subject distinct from the anaphor). This example therefore obeys Principle A of (48). Finally, (4c) is grammatical because, although the R-expression *John* is coindexed with *his*, there is no c-command relation between the two and so *John* is not bound by *his*, in conformity with Principle C of (48).

So we see that the binding principles give us a compact account of a wide range of distributional and interpretational properties of different NP-types. The binding principles are interpretative rules regulating the dependencies among NPs in structures generated by PS-rules in conformity with X'-theory, and appear to be quite distinct from movement rules (although they are sensitive to the operations of movement rules, as we will see in the next section).

6.7   Variables, Principle C and Movement

In our discussion of movement rules in Chapter 5, we arrived at the following general characterisation of movement:

(49)   Movement substitutes an element of type X into a higher position of type X, where X ranges over heads, wh-phrases and grammatical-function NPs. (See Chapter 5, (58).)

The reference to a 'higher position' here reflects the fact that we observed that movement always appears to be upwards. This can be seen in the following structures illustrating each kind of movement, again repeated from Chapter 5:

(50) a.   Head-movement:

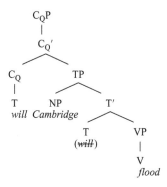

b.   NP-movement:

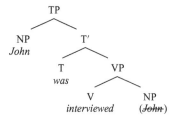

c.   Wh-movement:

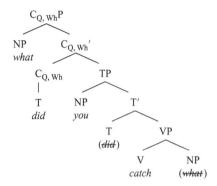

We can now observe that the correct notion of 'upwards' is defined by c-command: movement targets a c-commanding position. In each of (50a–c), the first branching node dominating the target position of movement dominates the trace/copy in the starting position. This is clear in (50b,c) where the moved category occupies the Specifier of the root node, so that the first branching node dominating it is the root node, which dominates everything. But it is also the case in (50a), where the first branching node dominating C_Q, the target of T-to-C movement, is C_Q', which dominates T.

So we can replace (49) with (51):

(51)   Movement substitutes an element of type X into a *c-commanding* position of type X, where X ranges over heads, wh-phrases and grammatical-function NPs.

If the moved category c-commands its trace, since c-command is part of the definition of binding, we can ask whether a moved category binds its trace/copy. In other words, is the moved category coindexed with its trace/copy? For NP-movement and wh-movement of NPs the answer to this question is clearly affirmative: if all NPs bear referential indices, then those indices will be copied as part of the copy/paste operation of movement, so coindexation automatically results. We may be able to extend the idea to head-movement and wh-movement of categories other than NP (although admittedly the notion of 'referential index' lacks a clear semantic grounding in these cases), but let us concentrate here on some interesting consequences of the conclusion that wh-NPs and moved NPs in passives bind their trace/copies.

There are good semantic reasons to think that wh-NPs bind their traces/copies quite independently of the fact that we can now see that the configuration created by wh-movement creates a binding relation between them given the definition of binding (c-command + coindexing) in (37). To see this, we need to look in a little more detail at the semantic properties of certain kinds of NPs.

We can start by comparing these two sentences:

(52) a.   Goona likes pizza.
      b.   Every student likes pizza.

The proper-name subject in (52a) is a standard kind of R-expression: it picks out a particular individual in the universe of discourse. The predication relation between this R-expression subject and the predicate can be construed as placing the referent of the R-expression in the set denoted by the predicate (VP): the set of pizza-likers. So (52a) is true if and only if Goona is a member of the set of pizza-likers, and false otherwise. This shows how we can combine an R-expression subject with a simple predicate and get the meaning, or the **truth conditions,** for the whole sentence.

Now look at (52b). The subject NP *every student* doesn't refer to a single individual (for binding-theory purposes it is nonetheless an R-expression subject to Principle C of (48); this is where the syntactic notion of R-expression and the semantic notion of reference come apart, as we hinted in Section 6.5). Because of the **quantifier** *every*, this NP is a quantified expression. To cut a long, complex and very interesting semantic story short, such NPs refer to a set of entities (students) and say that every member of that set is also in the set denoted by the predicate, the set of pizza-likers. (This is a subset relation: there can be pizza-likers who are not students but, if (52b) is true, there are no students who are not also pizza-likers.)

We can give a quasi-logical representation for (52b) as follows (if this were a proper semantics textbook, we'd have to use a much more mathematically precise formula here, but this is good enough for us):

(53)   For every x, if x is a student, then x likes pizza (or 'if x is in the set of students, then x is in the set of pizza-likers').

In (53), x is a variable, ranging over individuals in the domain of discourse. To get the full meaning of (52b), we have to 'plug in' individuals for x (technically, we assign values to the variable) and then see if that individual, say individual 23 = $John_{23}$, individual 5 = *the man next door*$_5$, individual 666 = *the pet shop boy*$_{666}$, etc., is a member of the set of students and a member of the set of pizza-likers. As long as we don't find any individuals who are in the set of students and not in the set of pizza-likers, then the sentence is true.

The above paragraph describes how we can give a precise semantics for NPs which are interpreted as quantified expressions. It is absolutely crucial for this account that the two occurrences of the variable x in 'if x is a student, then x likes pizza' (53) always have the same value. The semantics breaks down if we start asking whether if John is student, the man next door likes pizza. In logic and semantics, these variables are said to be bound by the quantifier, and so as we compute the semantics of the quantifier, plugging in values for the variables, the two variables always have the same value. This notion of binding is similar to what we have seen in syntactic binding theory: when a pronoun or anaphor is bound by an antecedent, it has the same referential value as that antecedent, i.e. it denotes the same (set of) individuals.

Now we can come back to wh-movement. Consider a simple wh-question in the light of what we've just seen regarding quantified expressions:

(54)   Which course$_i$ does Goona like t$_i$?

The crucial observation is that *which* is also quantificational rather than referential: the answer to the question could be 'none of them', showing that *which course* doesn't have to pick anything out in the domain of discourse. Like *every student*, *which course* applies to a set of entities (courses) and asks for the identity of a member of that set such that Goona likes it. In quasi-logic:

(55)   For which x, x a course, does Goona like x ?

So we see an important semantic similarity between wh-elements and quantifiers: both instantiate **operator-variable structures**. The **operator** (or **quantifier**) applies to a set of entities and specifies the subpart of that set we are dealing with (every member, some member, no member, or, in the case of wh-operators, find a member). The variable tells us where in the structure you would 'plug in' the specified domain in relation to the predicate so as to compute the relation to the predicate and see if the sentence is true or false. So, in relation to (55), we plug in different courses in the variable in object position as values of x, and ask if Goona is a member of the set of x-likers. As with the account of the semantics of *every*, it is crucial that the two x's following 'which x' in (55) always have the same value. So, *these variables are semantically bound by the wh-word*.

Leaving aside the syntactic counterpart of 'x a course' in (55), it is clear that the syntactic counterpart of the rightmost x in (55) is the trace/copy of wh-movement. So here we can conclude that syntactic binding, c-command and coindexation correspond exactly to the semantic binding involved in interpreting the wh-quantification. So now we really have a good answer for why wh-movement is always upwards: the wh-expression must be placed in a position from which it c-commands the trace/copy it is coindexed with in order for that trace/copy to be semantically interpreted as a variable.

So the relation between the wh-phrase and its copy/trace in (54) is a binding relation in good standing. The obvious question to ask now is which of the binding principles in (48) is the wh-copy/trace subject to? We can immediately conclude that it can't be Principle A, since the binding domain for the trace/copy is the finite TP [TP *Goona (does) like t$_i$*] and the wh-phrase is clearly outside this constituent (note in passing the importance of the copy of the finite T left by T-to-C movement for this conclusion). But is it Principle B or Principle C?

To answer this question, we need to introduce a pronoun into our example:

(56)   Who$_i$ did Goona say she likes t$_i$?

As we have seen, pronouns don't have to have linguistic antecedents, so *she* here could refer to some contextually given female individual distinct from Goona.

Equally, *she* can be coindexed with and therefore bound by *Goona* (since *Goona* c-commands *she*):

(57)   Who$_i$ did Goona$_j$ say she$_j$ likes t$_i$?

Principle B is respected here, since *she* is in a distinct binding domain from *Goona* (the deepest embedded TP is a BD by definition (41)). But now, if instead we assign index *i* to *she*, ungrammaticality results:

(58)   *Who$_i$ did Goona$_j$ say she$_i$ likes t$_i$?

The question in (58) cannot have the interpretation that *she* is the antecedent of *who* or its trace/copy. So the trace/copy cannot be an anaphor subject to Principle A, since it would be bound by *she$_i$* here, but that interpretation is unavailable. This leaves no alternative to Principle C.

Let us now look at the interpretation of (58). Since *she* is now coindexed with *who*, it is bound by *who*. Pronouns bound by quantifiers are semantically interpreted as variables (more on this below), so (58) has the interpretation in (59) (taking *who* to mean 'for which *x*, *x* a person'):

(59)   For which x, x a person, Goona said x likes x

The interpretation in (59) would correspond to a grammatical sentence like (60):

(60)   Who$_i$ did Goona$_j$ say t$_i$ likes herself$_i$?

It is clear, though, that (58) does not have that meaning. So what is the cause of the ungrammaticality of (58)? The pronoun *she* does not violate Principle B, as *who* is clearly outside its binding domain (the embedded TP). Therefore it must be the trace/copy. The trace/copy's binding domain is the embedded TP (the minimal XP containing the trace/copy, a subject and a finite T), which also contains *she*. So we could conclude that the trace/copy is subject to Principle B, which would then be violated here (and not, for example, in (57)).

However, if we swap the positions of *Goona* and *she* in (58), and maintain the indexing, ungrammaticality results again:

(61)   *Who$_i$ did she$_i$ say Goona$_j$ likes t$_i$?

The interpretation of (61) is (62a), which corresponds to the grammatical sentence (62b):

(62) a.   For which x, x a person, x said Goona likes x
     b.   Who$_i$ t$_i$ said Goona likes her$_i$?

The ungrammaticality of (61) cannot be attributed to Principle B applying to *she*, since the binding domain for *she* is the main-clause TP (the minimal XP that includes *she* and a finite T) and *she* is free in this domain. Neither can it be attributed to Principle B applying to the trace/copy, since *Goona*, which is in the trace/copy's binding domain, has a distinct index and *she* is now outside the trace/copy's binding domain. However, we could attribute it to Principle C applying to the trace/copy, since the trace/copy is bound by *she*.

Saying that traces/copies, at least of wh-movement, are subject to Principle C has one advantage and, at first sight, one major problem. The advantage is the connection with the semantics of variables described above. Variables are semantically substituted by expressions with constant values ($John_{23}$, etc.), as we saw, and so we can reasonably treat them as R-expressions. On the other hand, as we have also seen, variables are c-commanded by and coindexed with their wh-phrases, therefore they are bound by them. On the face of it then, they should always violate Principle C.

The solution lies in distinguishing two kinds of NP positions. In fact, we have already implicitly made the right distinction in our discussion of NP-movement in Section 5.6. There we characterised NP-movement in passives as moving NPs from one grammatical-function position (object) to another (subject). All our examples of binding have involved coindexation and c-command relations between grammatical-function positions, mainly subject positions and object positions, although in (13) and (33) indirect-object positions were involved. We can also count the complement of P as a grammatical-function position (either indirect object or oblique) and the Specifier of a possessive NP (NP_2 immediately dominated by NP_1 has the possessor function). Thus, the core cases of binding theory all involve grammatical-function positions. The target of wh-movement $SpecC_{Wh}'$, on the other hand, is not a grammatical-function position: as we saw in Chapter 5, XPs bearing any grammatical function (subject, direct object, indirect object, predicate) or none (e.g. temporal *when*, locative *where*, etc.) can appear there.

So we can distinguish grammatical-function, or **A-positions**, from non-grammatical-function or **A'-positions**. Now we can say that the binding conditions hold of binding relations from A-positions (**A-binding**) only. The A-positions are subject, object, indirect object, object of preposition and possessor. All other positions are A'-positions. In that case, binding of a trace/copy by a wh-phrase in SpecC' does not violate Principle C, as Principle C holds only of A-binding. On the other hand, the trace/copy in (61) is A-bound by *she*, so we can maintain that the traces/copies of wh-movement, as variables, are R-expressions subject to Principle C, and Principle C is violated in (61).

Examples like (61) where a trace/copy of wh-movement is A-bound in violation of Principle C are known as **strong crossover** (the idea being that the wh-phrase 'crosses over' the pronoun as it moves). There is also a phenomenon of **weak crossover**, illustrated by examples like (63):

(63)   ?*Who$_i$ does her$_i$ mother love t$_i$?

Here again, the pronoun *her*, since it is bound by *who*, is interpreted as a variable bound by it. So (63) has the interpretation:

(64)   For which x, x a person, x's mother loves x

Although the interpretation is coherent, (63) is somewhat unacceptable; compare *Who is loved by her mother*, which is acceptable with the interpretation in (64). The phenomenon is called 'weak crossover' precisely because the unacceptability is less strong than in strong-crossover cases such as (61).

What is wrong with (63)? Here there is no Principle C violation as *her* does not c-command the trace/copy. Neither is there a Principle B violation as *her* is not A-bound by anything here (it is A'-bound by *who*, giving rise to the bound-variable interpretation, but we have now excluded A'-binding from core binding theory). We will leave this question open, merely noting the phenomenon.

We have now seen some cases where pronouns are interpreted as variables bound by wh-phrases. Pronouns can also have bound-variable interpretations when bound by other quantified expressions, e.g. *every student* in (65):

(65)   Every student$_i$ thinks they$_i$ are the best.

The natural interpretation of (65) is (66):

(66)   For every x, if x is a student, then x thinks x is the best.

The expression in (66) can be interpreted by the procedure of plugging in values for variables described above.

There are two things to note about bound-variable pronouns. First, the interpretation depends on the quantified NP c-commanding the pronoun. So the interpretation is unavailable in cases like the following:

(67)   The man who talked to every student$_i$ thinks they$_i$ are the best.

Here the only interpretation available seems to be that where the man thinks that the set of students as a whole are the best; the bound-variable interpretation ('the man who talked to every x, x a student, thinks x is the best') is not available. This is because *every student* does not c-command *they* here.

Second, the bound pronoun obeys Principle B, as we would expect, since it is A-bound. Hence (68a) is ungrammatical on any interpretation, while (68b) shows that anaphors can also have bound-variable interpretations provided Principle A is satisfied:

(68) a.   *Every boy$_i$ admires him$_i$.
     b.   Every boy$_i$ admires himself$_i$.

As a corollary of obeying Principle B, a pronoun can have a bound-variable interpretation at a considerable syntactic distance from its quantified antecedent:

(69)   Every politician$_i$ betrays the people who vote for him$_i$.

Here, *him* is inside a relative clause, yet it is c-commanded by *every politician*, Principle B is not violated and the bound-variable interpretation is available.

As a final point, if traces/copies are bound by their moved antecedents, the traces/copies of NP-movement must be A-bound. So, again, we can ask which of the binding principles applies to them. Here the answer seems clear from a simple passive sentence like (50b), repeated here:

(50b)   John$_i$ was interviewed t$_i$.

The trace/copy is clearly in the same binding domain as *John*, and the sentence is grammatical. Therefore the trace/copy must be subject to Principle A. If the trace/copy were subject to either Principle B or Principle C, the sentence would be ungrammatical. This conclusion is supported by examples like those in (70):

(70) a.   *John was believed that (John) was bankrupt.
     b.   John was believed (John) to be bankrupt.
     c.   *John was believed Mary to like (John).

Here the object-to-subject movement relation looks similar to the antecedent-reflexive relation seen in examples (21), (25) and (28) in Section 6.3.

In this section we have made some connections between binding theory and movement. We have seen good reasons, both syntactic and semantic, to ana-lyse the trace/copy left by wh-movement as a variable. Making the distinction between A- and A′-binding, we can regard these variables as R-expressions subject to Principle C. This gives us an account of the strong-crossover phe-nomenon. We also noted that pronouns can function as variables bound by quantified antecedents and that the trace/copy of NP-movement is subject to Principle A. The question of the status of traces/copies of head-movement remains open. Since heads do not denote (sets of) individuals – only NPs do this – then the question may simply not arise; we will return to this point in Section 8.6.

6.8   Conclusion

This chapter completes our introduction to the central mechanisms of the theory of syntax. Now we have seen how structures are generated by PS-rules following the X′-template, how they can be modified by movement rules and how the rules of binding theory regulate distributional and interpreta-tive dependencies of various kinds. Obviously, very many questions have been left open, or barely addressed at all. Nonetheless, the core ideas and mechanisms are presented here.

One very major question needs to be addressed: how far are the mechanisms and phenomena they are intended to account for idiosyncratic to English? We have concentrated almost exclusively on English up to now, largely for exposi-tory convenience. But we said at the outset that we are trying to construct a gen-eral theory of syntactic structure, one that applies in principle to all languages. It is therefore necessary, now that the basic notions are in place, to try to apply the approach to some data from other languages. Unsurprisingly, it will emerge that other languages, to varying extents, are organised differently from English.

So a very important question emerges: how can we best account for syntactic variation across languages? This will be the topic of the next chapter.

Exercises

1.   Give the trees for the following sentences:

      a.   Sarah likes herself.
      b.   Mark said that Sarah should promote herself.
      c.   *Sarah said that Mark should promote herself.
      d.   *Sarah thinks that herself/himself is the best.
      e.   Sarah considers Mark to like himself/*herself.
      f.   Sarah's brother likes himself/*herself.

      Say why the ungrammatical examples are ungrammatical. Replace the reflexives with the corresponding non-reflexive pronouns, give your judgements as to the grammaticality and the possible interpretations of the resulting examples, and explain them as far as you can.

2.   In the following examples, take *each other* to be an NP with the structure [NP *each* [N' [N *other*]]]. There are two generalisations governing the distribution of this NP, one from binding theory and another concerning its intrinsic nature. Try to state both (hint: for the second one, try to make *friend* plural in (e) and see what happens):

      a.   The hippies love each other.
      b.   *Each other love the hippies.
      c.   I asked the hippies about each other.
      d.   *I asked each other about the hippies.
      e.   *The hippies' friend talked to each other.
      f.   *The hippies said that each other had left.
      g.   The hippies believe each other to be geniuses.
      h.   *John believes Mary to like each other.

For Discussion

1.   If you had to decompose the structure of NPs like *himself*, what would their internal structure look like?
      Think of (a) X'-theory and (b) the 1st- and 2nd-person reflexives *myself, yourself, ourselves*, etc., and non-standard forms like *hisself, theirselves*.

What would that structure suggest about (a) the morpheme *-self* and (b) pronouns? Can you think of any support for treating *self* as an autonomous morpheme?

Further Reading

Carnie, A. 2013. *Syntax: A Generative introduction*. Oxford: Blackwell, Chapters 4, 5, 15.

Haegeman, L. & J. Guéron. 1999. *English Grammar*. Oxford: Blackwell, Section 4.1.

Isac, D. & C. Reiss. 2008. *I-Language*. Oxford: Oxford University Press, Chapter 8.

Roberts, I. 1997. *Comparative Syntax*. London: Arnold, Chapter 3.

Sportiche, D., H. Koopman & E. Stabler. (2014). *An Introduction to Syntactic Analysis and Theory*. Oxford: Wiley, Chapter 7.

7   Syntax beyond English

7.1   Introduction and Recap

In the preceding chapters we have gradually put together the building blocks of the theory of syntax. We have seen that sentences can be broken down into their constituent structure, and how to represent this and test for it (Chapter 2). Then we saw how PS-rules can generate the well-formed structures (Chapter 3). Next, we replaced the rather general PS-rule format with the simpler and more abstract X'-theory (Chapter 4). Chapter 5 introduced and motivated movement rules, rules which modify structure rather than directly generating it. Finally, in Chapter 6, we introduced binding theory, which regulates the distribution and interpretation of certain syntactic dependencies including at least some cases of movement.

The topic of the current chapter is to investigate how far and in what ways the syntactic tools we have developed up to now, very much on the basis just of English data, can apply to other languages. Inevitably, our discussion will be limited; it is obvious that an exhaustive treatment of comparative syntax cannot even be seriously begun in this introductory context. But nonetheless, looking beyond English, even just a little bit, can be very revealing and can give us a sense of the task at hand. Certain useful ideas and important generalisations will emerge from our discussion, as we shall see.

7.2   Approaching Universal Grammar

As we said in the Introduction, Universal Grammar (UG) is the theory of the first factor which makes up the language faculty: our innate genetic endowment for language. In terms of this idea, it is natural to see specific I-languages as variations on a single theme. Therefore, all other things being equal, we want our syntactic representations of comparable (i.e. semantically matching, or at least highly similar) sentences in different languages to be as uniform as possible. Of course, things may very well not be equal quite a lot of the time, but we can perhaps apply a kind of comparative Occam's Razor when we start to do comparative work: do not multiply cross-linguistic differences beyond what is necessary.

In these terms, since the notion of constituent structure is well established on the basis of English, there is no reason to start out from the assumption that other languages are organised syntactically along radically different lines. It is

156

a perfectly reasonable assumption that all languages have constituent structure; this assumption is a consequence of the fact that the rule systems of all languages are fundamentally the same. Let us then make the hypothesis that all languages use PS-rules to generate constituent structure, and that X′-theory dictates a common cross-categorial structure. This, of course, does not imply that any and every structure that we assign to English sentences will be found in other languages, only that the building blocks of X′-theory are universal. We thus expect notions of head, complement and phrasal projection to be universal, along with, again all other things being equal, Specifiers and adjuncts.

So much, for now, for the category-neutral template. What about the categories themselves? We mentioned in Chapter 2 that the noun–verb distinction may well be universal, while adjectives and prepositions probably are not. We can further add that the inventories of functional categories and features undoubtedly vary across languages: English lacks grammatical gender features, while Italian and other Romance languages have them, for example. Many languages (almost all the Slavonic languages, Latin, Chinese, Japanese and many others) lack articles, Chinese may well lack Tense, it is uncertain whether Japanese really has complementisers (but see below), and so on. Conversely, other languages have grammatical categories, probably structurally realised as functional projections, that English lacks, such as nominal **classifiers**, **evidential markers** and many others.

However, a reasonable hypothesis concerning all this variation might be to say that there is a universal 'pool' of categories, and individual languages make a selection among these. There may be constraints on what the selection can be; for example, all languages have negation (and there may be functional explanations for those constraints). Certain categories, perhaps Nouns and Verbs, may fall outside of this pool, being absolutely required by UG. Remarkably little can be said with any confidence on these points, but the idea of a universal pool of some kind seems somewhat plausible.

More broadly, we could think of a universal pool of possible ways in which X′-theory, movement rules and interpretative rules like binding theory may operate. There may be a universal core to these aspects of syntax, with associated **parameters of variation**, specifying various options for how core processes can apply. This approach to syntactic variation has been fairly widely adopted since the 1980s, and we will see some examples of how it works in what follows. Whether this parameter-based approach will be able to account for all syntactic variation remains an open question. But let's begin with a simple example, involving an interesting set of differences between English and French.

7.3   Verb Positions in French and English

English and French are both Indo-European languages, and are structurally fairly similar. In particular, both languages show a basic subject-object-verb (SVO) word order, which we can see in (1) ((1b) is a word-for-word translation of (1a), and is fully grammatical):

(1) a.   Harry and Hermione follow Filch.
    b.   Harry et Hermione suivent Rusard.

The SVO order is 'basic' in the sense that although it can be changed by movement rules (e.g. wh-movement could place the object in the first position,
SpecC′), it is the neutral order for expressing simple declarative sentences without any particular emphasis on any constituent.

The structure of (1a) is given in (2):

(2)

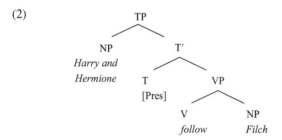

Our comparative Occam's Razor would lead us to assign exactly the same structure to the French sentence (1b). But consider the next pair of sentences:

(3) a.   Harry and Hermione often follow Filch.
    b.   Harry et Hermione suivent souvent Rusard.

Here we see a small but important difference in word order between the two
languages: while the adverb *often* precedes the Verb *follow* in English, the order
of their French counterparts is the opposite: *suivent* ('follow') precedes *souvent*
('often'). Moreover, in both languages the opposite order, i.e. the one found in
the other language, is ungrammatical:

(4) a.   *Harry and Hermione follow often Filch.
    b.   *Harry et Hermione souvent suivent Rusard.

For the English example (3a), it seems reasonable to treat *often* as an AdvP
adjoined to V′, since it provides extra information about the action of following
Filch. So we can give (3a) the structure in (5):

(5)

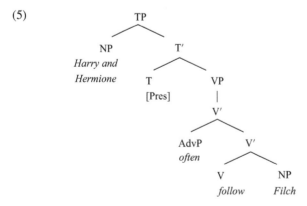

What should we say about the French sentence (3b)? We either have to say that there's something different about the Verb as compared to English or something different about the Adverb (we could say both are different, but that would clearly violate Occam's Razor). The adverb *souvent* means the same thing as English *often* and modifies the action described by V′ in the same way; there do not seem to be very good grounds for attributing the difference between the two languages to this element. On the other hand, the Verb *suivent* does differ from English *follow* in that it is overtly marked for present tense while *follow* does not show any overt marking for Tense (this does not mean that there isn't an abstract Tense affix; see Section 8.6). French verbs are also marked to varying degrees for person and number: this Verb has the third-person plural ending *-ent*. Forms of this Verb in the third-person plural in other tenses include *suivaient* (imperfect, 'used to follow'), *suivirent* (past, 'followed'), *suivront* (future, 'will follow') and *suivraient* (conditional, 'would follow'). As we saw when we compared the fish sentences in English and Italian in Chapter 2, English is rather poor in overt morphological marking of Tense, Mood and Agreement, while Italian is quite rich. We can see now that French is more like Italian in this respect (this isn't surprising, as French and Italian are both quite closely related Romance languages). Since we've been assuming all along that Tense information is present on T, we could propose that the French Verb moves to T. Keeping *souvent* in exactly the same V′-adjoined position as in English, this gives us the structure (6) for the French sentence (3b):

(6)

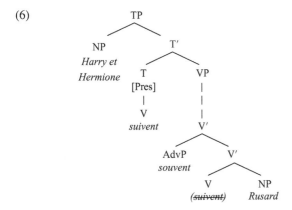

Substituting *suivent* into T[Pres] may force the two elements to combine as a single head, hence the correlation between V-to-T movement and morphological tense marking.

So we observe a difference between English and French, which we can call the **V-to-T Parameter**. This is a parameter defining a specific head-movement option, whether a given language has V-to-T movement or not. In English, this parameter is set to negative, so there is no V-to-T head movement. In French, it is set to positive: there is V-to-T head movement. The difference is not always apparent, as the examples in (1) show, but it emerges where adverbs like *often* are adjoined to V'. It also shows up in negative sentences and various other environments, but our illustration here will suffice for now. The parametric difference may well be connected to the richer verbal tense inflection of French as compared to English.

7.4   Word Order and X′-theory

We mentioned in the previous section that English and French are both SVO languages. Taking these three elements as basic to simple transitive clauses, a reasonable question is what other orders of these elements are found. A strongly universalist view might expect to find no variation; then the universality of SVO would need to be explained. However, it seems clear that the strong universalist view doesn't hold up in this case, since all six possible permutations of the three elements are attested in the world's languages. A strongly 'egalitarian' view might expect that all six orders are found roughly equally distributed across the world's languages, i.e. about a sixth of all languages show each order, or roughly 16–17 per cent of languages per order. That is not true either. Certain orders are frequent, others very rare, although, as already mentioned, all the possibilities are found.

According to the most recent data from the *World Atlas of Language Structures* (*WALS*; wals.info), an online database of 192 phonological, morphological, syntactic and lexical features of 2,662 languages, the basic word orders of Subject, Verb and Object in 1,376 languages pattern as follows:

(7)   SOV   *John cake ate.*   564   (e.g. Japanese)
        SVO   *John ate cake.*   488   (e.g. English)
        VSO   *Ate John cake.*   95   (e.g. Welsh)
        VOS   *Ate cake John.*   25   (e.g. Malagasy, Madagascar)
        OVS   *Cake ate John.*   11   (e.g. Mangarrayi, Australia)
        OSV   *Cake John ate.*   4   (e.g. Warao, Venezuela)
        (*World Atlas of Language Structures*, Feature/Map 81A; https://wals.info/
        feature/81A#2/18.0/153.1)

A further 189 languages are listed as 'no dominant order', i.e. either languages for which a single, 'basic' order cannot be discerned on the basis of available data, or for which more than one order is 'basic' depending on various factors. Leaving aside these languages, we see that 564 out of the remaining 1,187 languages (just over 47.5%) are SOV and 488 (just over 41.1%) are SVO. So together these two orders make up almost 90% (88.6%) of the world's languages. Among the other orders, the 95 VSO languages make up 8% of the total and just over 70% of the 135 non-SOV, non-SVO languages. The other orders are very rare, at 2.1% (VOS), 0.92% (OVS) and 0.37% (OSV) of the total.

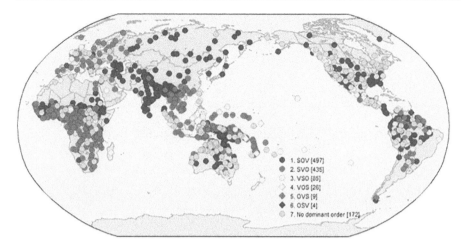

Map 7.1 Geographical distribution of 'basic' S, V, O orders (*WALS* Map 81A; https://wals.info/feature/81A#2/18.0/153.1)

The geographical distribution of the orders is shown on Map 7.1.

Here we can see clear areal patterns for SOV (the Indian subcontinent, most of Asia except the South-East, a belt across Central Africa and a preponderance in North America) and SVO (Europe, South-East Asia, Sub-Saharan Africa and Indonesia/Papua New Guinea), with pockets of VSO languages in the British Isles (the Celtic languages), the extreme North-West of Africa, the Philippines, the Pacific North-West of North America and Mesoamerica. It is not easy to see areal patterns for the other orders, since they are so rare, although the majority of O-initial languages are found in Amazonia. Various explanations have been proposed for these patterns, but we will not go into those here. What is clear is that two patterns, SOV and SVO, are much more common than all the others, so the variation is not random.

Let us compare an SOV and an SVO language, taking Japanese as our SOV language and French as our SVO one. The simple sentences in (8) illustrate the different orders:

(8) a.   Thierry   écrivit   la   lettre
           Thierry   wrote   the   letter
           S   V   O
     b.   Taroo-ga   tegami-o   kaita
           Taroo-NOM   letter-ACC   wrote
           S   O   V

Clearly, the basic difference is whether the Verb appears to the left or to the right of the object. We could say, then, that French has the order V – NP in V′, Japanese has the opposite order:

(9) a.   French: V'
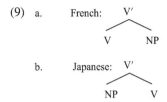
                   V   NP

     b.   Japanese: V'

                   NP   V

In terms of the category-neutral X'-template, we could generalise from (9) to (10):

(10) a.   French: X'

                   X   YP

     b.   Japanese: X'

                   YP   X

If French generalised the **head-initial** pattern in (10a) across categories, then we would expect to find that P precedes its complement, i.e. ***Prepositions***. This is what we indeed find in French:

(11)   sous l'océan
            'under the sea'

On the other hand, (10b) predicts that in Japanese the complement of P should precede it, i.e. we expect to find ***Post*positions** in Japanese, and we do:

(12)   Nihon   kara
            Japan   from
            'from Japan'

We could expect the same with functional categories, so in French T is expected to precede VP. We showed this order in the structure in (6), but, assuming that auxiliaries appear in T (without moving there from V), then we expect to find the order Aux – V in French, which we do:

(13)   Thierry   a écrit   la   lettre.
            Thierry   has written the   letter

Again, in Japanese we expect to see VP-T order. It is a little difficult to discern auxiliaries in Japanese, but the following example may suffice:

(14)   John-ga   Mary-to   renaisite iru.
            John-NOM   Mary-with   in-love   is
            'John is in love with Mary.'

Furthermore, we expect C to precede TP in French. Again, this is clearly the case:

(15)   J'   ai   entendu [CP que [TP Muriel travaille   au   musée]]
            I   have   heard   that   Muriel works   at.the   museum

In Japanese C should follow TP, i.e. complementisers are expected to follow the embedded clause:

(16)   Bill-ga [CP [TP Mary-ga [VP John-ni [NP sono hon-o] watasita] to] itta
            Bill-NOM   Mary-NOM John-DAT that book-ACC hand-PST that said
            'Bill said that Mary handed that book to John'

So we can define the **Head Parameter** in X′-theoretic terms as follows:

(17)   Does X precede or follow its complement in X′?

(It is a useful convention to formulate parameters as yes/no questions since this brings out their binary nature and suggests how the acquirer might interrogate the data it is exposed to.) We see that French is head-initial, taking the 'precede' option in (17). It therefore has VO order (8a), Prepositions (11), Aux-VP order (13) and C-TP order (15). Japanese, on the other hand, is **head-final**, taking the 'follow' option in (16). It therefore has OV order (8b), Postpositions (12), VP-Aux order (14) and TP-C order (16). These are the **harmonic word-order patterns** predicted by the X′-parameter in (17). Moreover, since subjects occupy a Specifier position, they are not affected by (17). If the universal, non-parametrised position of the subject is SpecT′, then (17) predicts SOV and SVO orders. These assumptions appear to be correct at first sight for 88.6 per cent of the languages assigned dominant basic word-order patterns in *WALS*, as we saw in (7). We can assume that the four minority patterns involve various **marked** options, which we do not need to go into here.

WALS does not give data on Aux-VP or C-TP orders. It does, however, give data on Pre- and Postpositions in 1,089 languages, shown in Map 7.2.

As with SOV and SVO order in Map 7.1, we see clear areal clusters: postpositions are predominant in the Indian subcontinent and in Asia as a whole, except for South-East Asia, as well as in the Americas, West Africa and most of Australia, while prepositions dominate in Europe, Sub-Saharan Africa, South-East Asia, Indonesia/Papua New Guinea, Mesoamerica and the Pacific North-West.

Table 7.1 gives the data from *WALS* (Maps 83A Order of Object and Verb, and 85A Order of Adposition and Noun Phrase), showing the correlation of OV with Postpositions and VO with Prepositions.

Here the total number of languages is 982, and so the figures almost correspond to percentages to one decimal place. We see the predicted harmonic patterns, OV and Postpositions and VO and Prepositions, in 928 of the 982 languages, 94.5 per cent of the languages.

So we see that the X′-based Head Parameter of (17) makes quite good predictions both for the verb-object/adposition-order case and for the general

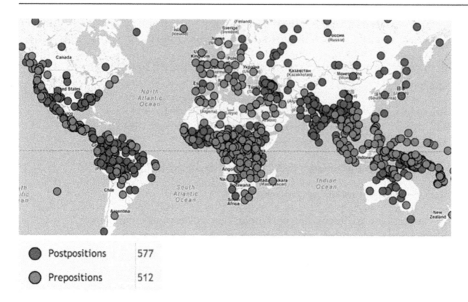

Postpositions   577

Prepositions   512

Map 7.2 Distribution of postpositional and prepositional languages (*WALS*
Map 85A; *https://wals.info/feature/85A#2/16.3/153.1*, inpositions, no
dominant order and no-adpositions omitted)

Table 7.1 *Correlations between Order of Object and
Verb and Order of Adposition and Noun Phrase (based
on WALS Maps/Features 81A and 85A).*

OV & postp.	472
OV & prep.	14
VO & postp	42
VO & prep.	456
TOTAL	982

preponderance of SOV and SVO orders, although the disharmonic and minority patterns
must of course be accounted for. The parameter in (17) also makes predictions about the
order of Nouns and their complements and of Adjectives and their complements, which
we have not gone into at all here. The parameter-based approach to accounting for the
distributions of some of the major word-order patterns in the world's languages, based
on the X′-parameter in (17), certainly shows some initial promise. We will return to
this matter in detail in Volume III, armed with a much more sophisticated approach to
word-order variation.

We have concentrated here on harmonic head-initial or head-final languages, as
defined by (17), taking French and Japanese as our respective case studies. Clearly,
though, there are quite a number of languages with no dominant order, in *WALS* terms,
or with disharmonic order. In the next section we will look at a well-known case of this
kind: German.

7.5   A Case Study: German

German is classified by *WALS* as 'No Dominant Order' under Map/ Feature 81A (Order of Subject, Object and Verb), and as displaying both SOV and SVO order under Map/Feature 81B (Languages with Two Dominant Orders of Subject, Object and Verb). The sentences in (18) illustrate these orders:

(18) a.   Hermann schreibt den Brief.
        Hermann writes   the letter
        S   V   O

   b.   Ich weiß   daß   Hermann den Brief schreibt.
        I   know   that   Hermann the letter writes
                     S   O V

The structure of the SOV embedded clause in (18b) is (19):

(19)

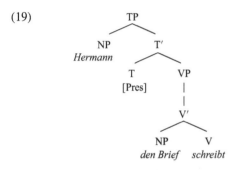

If this is the correct structure, then the question of how (18a) is related to it immediately arises. In fact, as pointed in the commentary text to *WALS* Feature 81B, German is **verb second** rather than SVO in main clauses, while it is clearly SOV in embedded clauses. We now look at the difference between SVO and V2.

   The V2 nature of German main clauses can be seen from the following examples:

(20) a.   Am Tisch   schreibt   Hermann den Brief.
        on table   writes   Hermann the letter
        'Hermann writes the letter on the table.'

   b.   Was   schreibt   Hermann?
        what   writes   Hermann
        'What does Hermann write/what is Hermann writing?'

   c.   Einen   Brief   schreibt   er.
        a   letter   writes   he
        'He is writing a letter.'

   d.   Gestern   hat   Hermann   den   Brief   geschrieben.
        yesterday has   Hermann   the   letter   written
        'Hermann wrote the letter yesterday.'

e.   Hermann hat den Brief geschrieben.
        Hermann has the letter written
        'Hermann has written the letter.'

Alongside the subject-verb order in (18a), what we see here is PP-verb in (20a), wh-phrase verb in (20b), object-verb order in (20c), adverb-auxiliary order in (20d) and subject-auxiliary order in (20e). In each case, exactly one XP precedes the finite verb, i.e. the verb occupies the linear second position. Examples (20d) and (20e), where we have a combination of finite auxiliary and a verbal participle, show that it is the finite element, not strictly speaking the lexical verb, which occupies second position. Here, the main verb is final, following its object, and so we have OV order.

Furthermore, the V2 constraint is very strict. Orders where two XPs precede the finite verb in main clauses are, with certain well-defined exceptions which we need not go into here, ungrammatical. So the word-for-word counterpart of a simple English sentence like (21a) is ungrammatical in German, as (21b) shows. Instead, either the subject or the adverb has to occupy a postverbal position, as seen in (21c) and (21d):

(21) a.   Yesterday John wrote a letter.
     b.   *Gestern Johann schrieb einen Brief.
     c.   Gestern schrieb Johann einen Brief.
     d.   Johann schrieb gestern einen Brief.

So we have two questions to answer about German. First, how do we account for the V2 order in main clauses? Second, how do we account for OV order in subordinate clauses (and when the main verb is non-finite in a main clause, as in (20d) and (20e))?

In order to understand V2, we need to know what the initial XP-position is. Here the wh-question in (20b) gives us an important clue. We saw in Chapter 5 that wh-phrases raise in English to SpecC$_{Wh,Q}'$, as in (22), repeated from (30) in Chapter 5:

(22)

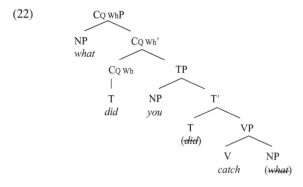

Let us assume that wh-movement behaves in the same way in German. Then the first position in (20b) is SpecC' and the Verb *schreibt* is in C. We can think that XP-movement to SpecC′ in German and V-to-C movement don't depend on C_{Wh}, but are operations that take place in any root CP. So we conclude that the initial XPs in (20) are all in SpecC′. By this logic, the same goes for the subject in (18a).

If the XP is in SpecC′, then we can get the 'second-position effect' directly from the fact of X′-theory that there is just one Specifier per head (cf. PS-rule (2a) of Chapter 5), as long as V is in C. Moreover, we already have the analytical tools to guarantee that V gets to C in German. We saw in Section 7.3 that there is a parameter regulating whether V raises to T. This parameter is positive in French, but negative in English, as we saw. Suppose it is positive in German; this is actually much more difficult to demonstrate for German than it is for French owing to the V2 nature of main clauses and the OV nature of embedded clauses in German, but let us make the assumption in any case. In Section 5.2, we saw that English has a rule raising T to C, giving subject-auxiliary inversion in questions, for example. In a language with the positive value of the V-to-T parameter, T-to-C movement could place a main verb which has moved to T in C. In fact, we see this in French, in direct questions like (23):

(23)   Suivent-ils souvent Rusard?
          Follow they often Filch?
          'Do they follow Filch often?'

So we can say that French is just like English is having C_Q cause T-to-C movement. The difference between French and English is that main verbs like *suivent* in (23) can raise to T, and from there move on to C (where C has the right features). English, lacking V-to-T movement, has to use the dummy auxiliary *do* here.

Coming back to German, we can say that German resembles French in having both V-to-T and T-to-C, but it differs from French (and English) in that T-to-C does not depend on C_Q; it seems that any root C-type can trigger T-to-C. In other words, this property generalizes to all (root) Cs in German, as does the triggering of XP-movement to SpecC′, as we saw. In this way, we arrive at a full account of V2.

Turning now to OV order, we can account for this in terms of the OV-VO parameter in (9) in the previous section, repeated here:

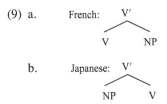

(9) a.   French: V′
               V   NP

    b.   Japanese: V′
               NP   V

If we say that German, like Japanese, chooses (9b), then V will follow the object.

All of this will give us the structure in (24b) for the sentence in (24a):

(24) a.   Hermann hat den Brief geschrieben.
            Hermann has the letter written
            'Hermann has written the letter.'

b.

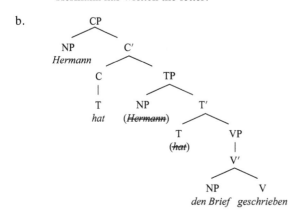

In (24b) we see three important aspects of this kind of V2 sentence, with an initial subject and a periphrastic tense (consisting of the auxiliary *hat* and the participle *geschrieben*). First, the subject *Hermann* raises from SpecT' to SpecC'; this is comparable to what we saw in Section 5.4 with subject wh-movement in English, except that, thanks to the raising of T to C, the movement is not string-vacuous here (compare (30) and (33) in Chapter 5). Second, we see T-to-C movement, exactly as in English and French, except that the movement is not sensitive to an interrogative feature of C, but applies in all root clause types. Third, we see head-final order in V': the object *den Brief* precedes the main verb *geschrieben*. This is a good example of how mechanisms with an independent existence in other languages (T-to-C movement as in English and French, OV order in V' as in Japanese, XP-movement to SpecC' as in English) combine to give the specifically German sentence-type we see here. Aside from extending T-to-C movement and XP-movement to SpecC' to non-interrogatives, we have introduced no new mechanisms in our analysis of German V2; we have merely combined independently needed mechanisms in a new way.

We can account for the root nature of V2 in terms of the idea that a complementiser is always present in finite, non-root CPs. The complementiser occupies C and thereby prevents T-to-C movement. The fact that where there is no T-to-C movement there is no XP-movement to SpecC' suggests that the latter operation somehow depends on the former, although this is poorly understood.

To complete the picture, (25a) and (25b) represent the case of V2 where no auxiliary is present and the main verb raises to T and C:

(25) a.   Hermann schreibt den Brief.
          Hermann writes   the letter

b.

Everything is as in (24), except that the main verb *schreibt* moves first to T (as in French, see Section 7.3) and then T-to-C movement raises it to C.

We see in (25b) that German has the order OV in V′. As we mentioned above, this corresponds to the Japanese choice in (9b). However, German clearly does *not* take the general category-neutral option of (10b), repeated here, unlike Japanese:

(10b)

For example, we can see from our V2 examples and from the structures in (24b) and (25b) that C precedes TP. This is confirmed by the position of complementisers like *daß* ('that'), which precedes TP, as we saw in (18b), repeated here:

(18b)   Ich weiß [cp daß Hermann den Brief schreibt].
           I   know   that Hermann the letter writes

In fact, it may be correct that T follows VP, contrary to what is shown in (24b) and (25b). If auxiliaries such as *hat* are in T, then the fact they follow the main verb in non-V2 clauses indicates this. This is illustrated in (26a), with the structure in (26b):

(26) a.   ... daß Hermann den Brief geschrieben hat.
          ... that Hermann the letter written   has
          '... that Hermann has written the letter'.

b.
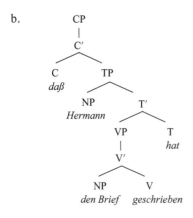

If we flip the order of VP and T inside T′ in (24b) and (25b), it makes no difference to the eventual surface word order, since T is in both cases occupied by the trace/copy of the auxiliary or the verb.

So German is head-final in VP and TP, but head-initial in CP. Furthermore, German is head-final in A′:

(27)   sich   seiner   Sache   sicher
          oneself.DAT one's   subject.GEN certain
          'to be sure about something'

Strikingly, German has mixed order in adpositional phrases. It is head-initial with most Ps, but there are several postpositions:

(28) a.   nach Berlin
           to   Berlin

     b.   den Fluss entlang
           the river along
           'along the river'

So German is a good example of a mixed word order, disharmonic language. It is certainly not the only one; Latin has quite similar overall word patterns to German (although Classical Latin was not V2), and Mandarin Chinese is disharmonic but in quite a different way from German or Latin. This shows that we cannot deduce all word-order properties in all languages from the Head Parameter in (17); in some languages we need to look at subcases of (17). However, in very many languages, as we saw with our examples from French and Japanese in the previous section, (17) makes the right predictions.

To sum up, German has the following positive parameters:

(29) a.   Head-initial: C, P (partially); Head-final: V, T, A, P (partially)
     b.   V-to-T movement
     c.   T-to-C movement in all main clauses
     d.   XP to SpecC′ movement in all main clauses

Compare (29) with the English parameters in (30):

(30) a.   Head-initial
    b.   No V-to-T movement
    c.   T-to-C movement in main-clause interrogatives
    d.   Wh-XP to SpecC′ movement in wh-interrogatives

French is like English except it has V-to-T movement; in this respect it is like German, as we have seen. In the next section, we will look at an example of a language lacking wh-movement.

Here we have gone into some detail on German syntax, although of course there is much more to say and we have simplified a couple of points. The purpose of the discussion was to illustrate how various parameters combine to give us the particular properties of German, such as V2 and OV order non-V2 clauses. We also saw that German is disharmonic in relation to the Head Parameter, indicating that there is more to say about word-order parameters than (17), although (17) does a lot of work in a lot of languages. In general, we see how the parametric approach can be applied; in principle, it could be applied in this way to any language.

7.6   The Wh-Movement Parameter

There are quite a few languages which apparently lack wh-movement; *WALS* (Map/Feature 93; https://wals.info/chapter/93) states that 615 of 902 languages surveyed lack obligatorily initial wh-phrases, which we can at least tentatively take to mean that wh-movement to SpecC′ (the initial position in direct questions) is not required. Mandarin Chinese is a well-known example of a language lacking wh-movement, as the following examples illustrate:

(31) a.   Zhangsan xiang-zhidao [CP Lisi mai-le   shenme].
    Zhangsan wonder   Lisi buy-Perf(P) what
    'Zhangsan wonders what Lisi bought.'

    b.   Ni   weishenme bu   qu   ne?
    You why   not go   wh
    'Why aren't you going?'

As the English translation shows, and as we saw in Chapter 5, in English wh-movement to SpecC′ is required in both direct and indirect interrogative clauses.

Of course, we can easily add a further movement parameter to our inventory. We have seen two head-movement parameters: V-to-T movement and T-to-C movement, and we have seen variation with respect to both in that English lacks V-to-T movement and T-to-C movement takes place in a wider range of contexts in German than in English or French. So we can easily add a **wh-movement parameter** to describe the difference between Chinese and English that we observe in (31).

However, if Chinese lacks wh-movement, two questions arise. First, how, if at all, does Chinese mark wh-interrogatives? Second, if, as we saw in Section 6.7, wh-movement takes place in order to bind the trace/copy as a variable so that the wh-quantifier can be semantically interpreted, how does this happen in a language without wh-movement? Here we will answer the first of these questions, but we will defer answering the second to the next chapter.

There is evidence that Chinese marks wh-interrogatives as a clause type, in other words that Chinese has C_{Wh} in the terms introduced in Chapter 5. First, in main clauses, a special sentence-final particle can appear to mark the clause as a wh-question; this is *ne* in (31b). We could treat *ne* as occupying a final C_{wh}, as shown in (32):

(32)

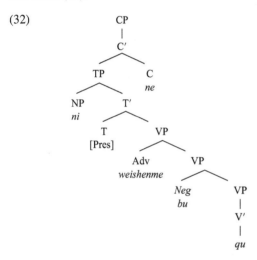

This analysis implies that Chinese C follows TP in C′, like its Japanese counterpart, as we saw in Section 7.4; we mentioned at the end of the previous section that Chinese has disharmonic word order, though, so this does not imply that Chinese is fully head-final the way Japanese is. This particle, which is optional, contrasts with the yes/no particle *ma*:

(33) a.   Ni   shuo Zhongwen.
           You speak Chinese.
           'You speak Chinese.'

     b.   Ni   shuo Zhongwen   ma?
           You speak Chinese   Q
           'Do you speak Chinese?'

So we could say that, for root clauses, *ne* optionally realises C_{Wh} and *ma* realises C_Q. This is evidence that C is present, and that it can function, as in English, to type a clause as an interrogative of one kind or another.

Second, there is evidence from how clauses containing an unmoved (or *in-situ*) wh-phrase are interpreted which shows that C_{Wh} is present. We saw in Chapter 5 that in English verbs like *wonder* require an indirect-question complement, i.e. they obligatorily c-select C_Q or C_{Wh}. Furthermore, verbs like *think* do not allow such a clausal complement, instead obligatorily selecting declaratives. There is also a third class of verbs, exemplified by *remember*, which optionally take an interrogative complement. In English, these differences can be clearly seen from the possibilities of placing a wh-phrase which originates inside the complement clause in the Specifier of the CP selected by the verb:

(34) a. We wonder what you bought.
　　　　?*What did you wonder (that) I bought?

 b. *I think what you bought.
　　　　What did you think (that) I bought?

 c. I remember what you bought.
　　　　What did you remember (that) I bought?

The possible positions for the wh-phrase reflect the c-selection properties of each verb class, i.e. whether the embedded C is $C_{wh, Q}$. Furthermore, since the presence of a wh-phrase implies an accessible SpecC$_{wh}$', where the selected C is not C_{Wh}, as obligatorily in the complement of *think* and optionally in the complement of *remember*, the root C is C_{wh}. Hence the **scope** of the interrogative (whether the main or embedded clause counts as a question, i.e. whether the main or the embedded clause has C_{wh}) is indicated by wh-movement.

The striking fact is that the corresponding sentences in Chinese have exactly the same range of possible and impossible interpretations, despite the absence of wh-movement:

(35) a. Zhangsan xiang-zhidao [$_{CP}$ Lisi mai-le   shenme].
　　　　Zhangsan wonder   Lisi buy-PERF what
　　　　'Zhangsan wonders what Lisi bought.'

 b. Zhangsan yiwei [$_{CP}$ Lisi mai-le   shenme] ?
　　　　Zhangsan think   Lisi buy- PERF what
　　　　'What does Zhangsan think that Lisi bought?'

 c. Zhangsan jide   [$_{CP}$ Lisi mai-le   shenme] ?
　　　　Zhangsan remember   Lisi buy- PERF what
　　　　'Zhangsan remembers what Lisi bought.' **Or**
　　　　'What did Zhangsan remember that Lisi bought?'

Clearly, the wh-phrase *shenme* is in the same position in all three cases (the direct object position of the subordinate clause), but the interpretations vary as a function of the main verb in exactly the same way as in English. This shows us that Chinese has C_{wh}. The difference between Chinese and English does not lie in the interpretation or clause-typing of wh-questions, or in the classes of verbs that c-select C_{wh} optionally or obligatorily, but much more narrowly in whether a C_{wh} triggers movement to its Specifier. The difference, then, is purely syntactic, having to do with whether a movement operation takes place in a given context or not (in this respect the wh-parameter is hardly different in principle from the V-to-T parameter we saw in Section 7.3). Of course, to all appearances, the lack of wh-movement means that there is no variable for the wh-quantifier to bind in examples like (33), raising the question of how wh-questions are interpreted in languages like Chinese. As already mentioned, we will revisit this question in the next chapter.

In this section, we have introduced a further parameter, the wh-movement parameter. Although very simple in itself, this parameter has interesting implications for clause-typing and for the interpretation of wh-expressions. Chinese is a standard example of a language without wh-movement, although it is by no means the only one. In fact, the data from *WALS* cited at the beginning of this section suggest that this may be the majority pattern.

7.7   Conclusion

In this chapter, we have taken a first look at how the theory of syntax developed in the earlier chapters can be made into a cross-linguistically general theory. This is of course the overall goal of our enterprise, as we want ultimately to construct an account of the human language faculty (or at least the central syntactic part of it). Our theory must therefore have universal scope. Although we may still be some way off that ambitious goal, we can see the general shape of the approach.

The central idea is that there are universal mechanisms and principles: X′-theory, the binding principles and movement as an upward copy/paste operation. These universal features of the language faculty are subject to parametric variation. Here we saw two types of parameters: one concerning the presence or absence of particular movement rules (V-to-T, wh-movement) and the Head Parameter (which may hold in maximally general form as in (17) or, for disharmonic languages like German, in a more attenuated form). What the full range of possible parameters might be is a matter for ongoing research which we will come back to in the later volumes, particularly Volume III. We can ask one simple question here though: if there are head-movement parameters (e.g. V-to-T) and wh-movement parameters (see Section 7.6), then are there NP-movement parameters? The only case of NP-movement we have seen here is the passive (see Section 5.2). So even our highly limited look at parameters leads us to ask whether there are languages without passives, and the answer is positive: *WALS* (Map 107A; https://wals.info/feature/107A#2/18.0/148.9) cites 211 languages lacking passives as opposed to 162 in which passives are found. Maybe, then, the answer to our question is positive: there is an NP-movement parameter of some kind.

What we have also seen here, particularly in our discussion of German in Section 7.5, is that different languages can combine the same (or almost the

Table 7.2 *Summary of languages and parameters discussed in this chapter*

	English	French	German	Chinese	Japanese
V-to-T	No	Yes	Yes	No	No?
Head Parameter	Initial	Initial	Mixed	Mixed	Final
Wh-movement	Yes	Yes	Yes	No	No

same) parameters differently and quite distinct grammatical systems emerge. This is a very important and attractive aspect of the parametric approach, which can obviously be taken significantly further than we have done here; again, this approach to cross-linguistic variation is the object of much ongoing research and is yielding some very interesting results.

As a final point on cross-linguistic variation (for now), let us look at the three parameters we have introduced and exemplified here in relation to the five languages we have taken examples from. The parameters are V-to-T movement, the Head Parameter and wh-movement; the languages are English, French, German, Chinese and Japanese. Table 7.2 gives the value of each parameter for each language:

We have seen the evidence for almost all of these parameter settings in the foregoing. Of course 'mixed' is not really a setting of the Head Parameter, rather an indication that the language is disharmonic in that some heads precede and some follow their complements; we saw some of the evidence for the mixed nature of German head-complement orders in Section 7.5, but a full description of Chinese would take us too far afield here (it should also be noted that Japanese has some head-initial order, and so Table 7.2 slightly oversimplifies things). The absence of V-to-T in Chinese is indicated by the fact that almost all adverbs, as well as clausal negation, precede the verb. We can see this for negation in (31b), repeated here:

(31b)   Ni   weishenme bu qu ne?
           You why   not go wh
           'Why aren't you going?'

The negator *bu* is probably located in between T and VP in Chinese, as is English *not* and French *pas*, and the verb always follows it, as *qu* ('go') does here. Compare this with French, where the finite verb precedes *pas* (we give a declarative example to avoid the complication of T-to-C movement in interrogatives):

(36)   Vous n'allez pas à   Paris.
           You   neg-go not to Paris
           'You aren't going to Paris.'

The status of V-to-T movement in Japanese is debated, and so I will leave it aside here.

The only other cell of Table 7.2 we have not illustrated concerns the lack of wh-movement in Japanese. This is a well-known property of Japanese, illustrated by examples like (37):

(37)   Boku-wa [CP [TP John-ga   nani-o   katta] ka]   shiritai.
         I-TOP   John-NOM what-ACC bought Q   want-to-know
         'I want to know what John bought.'

In Table 7.2, we see that each language has its own set of parameter settings; this reinforces the idea that each language takes essentially the same set of building blocks for a grammar but puts them together in its own distinct way. This is the key to understanding the unity in diversity that we find when we try to reconcile cross-linguistic diversity with the idea that there is a Universal Grammar. If we can multiply Table 7.2 by many orders of magnitude, adding thousands of languages and hundreds of parameters, then we may be able to get an inductive idea of the true diversity of the world's languages, whilst at the same time sticking to a clear universalist perspective. That is one of the goals of parametric comparative syntax.

We have been concentrating on the details of the theory of syntax in the last few chapters. Now it is time to return to a wider perspective and try to see how everything we've seen (constituent structure, X'-theory, movement, binding, parameters) fits together and fits with the overall architecture of the language faculty, including phonology and semantics. That is the goal of the next and final chapter.

Exercises

1.   We mentioned in the text that finite verbs precede the negator *pas* in French. What do we conclude from the following infinitives in French?

         (i) a.   *Ne sembler pas content est une condition pour écrire des romans.
                    'To seem not happy is a condition for writing novels.'

            b.   *Ne posséder pas de voiture en banlieue rend la vie difficile.
                    'To possess not a car in the suburbs makes life difficult.'

            c.   Ne pas sembler content est une condition pour écrire des romans.
                    'To not seem happy is a condition for writing novels.'

            d.   Ne pas posséder de voiture en banlieue rend la vie difficile.
                    'To not possess a car in the suburbs makes life difficult.'

         Now consider these examples:

         (ii) a.   N'être pas content est une condition pour écrire des romans.
                    'To not be happy is a condition for writing novels.'

b. N'avoir pas de voiture en banlieue rend la vie difficile.
'To not have a car in the suburbs makes life difficult.'
What is the generalisation regarding V-to-T movement of
infinitives in French?

2. Here is some Danish data (from Vikner 1995):[1]
(i) a. Jeg tror at   Johan ikke købte bogen.
I believe that John   not   bought book-the
'I believe that John didn't buy the book.'
b. Hvorfor købte   Johan ikke bogen?
Why   bought John   not   book-the
'Why didn't John buy the book?'
c. Derfor   har Peter uden   tvivl ikke læst den.
Therefore has Peter without doubt not   read it.
'Therefore Peter has without doubt not read it.'
These examples suffice to situate Danish in Table 7.2. Show how
Danish fits in. Now add a further parameter to Table 7.2: verb sec-
ond. State the values of this parameter for the languages in Table
7.2. The following examples, along with (ic), suffice to tell you the
value of this parameter in Danish:
(ii) a. Denne film har   børnene   set.
This   film have children-the seen
'The children have seen this film.'
b. I går   så børnene   filmen.
Yesterday saw children-the film-the
'Yesterday the children saw the film.'
c. Børnene   så   filmen.
Children-the saw   film-the
'The children saw the film.'

3. Now consider Icelandic. The examples in (iii) (also from Vikner
1995) correspond to the Danish ones in (ii) and clearly show that
Icelandic is V2:
(iii) a. Þessi mynd hefur börnin   séð.
This film   have children-the seen
'The children have seen this film.'
b. Í gær   sáu börnin   myndina.
Yesterday saw children-the film-the
'Yesterday the children saw the film.'
c. Börnin   sáu myndina.
Children-the saw film-the
'The children saw the film.'

[1] S. Vikner (1995), *Verb Movement and Expletive Subjects in the Germanic languages*, Oxford: Oxford University Press.

(iv)   Now consider the Icelandic translation of (2(i)a):
            Ég held að Johan keypti ekki bókina.
            I believe that John bought not book-the
            'I believe that John didn't buy the book.'

You should now be able to add Icelandic to your expanded Table 7.2.

For Further Discussion

At the end of Chapter 1, we raised the following questions about I-language (see (57) of Chapter 1):

(i) a.   how does a given I-language relate to UG?
     b.   how does adult I-language result from acquisition?
     c.   how is I-language related to general cognition and the third factors?

Consider how parameters of the kind illustrated in Table 7.2 may provide answers to these questions.

Further Reading

Adger, D. 2003. *Core Syntax: A Minimalist Approach*. Oxford: Oxford University Press.

Haegeman, L. & J. Guéron. 1999. *English Grammar: A Generative Perspective*. Oxford: Blackwell, Chapter 6.

Larson, R. 2010. *Grammar as Science*. Cambridge, MA: MIT Press, Unit 28.

Roberts, I. 1997. *Comparative Syntax*. London: Arnold, Chapter 5.

You should also take a look at the website of the *World Atlas of Language Structures*: www.wals.info.

8   The Architecture of Grammar

8.1   Introduction and Recap

Starting from Chapter 2, where our real investigation of the theory of syntax began, we have looked at constituent structure (Chapter 2), PS-rules (Chapter 3), X'-theory (Chapter 4), movement (Chapter 5), binding (Chapter 6) and parameters (Chapter 7). In this final chapter of this volume, the aim is to see how all this fits together and, returning to the broader perspective of the discussion in the Introduction, to consider these components of the theory of syntax in relation to the overall architecture of grammar. Ultimately, this should be a model of I-language, Universal Grammar.

We will begin by describing a particular overall model of the grammar, which has five components and a fairly clear specification of how those components interact. We will then look at each component in turn. To some extent, we will revisit topics we have already seen in earlier chapters, but often from a slightly different perspective.

8.2   A Model of Grammar

The organisation of the grammar we will assume has the form in (1):

(1)

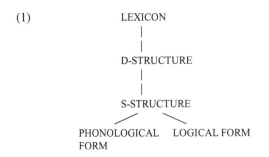

Here I briefly describe each component in turn, before going on to a more detailed discussion of each one in the sections to follow.

The **lexicon** is a list of words and morphemes, a kind of mental dictionary (although of course the entries aren't alphabetised and definitions may be given in terms of concepts rather than other words). A native speaker of a given I-language has, stored in long-term memory but readily accessible at a millisecond's notice, a collection of lexical items which include idiosyncratic information, i.e. information that cannot be predicted by any linguistic rule. Estimates as to the size of the average adult's vocabulary vary, but they are invariably in the tens of thousands. An important aspect of the lexicon for syntax is that it contains functional elements such as auxiliaries, complementisers, etc. The lexicon is important for what we have seen in the foregoing chapters in that it interacts with X'-theory in specifying the syntactic categories of lexical items, with movement theory in specifying the presence and nature of movement-triggering features such as Wh, Q, etc., and with binding theory in specifying which elements are anaphors, pronouns and R-expressions (i.e. which lexical items are subject to which binding principles).

D-structure, or **deep structure**, is a syntactic representation built by PS-rules in conformity with X'-theory. No movement rules apply in the derivation of D-structure, however. This is the level where thematic roles such as Agent, Patient, etc. (which we briefly saw in Section 5.2) are structurally represented.

S-structure, or **surface structure**, is a further syntactic representation derived from D-structure by movement rules. After S-structure, the derivation divides into two distinct parts: **Phonological Form (PF)** and **Logical Form (LF)**. The importance of this division will become apparent below. The respective roles of PF and LF are apparent from their names. PF is the level of representation which converts a syntactic representation (a tree or labelled bracketing) into a representation which can be input to phonological and, ultimately, phonetic rules and representations. LF is the level of representation which converts the syntactic representation into a representation which can be the input to the semantic representation which, in standard theories of semantics, is capable of bearing truth conditions, i.e. of being evaluated as true or false. Collectively, we refer to PF and LF as the **interface levels**, as they connect syntax to aspects of the grammar which are external to syntax, i.e. phonology and semantics respectively. The split is required because phonological features cannot be interpreted at the semantic level and non-phonological features cannot be interpreted by the phonological level.

We now look at each component in more detail. It should be borne in mind throughout that, aside from the lexicon, each component represents a stage of the derivation of a sentence; since the derivation splits after S-structure, the derivation has two outputs: a PF one and an LF one.

8.3   The Lexicon

In order to see the role of the lexicon, consider the following examples:

(2) a. John dined at 8.
   b. *John devoured at 8.
   c. *John dined the sandwich at 8.
   d. John devoured the sandwich at 8.

What accounts for the grammaticality contrasts here? In (2a,b) we have a V′ containing just V (the adjunct *at 8* is adjoined to V′ or T′, which one is immaterial here). In (2c,d) V′ contains V along with a complement NP. Either structure is allowed by the X′-template, and so in this sense the examples are all well-formed. What we can see from (2), though, is that *dine* is intransitive, i.e. it does not allow an NP complement, and *devour* is transitive, i.e. it requires an NP complement. Both *dine* and *devour* entail eating, each one adding a particular specification as to the manner of eating. The more generic verb *eat* is optionally transitive:

(3) a. John ate at 8.
   b. John ate the sandwich at 8.

All of this indicates that it is difficult to predict the precise syntactic requirements a verb may have (e.g. NP-complement or not) from its meaning. This idiosyncratic information is stored in the lexicon, which specifies (among other things) categorial selection (c-selection) and semantic selection (s-selection) properties of lexical items. Together, these selection frames specify the argument structure for each verb, i.e. who's doing what to whom. For the three verbs we have been looking at here, then, the c-selection and s-selection properties are specified as shown in (4):

(4) a. *devour* (V): __ NP <Agent, Theme>
       e.g. John devoured the pie at 5 pm.

   b. *dine* (V): __ <Agent>
       e.g. Larry always dines at 5 pm.

   c. *eat* (V): __ (NP) <Agent, (Theme)>
       e.g. John ate (the pie) at 5 pm.

These entries give information as to the word's category (V in each case here), the c-selection frame, i.e. the syntactic material that must appear in X′ as its sister, and the s-selection frame, i.e. the thematic roles the word's arguments bear. Optional material is in brackets in both the c-selection and the s-selection specification.

The c-selection frame only specifies the arguments that appear in V′: the **internal arguments**. Subjects are not c-selected, since they occupy a Specifier position, which is always available independently of the specific properties of any lexical item. General information of this kind, which is not specific to lexical items, is not specified in the lexicon. Instead, the PS-rules always generate subject positions. Verbs do differ, however, in the thematic roles they assign to subjects. Some verbs which describe mental states or emotions, known as **psych-verbs**, assign an **Experiencer** thematic role to their subjects, e.g. *love* in (5):

(5)   John loves Mary.

If John loves Mary, John doesn't have to actually do anything (although of course he might do absolutely *anything*); the verb simply describes his emotional state in relation to Mary. So the lexical entry for *love* might look like (6):

(6)   *love* (V): __ NP   <Experiencer, Theme>

By convention, the leftmost thematic role in the s-selection frame is assigned to the subject, which we can also think of as the **external argument**, i.e. the argument which occupies a non-c-selected Specifier position outside the core predicative category consisting of V and its c-selected complements (we will see in Volume II that this position does not have to be SpecT' but could be a lower Specifier position, perhaps in VP). So the subject of the Verbs in (4a–c) bears the Agent role, while (6) specifies that the subject of *love* receives the Experiencer role.

There are also verbs that assign no subject/external thematic role at all. This is true of verbs like *seem*, for example. With these verbs, the subject position is nonetheless filled by a dummy, or expletive, element *it*. This element has no semantic interpretation, bears no thematic role and appears to be present purely in order to fill the subject position:

(7)   It seems that the world is round.

This shows that the subject position is not c-selected; it appears even where the verb imposes no lexical-semantic requirement for its presence at all, i.e. it is not s-selected either. This is a fundamental difference between subjects/external arguments and internal arguments: internal arguments appear as a function of c-selection and s-selection properties of lexical items (i.e. heads in X' terms), while subject positions always appear and they may, but do not have to, house external arguments s-selected by a lexical head. If some verbs do not s-select an external argument, the convention that the leftmost s-selected thematic role is assigned to the external argument will not suffice. For most verbs, two conventions will suffice:

(8) a.   Agents are always lexically external arguments.
    b.   Themes are never lexically external arguments.

These statements capture redundancies in lexical entries. For psych-verbs, the convention that the leftmost thematic role is assigned to the external argument is still valid.

In Chapter 4 we saw the following examples of c-selection frames for various English verbs (changing the original S' to CP in the case of *say*):

(9) a.   *watch* (V) ___ NP
    b.   *rely* (V) ___ PP
    c.   *put* (V) ___ NP PP
    d.   *say* (V) ___ CP

To these we can now add the s-selection frames for each verb as in (9′):

(9′) a.   *watch* (V) ___ NP   <Agent, Theme>
    b.   *rely* (V) ___ PP   <Agent, Theme>
    c.   *put* (V) ___ NP PP   <Agent, Theme, Location>
    d.   *say* (V) ___CP   <Agent, Theme>

Here we see further divergences between c-selection and s-selection, in particular in that the Theme role can be borne by a direct-object NP, as with *watch* and *put*, and by a CP in the case of *say*.

Other semantic features are associated with thematic roles and so are also s-selected. Agents and Experiencers are always animate, while Themes may be animate or inanimate. Hence we can observe contrasts such as the following:

(10) a.   Sincerity delights John.
    b.   ?*Sincerity relies on Mary.
    c.   Mary relies on sincerity.

Examples like (10b) may be found in poetry or perhaps other registers in which aspects of word meanings are 'stretched' for literary or aesthetic effect, and so it may not be strictly correct to treat them as ungrammatical. We can in fact regard them as syntactically well-formed in that they can be generated by X′-theory (along with whatever movement rules might be necessary). The anomalous nature of such examples, at least in most registers, is due to a violation of an s-selection requirement. On the other hand, c-selection violations, as in (11), give rise to genuine ungrammaticality, i.e. syntactic ill-formedness:

(11) a.   *Sincerity delights that the world is round.
    b.   *Mary relies sincerity.

The contrast in (12), which we mentioned in Chapter 1, also reflects s-selection:

(12) a.   Colourless green ideas sleep furiously.
    b.   Revolutionary new ideas spread quickly.

As we pointed in Chapter 1, (12a) is grammatical in the sense that it is generated by the syntactic rules. However, we can see that the s-selection property of *sleep* that it requires an animate external argument (whether this is best described as an Agent is another matter) is violated here, among other things.

Verbs have the richest argument structure of all lexical categories, but the other categories also impose c-selection and s-selection requirements, as illustrated in (13):

(13) a.   *picture* (N) ___ (PP)   \<Theme>
      b.   *angry* (A) ___ (PP)   \<Experiencer, Theme>
      c.   *beyond* (P) ___ NP   \<Location>

It is debatable whether Prepositions ever have external arguments; clearly the
Location role is borne by the sole NP argument of *beyond* in (13c). The internal
arguments of Nouns and Adjectives are typically optional. Moreover, some lexical
items may lack argument structure altogether: a simple common Noun like *dog*
or *cat* does not appear to have either an external or an internal argument. On the
other hand, it is unclear whether there are any Verbs which entirely lack argument
structure. Meteorological Verbs such as *rain* and *snow* may be a case in point, as
they can appear with an apparently expletive subject *it* and no internal argument:

(14)   It's raining.

This is debatable however; *rain* can take an internal argument as in (15), although
this might be a fixed, idiomatic expression:

(15)   It's raining cats and dogs.

We will leave the very interesting question of the argument structure of meteorological Verbs aside.
    Some reason to think that Nouns do not have to have argument structure while
Verbs do comes from a reconsideration the fish sentences from Chapter 1:

(16)   Fish$_N$ fishv.

    Here the Noun *fish* acts like a typical common Noun and appears to have no
argument structure. The Verb *fish*, on the other hand, presumably has the argument structure given in (17):

(17)   *fish* (V) ___ (NP) \<Agent, (Theme)>

So the Verb *fish* has an Agent external argument and an optional Theme internal
argument, realised as an NP. The latter option is taken in the three-fish example:

(18)   Fish fish fish.

The Noun *fish*, on the other hand, appears to have no argument structure at all.
Perhaps here we are seeing a fundamental difference between Verbs and Nouns.
    As we mentioned above, functional categories are also listed in the lexicon.
We can give the lexical entries for some English auxiliaries as follows:

(19) a.   *can* (T): ___ VP
      b.   *have* (Perf): ___ V-enP
      b.   *be* (Prog): ___ V-ingP

These lexical entries specify the c-selection properties of each auxiliary, including the information in (19b), for example, that perfect *have* requires the head
of the selected VP to be a perfect participle, here roughly indicated as V-en.
Similarly, progressive *be* requires the selected VP to be a progressive participle
in -*ing*. (Of course, there are other kinds of *have*, e.g. the possessive, and other

kinds of *be*, e.g. the copula; (19) implies that these are actually distinct lexical items with their own lexical entries.) Modals such as *can* select a bare V. It is fairly straightforward to state the c-selection requirements of these auxiliaries, but what about s-selection? The auxiliaries appear to have semantic content, but it is not clear that they are associated with thematic roles, at least not thematic roles of the Agent, Experiencer, Theme (etc.) type. This is a major open question for our understanding of auxiliaries and perhaps other functional categories.

We also stated that functional features may have their own lexical entries. For example [Present] and [Past] may have entries like the following:

(20) a.   [Present] (T): __ VP
      b.   [Past] (T): __ VP

These lexical entries simply specify that these features are realised on T and c-select for VP. As with the auxiliaries in (19), they clearly have semantic content, but the question of their s-selection properties is a difficult one.

Up to now we have concentrated on the categorial, c-selection and s-selection specifications in lexical entries. But, as with conventional dictionaries, lexical entries must also provide phonological and semantic information. For entries like (6), (13a) and (19a), we can take the phonological specification to simply be a phonemic representation of the word, e.g. /lʌv/, /pɪktʃə(r)/ and /kæn/. But for (20) we need to specify that these lexical items are realised as affixes. For [Past], for example, we could perhaps try to specify something like /+d/, with the +-sign indicating that it is obligatorily realised as an affix. This is adequate for the majority of regular Verbs, it does not take into account the existence of irregular past-tense forms like *sang*, *went*, etc. It is impossible for a lexical item such as [Past], a member of the category T, to change its phonological form as a function of the particular lexical item in V. The fact that *sing*, *go* and about 150 other English Verbs have irregular past tenses can only be listed in the lexicon. Therefore, these Verbs have to be lexically specified for their past-tense forms, roughly as in (21) for *sing*:

(21)   *sing* (V): __ (NP, PP) <Agent, Theme, Goal>. PF: /sɪŋ ~ sæŋ[Past]/.

For regular verbs, we can maintain that the PF form of [Past] is /d/. This default (or **elsewhere**) realisation of [Past] is blocked by the lexically pre-specified form for *sing*. The idea that a more specific realisation of a formative, such as the particular realisation of [Past] when combined with *sing*, blocks the default/elsewhere realisation, is known as **disjunctive ordering**, and plays a pervasive role in morphology and phonology. All of this of course presupposes that V and T combine when T is [Past]. This must be specified in some way in the lexical entry, perhaps by means of a simple diacritic like '+', as part of the PF-representation. Since English lacks V-to-T movement, as we saw in Section 7.3, it must have T-to-V movement, a rare case of a 'downward' movement rule (recall that we concluded in Section 6.7 that it is not clear that head-movement must result in a binding relation, hence downward head-movement, unlike wh- or NP-movement, may be possible). The downward-movement option applies to lexical items specified as '+' where upward movement is ruled out by the negative setting of the V-to-T parameter.

Lexical entries must also give a specification of the semantics of lexical items. It is difficult to illustrate this properly here without providing an introduction to semantics. For many verbs, a kind of 'action schema' related to the thematic roles can be given. Very approximate 'action schemata' for three common English Verbs are given in (22):

(22) a.   *say*: 'the Agent causes a propositional Theme to exist by speaking'
     b.   *eat*: 'the Agent consumes the Theme by oral ingestion'
     c.   *give*: 'the Agent causes the Theme to become located at/possessed by the Goal.

These are of course just approximations to the meanings of these Verbs. Obviously, there's a lot more to say, but it would take us too far afield here.

Many functional items have logical or quasi-logical semantics. The quantifier *every*, for example, which we saw in Section 6.7, has a semantics which approximates closely to that of the **universal quantifier** of standard logical systems, usually written with the symbol $\forall$. There is also the question of real-world, encyclopedic knowledge. For example, the lexical entry for the proper noun *Paris* may specify that the word refers to the capital of France. Obviously, there is much much more to say about all of this.

Here, as sample lexical entries, are the full entries for the Noun *fish* and the Verb *fish*:

(23) a.   *fish* (N): __.   PF: /fɪʃ/. LF: λx [fish (x)]
     b.   *fish* (V): __ (NP). <Agent, (Theme)>. PF: /fɪʃ/. LF: HUNT(Agent) [FISH (Theme)]

(The formula in (23a) says 'the set of individuals such that they are fish'; a similar, much more complex formula, can be given for the LF in (23b), but this is not necessary here. The semantics must also somehow specify the intrinsic content of 'fish' as an aquatic animal or whatever, a matter at least partially bearing on world knowledge which we can safely leave aside here.) What we see here is that the Verb *fish* has a more complex lexical entry than the corresponding Noun, and that the Verb's lexical entry makes reference to the Noun's: the occurrence of the term FISH in the LF for the Verb *fish* must be connected to that of the Noun in order to avoid unnecessary redundancy in specifying the meaning of the concept 'fish' (presumably λx *[fish (x)]*) twice over. As we already hinted, an intriguing question concerns the extent to which the greater complexity of the lexical entry of the Verb is due to the fact that it is a Verb. Fully exploring this question would take us too far afield here.

As a last point, here are the lexical entries for the Italian counterparts to the English Noun and Verb *fish*, which we saw in Chapter 1:

(24) a.   *pesce* (N; Gender: Masc): __.   PF: /'peʃe/. LF: λx [fish (x)]
     b.   *pescare* (V; Conj: 1): __ (NP). <Agent, (Theme)>. PF: /pes'kare/. LF: HUNT(Agent) [FISH (Theme)]

Here, the phonological information is obviously different compared to English. The semantic information, however, is identical to English. The syntactic information is similar, but two extra pieces of lexical information need to be added in Italian: for Nouns, the grammatical gender must be specified (in (24a), this is 'Gender: Masc'), and for Verbs, information about conjugation class ('Conj: 1' in (24b)). This information corresponds exactly to what we suggested in Chapter 1 should not be specified by silent functional categories in English (unlike, for example, Agreement information; see the discussion of examples (14–21) of Chapter 1). In fact, we already pointed out in Chapter 1 that the syntax of English and Italian are '(near-)uniform and the semantics entirely uniform'; comparison of the lexical entries in (23) and (24) shows this to be the case.

In this section we have taken a look at aspects of lexical entries. The most important notions are those of c-selection and s-selection, argument structure, including thematic role and the distinction between external and internal arguments. We have also looked briefly, and rather inconclusively, at the lexical entries of functional categories. Here the issues connected to the representation of irregular forms and default/elsewhere realisations are important, as is the PF specification of certain formatives as inherently affixal. We also took a very sketchy look at the semantic part of lexical entries. Without bringing in a great deal more semantic theory, it is difficult to give a clearer picture of this aspect of lexical entries, but we saw that verbs, at least, might be represented by 'action schemata' of the kind in (22). Finally, we gave the lexical entries for the Noun and the Verb *fish* in (23); these suggest some intriguing connections between the semantics and selectional properties of Nouns and Verbs.

We will leave our discussion of lexical entries here, with many matters left unresolved. What is important now is to see how this static, dictionary-like list is connected to the generative rules of syntax.

8.4   D-structure

As we said in Section 8.2, D-structure is a syntactic representation built by PS-rules in conformity with X'-theory. No movement rules apply in the derivation of D-structure, however. This is the level where the c- and s-selection requirements of lexical items are directly represented structurally. But how do the Lexicon and Syntax 'communicate'? How is the information regarding c- and s-selection of the kind we saw in the previous section transmitted from the lexical entries to the syntactic structures?

This is achieved by the **Projection Principle**, which can be stated as follows:

(25)   All and only featural information that is stored in the Lexicon must be reflected in the Syntax, at all levels of representation.

Looking at (23a), for example, we can take the effect of the Projection Principle to mean that the Noun *fish* can only undergo **lexical insertion** into an N-node. Since its c-selection and s-selection frames are null, this Noun cannot have a complement. This accounts for the ungrammaticality of NPs such as (26):

(26) a.   *a fish of physics (with large fins)
     b.   *every fish about/on Ancient Greece

On the other hand, Nouns like *student* are specified for an optional PP complement headed by *of*, with an associated Theme thematic role, and Nouns like *book* are specified for an optional PP complement headed by *about* or *on*:

(27) a.   a student (of physics)
     b.   every book (on/about Ancient Greece)

Adjuncts, such as *with large fins* in (26a), and Specifiers, e.g. the determiners *a* and *every* here, are not c-selected and hence the Projection Principle neither requires nor forbids their appearance in syntax. This is not to imply that there are no constraints on adjuncts or Specifiers: *a student of physics with large fins* conjures up a possibly anomalous image, but this is a matter of world knowledge rather than grammar or syntax (and this, as we saw with (10b), may depend on register in that such an NP would not necessarily be anomalous in a science-fiction context, for example). One important lexical property of Nouns does relate to what kind of Specifier they are compatible with: whether they are count or mass. We introduced this distinction in Section 2.2, pointing out that mass nouns do not have plurals. The Noun *fish* can function as both a mass and a count noun, but this is hard to see with plural marking since, as we saw in Chapter 1, the usual plural of *fish* (except in the sense of 'species of fish') has a null ending and so looks the same as the singular; see (21) of Chapter 1. In English, mass nouns can appear in the singular with no determiner, but count nouns cannot, while count nouns can appear with the indefinite article but mass nouns cannot. The Noun *fish* can appear in either context; compare the obligatorily mass Noun *water* and the obligatory count Noun *ant* in (28):

(28) a.   Fish/water is good for you.
     b.   A fish/an ant is on your plate.

So we see that mass or count nature of a Noun, which should also be stated in its lexical entry (although we have not seen exactly how), interacts with what can appear in its Specifier. This, too, is arguably a matter of semantics, since the distinction has to do with countable instances of something as opposed to undifferentiated quantities of something. As we mentioned in Section 2.2, many mass nouns can be 'coerced' into count readings, including *water* if one is concerned with distinguishing different types of water (cf. *a fine water from the foothills of the Alps*), but *fish* cannot really be coerced into giving coherent readings where its c-selection property is violated in examples like (26).

   As we said in the previous section, many common Nouns like *cat*, *dog* and *fish* lack external arguments. This is implicit in the lexical entry in (23a), since no Agent or other potential external argument is specified.

The PF and LF specifications in (23a) only become relevant at the PF and LF levels. However, we can think of them as 'carried along' with the lexical item through the syntactic parts of the grammar. The symbols which make up these specifications (e.g. phonemes like /f/, the λ-operator) are illegible to the syntax and so they are ignored until the derivation reaches the level of representation which can 'read' them. An analogy from cookery might help here. Pasta requires boiling water in order to cook, but you can put pasta in water before the water boils and nothing will happen to it. We could say that pasta can't 'read' water at less than 100°C, but water is water with the physical and chemical properties it has, below and above 100°C. Similarly, we can insert a lexical item at D-structure complete with PF and LF symbols, but nothing happens to those symbols until the derivation reaches the relevant level of representation while the lexical item remains what it is throughout the syntactic derivation. In fact, a strong interpretation of the Projection Principle guarantees this, in that it prevents us inserting *fish* at D-structure and giving it the PF form /kæt/ and the LF representation λ*x [dog (x)]*, possibilities we clearly need to rule out (this entails treating the PF and LF specifications in the Lexicon as featural).

Turning now to the Verb *fish* whose lexical entry is given in (23b), we see that it optionally c-selects an NP complement, corresponding to an optionally s-selected internal Theme argument, and obligatorily s-selects an external Agent argument. The Projection Principle therefore allows this Verb to appear in the contexts in (29) and rules out those in (30):

(29) a.   John fishes (in the pond).
     b.   Fish fish fish.

(30) a.   *It fishes that the world is round.
     b.   *There fished.
     c.   *John fished a book to Mary.
     d.   *The economy fishes John.

Again, the occurrence of adjuncts is independent of the Projection Principle, hence *in the pond* is optional in all these examples and does not affect their grammaticality. As before, I will leave aside the question of the content of SpecV′.

We can see further effects of s-selection in examples like (31). Inanimate nouns cannot be Agents and abstract nouns cannot be the Themes of Verbs like *fish*:

(31) a.   ??Philosophy fishes fish.
     b.   ??John fished sincerity.

As usual, metaphorical or poetic interpretations may be possible here, unlike in (30). It does seem that an inanimate external argument is possible with the interpretation that it bears the role of Instrument:

(32)   The new Ocean-Depleter 1000 ships will fish (our seas) more efficiently than ever.

This suggests that we may need to modify (23b) as regards the thematical roles s-selected as external argument. Of course, there are various further possible additions to be made to (23b), but what we have seen here suffices to illustrate the role of the Projection Principle.

D-structure, then, is the syntactic level at which lexical items are inserted into phrase markers generated by X'-theory in conformity with the Projection Principle. This means that (29b) has the D-structure in (33), where the c- and s-selection properties of all lexical items (including the functional item [Present], see (20a)) are satisfied:

(33)

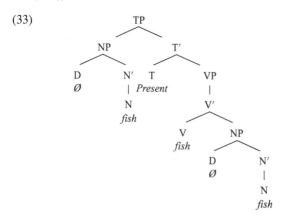

The Projection Principle also guarantees that the external argument *[NP [D ø] [N' [N fish]]* is interpreted as the Agent and the structurally identical internal argument is interpreted as the Theme in relation to the action schema in (23b) at LF. It also ensures that the correct PF representations are associated with each category, including null representations for D and T. We see that the two operative constraints at D-structure are X'-theory and the Projection Principle, with the latter guaranteeing the connection between the lexicon and independently generated phrase structure.

8.5   S-structure

In terms of the architecture of grammar shown in (1), the next stage of the derivation is S-structure. As we said above S-structure is derived from D-structure by movement rules. We introduced movement rules in Chapter 5. There we saw three types of movement rules: wh-movement, head-movement and NP-movement. Let us briefly look again at each of these, in the light of what we have seen in this chapter regarding the lexicon, D-structure and the Projection Principle.

Let us look first at wh-movement. The structure in (34), corresponding closely to (30) of Chapter 5, is an example of an S-structure derived by wh-movement:

(34)

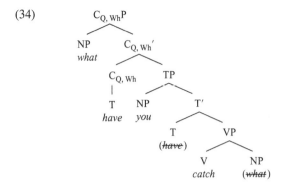

Here we see that the wh-NP *what* moves from the object position, complement of V, to SpecC$_{Q,Wh}$'. The D-structure from which (34) is derived is (35) (here head-movement of T to C has not taken place either, a point I return to directly):

(35)

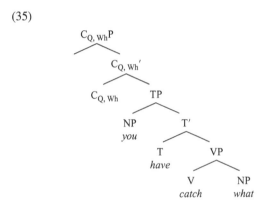

As a transitive verb, *catch* has a lexical entry similar to that of *fish* in (23b) but without the specification that the complement NP is optional:

(36)   *catch*(V): ___ NP. <Agent, Theme>. PF: /kætʃ/. LF: HUNT(Agent)
                [CONCRETE-OBJECT (Theme)]

In (35), *what* satisfies the c- and s-selection properties that *catch* imposes on its internal argument, and the external argument *you* is the s-selected Agent.

C$_{Q, Wh}$ c-selects finite TP, like any root C. As we saw in Chapter 5, it also has the property of triggering wh-movement. So, in the derivation from D-structure to S-structure, the wh-NP *what* moves to SpecC$_{Wh, Q}$', as seen in (34). Since the Projection Principle requires lexical properties to hold at all levels of the grammar (as given in (1)), the c-selection property of *catch* that it has a complement NP must be satisfied at S-structure. This is why there must be a trace or copy of *what* in that position. We did not take a position on which of these it is in Chapter 5, but we can now observe that positing a copy seems a simpler option than positing a trace, at least at S-structure, since the latter involves deleting the copy of *what* left by movement and inserting a trace in its place, while the former may not affect the direct-object position at all. X′-theory generates the landing site of wh-movement, SpecC$_{Q, Wh}$′. The S-structure in (34) forms the input to PF and LF, whose properties in relation to wh-movement we will look at in the next two sections.

Comparing the S-structure in (34) with the D-structure in (35), we can also see that head-movement from T to C takes place in the derivation of (34) from (35). We know from yes/no questions, as already discussed several times in earlier chapters, that C$_Q$ triggers T-to-C movement in main clauses whether the wh-feature is present on C or not:

(37) a.   Will Cambridge flood as a consequence of global warming?
      b.   Did Cambridge flood after the heavy rain last year?

We can also see that, where there is no other auxiliary present, *do* appears in T in main-clause interrogatives and various other environments (e.g. negation and VP-ellipsis). We can clearly assign *will* a lexical entry like the one given for *can* in (19a), as a T-element c-selecting VP (leaving aside the difficult question of the s-selection properties of modals, as we mentioned there). Then C$_Q$ will trigger T-to-C movement. But in (34) and (35), T is occupied by the feature [Past]. In our discussion of the PF properties of [Past] in Section 8.3, we said that it must combine with V by the 'downward' movement rule T-to-V. The operation combining T with V is somehow prevented from applying in main-clause interrogatives, and so the meaningless auxiliary *did* is inserted as the realisation of [Past]. If T-to-C movement places T in a position too distant from V to allow the PF T-to-V rule to take place, then this may be why *do*, in the form of *did*, is inserted. This implies that at D-structure and S-structure, T is simply [Past], with the default PF form /d/ as discussed in Section 8.3. (We will come back to *do*-support in more detail in the next section and slightly revise what we have said here.)

The Projection Principle, X′-theory, wh-movement, head-movement and the sketch of *do*-support just given, along with the lexical entry for *catch* in (36), together account for the paradigm in (38):

(38) a.   What have you caught (what)?
      b.   You caught a fish.
      c.   *What have you caught a fish?
      d.   You caught WHAT?

In (38a), we have wh-movement from the complement position of V, T-to-C movement triggered by C$_Q$ and copy-deletion. In (38b), we have T-to-V movement (and note that *catch* must be specified for its irregular Past form *caught* (/kɔːt/), which we omitted in (36)). Sentence (38c) is ungrammatical because the wh-phrase cannot be directly inserted into SpecC′, as there is no head to select it there, and there is no c-selected position inside TP from which it can have moved, as *a fish* occupies the object position c-selected by *catch*. In the echo question in (38d), there is neither wh-movement nor T-to-C movement.

The third type of movement we have seen is passives, as in (39) (repeated from Chapter 5):

(39) a.   Oprah interviewed John.   (active)
     b.   John was interviewed (by Oprah).   (passive)

As we saw in Chapter 5, *interview* has the c-selection frame in (40), to which we add the standard s-selection specification for a transitive verb:

(40)   *interview* (V) ___ NP. <Agent, Theme>.

These selection requirements are clearly satisfied in (39a), where *Oprah* is the Agent external argument and *John* the c-selected NP complement bearing the Theme thematic role. In the passive (39b) we see the same NP *John*, with the same thematic role of Theme, in SpecT'. We account for this by saying that this NP moves from one position to the other. The relationship can be captured by the trees in (41) (again repeated from Chapter 5):

(41) a.

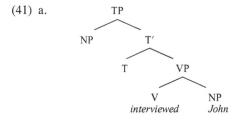

b.

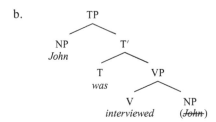

Here *John* moves to the subject position, which we defined as an A(rgument)-position in Section 6.7. As we saw there, this means that there is an A-binding relation between *John* and its copy in (41b). In some sense, then, this copy is able to 'count' as an anaphor for binding theory purposes, if we want to maintain that movement always entails binding of the copy; we will leave this important and tricky question aside here.

The Projection Principle forces the copy of *John* to remain in the c-selected complement position in (41b). But what of the s-selected external Agent argument in the passive? One clue comes from the optional *by*-phrase in (39b); here *Oprah* clearly bears the s-selected external Agent thematic role. The *by*-phrase is an adjunct and, like all adjuncts, is optional. Since there is no c-selection requirement for the external argument, there is nothing that actually requires that argument to be realised in subject position (SpecT'). Hence it may be free to be realised in a *by*-phrase. However, the Projection Principle requires s-selection for the external argument to be satisfied. In fact, there is evidence that this argument is present even in 'short' passives where the *by*-phrase is absent. A full discussion of this evidence would take us too far afield here; perhaps the most important observation is that in (39b) where the *by*-phrase is absent, the interpretation of the sentence is 'someone interviewed John', where 'someone' clearly functions as the s-selected external argument of *interview*. So in short passives the external argument is interpreted as an **arbitrary implicit argument**, a silent (or implicit) version of 'someone', referring to an arbitrary individual or individuals. The presence of this argument is presumably required by the Projection Principle. The precise structural realisation of the arbitrary implicit external argument is much debated; arguably the simplest approach would be to treat it as a silent version of the *by*-phrase, as a silent adjunct which, unlike typical adjuncts, is not optional because of the Projection Principle.

Here we have illustrated how S-structure is derived from D-structure by three different kinds of movement rules. The Projection Principle requires lexically specified c- and s-selection requirements to be satisfied at this level, as at all others. The principal consequence of this is that copies must be present in the positions vacated by movement; we also saw that the implicit external argument of passives must be in some sense present.

Let us now look again at the architecture of the grammar in (1):

(1)

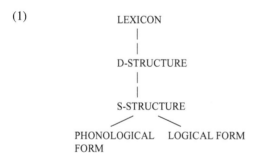

Here we see that the derivation splits into two paths after S-structure, one path leading to Phonological Form (PF) and the other to Logical Form (LF). As we will see in more detail in the next section, PF ultimately converts the representation of the sentence into a phonological and a phonetic form; this is what we hear. LF, on the other hand, converts the syntactic representation, which is a purely formal object, into a representation which can be the input to semantic interpretation (in standard semantic theory, this means a representation which can be read as a proposition bearing truth conditions, capable of being evaluated as true or false); this is what we understand. It is very important to see that the level of representation we hear (PF) and the level of representation we understand (LF) are distinct and that *they do not directly interact* in that neither is directly derived from the other. The 'bridge' between the two is constituted by the earlier levels of representation D-structure and S-structure, which we can collectively designate as the **narrow syntax**, and the Lexicon. The Projection Principle plays a vital role too, in that, as we saw, it prevents PF /kæt/ from corresponding to LF $\lambda x\ [\ dog(x)\ ]$ (as long as PF and LF specifications in lexical entries are taken to be featural).

The split in the derivation seen in (1) allows us to account for the ubiquitous fact that we understand more than we hear; as we have repeatedly emphasised, a great deal of syntax is covert, hence silent. In terms of the architecture of grammar in (1), aspects of narrow syntax feed into LF representations but are inert at PF. The opposite is also true: there are syntactic elements which we hear but which play no role at LF, e.g. the dummy English auxiliary *do*. Additionally, phonological and semantic aspects of lexical entries are inert in narrow syntax but active at their respective interfaces, as we mentioned earlier. We will see examples of PF/LF mismatches in the next two sections. These examples motivate the split derivation of sentences entailed by the architecture in (1).

8.6   Phonological Form (PF)

As we have said, PF interprets the representation sent to it by the narrow syntax (D-structure and S-structure) and converts it into phonological form. In other words, it converts (42a) to something like (42b):

(42) a.

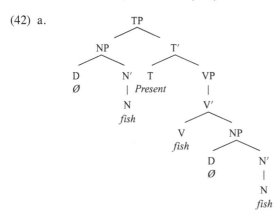

b.   fɪʃ fɪʃ fɪʃ

The PF in (42b) is seriously incomplete, in that only the segmental aspects of the phonological representation are specified; at the very minimum the third /fɪʃ/ receives greater accentual prominence than the preceding two (this is the English Nuclear Stress Rule).

Clearly, large parts of the S-structure representation in (42a) have no counterpart in (42b). None of the phrase structure determined by X′-theory appears to have a PF counterpart, although this may be a little too hasty a conclusion, as phrase structure information is required in order to determine the Nuclear Stress, i.e. the greater accentual prominence of the third /fɪʃ/ just noted. Of the lexical items in (42a), only the occurrences of the noun *fish* and the verb *fish* have any PF realisation, the former twice over. The plural indefinite D and Present Tense are null, as a matter of lexical specification. Different values of

D, e.g. singular indefinite *a*, and of T, e.g. Past /d/, do have PF realisations as shown in (43):

(43)

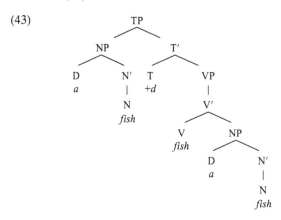

Here the singular indefinite D *a* is straightforwardly realised as /ə/ (in unstressed positions, where it normally occurs). The realisation of Past /d/ is more complex, though. First, it must undergo T-to-V movement, attaching it to *fish*, giving *fish+d*. Then there is a regular phonological assimilation rule which converts a voiced obstruent to its voiceless counterpart immediately following a voiceless obstruent in the same word: this rule converts /d/ to /t/ here. There is absolutely no doubt that the latter operation is a productive phonological rule of English (a variant of it converts the voiced obstruent marking plural, /z/, to its voiceless counterpart /s/ in *cats* /kæts/ but not in *dogs* /dɔgz/) and as such belongs firmly in the PF component. But what about the T-to-V operation? This appears to be a case of head-movement, the opposite of the French and German V-to-T rule we discussed in Sections 7.1 and 7.5.

In our discussion of the PF properties of [Past] in Sections 8.3 and 8.5, we said that the T-to-V rule takes place in the derivation from S-structure to PF, while the T-to-C rule triggered by C$_Q$ in root interrogatives, which gives subject-auxiliary inversion, takes place in the derivation from D-structure to S-structure. Let us now look more closely at this idea, in order to get an idea of some of aspects of how PF might interact with narrow syntax.

In Section 6.7 we gave the following general definition of movement:

(44)   Movement substitutes an element of type X into a **c-commanding** position of type X, where X ranges over head, grammatical-function NP and wh.

We suggested there that movement creates binding configurations, since indices are copied as part of the copy/paste operation, and explored the consequences of this idea for wh-movement especially; we will return to this idea in the section on LF to follow. We also observed that the notion of referential index is not so natural in the context of head-movement.

Since PF is entirely independent of LF, and binding and coindexation are relations with impact at LF since they affect semantic interpretation, it is possible that downward movement is allowed in PF since there is no associated binding requirement. If so, then T-to-V movement must be a PF operation: if it applied in narrow syntax, it would be fed to LF where the ensuing ill-formed binding relation leads to ungrammaticality. We also suggested in Section 8.3 that certain lexical items are specified as inherently affixal, marked with the diacritic '+'; this is true for Present and Past Tense in English. So we can add the PF properties of Present and Past to the lexical entry we gave in (20), as follows (still leaving aside the s-selection and semantic specifications, which are not directly relevant here in any case):

(45) a.   [Present] (T):   __ VP.   PF: /+ø/
     b.   [Past] (T):   __ VP.   PF: /+d/

If T is not raised to C in the narrow syntax, then Present/Past satisfy their affixation requirement at PF by lowering to V. This gives the following derived structure for (43):

(46)

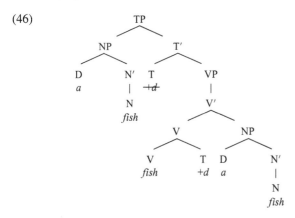

Here we see *[T +d]*, i.e. Past Tense, lowered to V (and in fact adjoined to it). Various PF rules now apply: the copy of *[T +d]* in T is deleted by regular copy deletion, on which see more below; and the derived *[v [v fish][T +d]]* is realised ('spelled out') as /fɪʃ+d/ and input to the assimilation rule we described above, converting /d/ to /t/. Phonological realisation of *[T +d]*, i.e. 'spell out' as /d/, is blocked by disjunctive ordering where the lexical entry of the verb is specified as having a special past-tense form, as we saw in the case of *sing* in (21): the availability of *sang* (/sæŋ/) as *sing*+Past overrides *singed* (/sɪŋd/).

    Where C$_Q$ attracts T in the narrow syntax, T-to-V lowering cannot take place. This is presumably because T in C is too distant from V. In that case, the affixal property of T is satisfied by insertion of *do* at PF, which combines with +d to give /dɪd/, again overriding the default form, which would presumably be /duːd/.

    '*Do*-support' is also required in negative contexts. Here it is presumably the presence of the negation, *not/n't*, which prevents T-to-V lowering. It is tempting to attribute this to linear adjacency, but other adverbs, including negative adverbs such as *never*, can intervene linearly between T and V without causing *do*-insertion:

(47) a.   John did not go on holiday in Bangor.
     b.   John often went on holiday in Bangor.
     c.   John never went on holiday in Bangor.

As we saw in our comparison of English and French verb positions in Section 7.3, *often* can be analysed as left-adjoined to V′; *never* is semantically similar to *often* in that it modifies the action described by V′, adding intrinsically negative content. Nonetheless, it does not block T-to-V lowering, as (47c) shows. What is the generalisation over T-to-C raising and *not*-insertion which blocks T-to-V lowering in both cases?

It is clear that, after T-to-C raising, a head, namely the copy of the raised T, sits in between T in C and V. Similarly, we can treat the clausal negator *not* as a head; one piece of evidence for this is that in its contracted form it raises to T, giving forms such as *won't*, *can't*, etc., which can then raise further to C giving sentences like (48):

(48) a.   Won't Vurdy talk to Goona?
     b.   Can't you understand this?

(This shows, incidentally, that *n't*-raising is a narrow-syntactic operation, not a PF one.) So, in negative sentences, we have a structure along the lines of (49) (omitting Neg′ and V′ for convenience and glossing over the c-selection properties of T this structure appears to introduce):

(49)

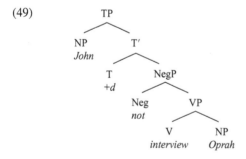

Compare (49) with the representation of a subject-auxiliary inversion example in (50):

(50)

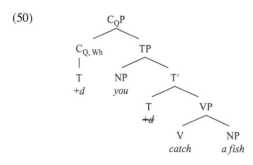

In both cases, we see that there is a head in between T and V: Neg in (49) and the copy of T in (50). So we can conclude that T-to-V lowering is blocked if a head intervenes between T (containing +*d*) and V; this prevents T lowering from C to V here. In Volume II, we will see that this is a subcase of a much more general constraint on movement in general.

Where T is Present, everything is the same as with Past. But there is one important difference, which shows us that PF is quite an abstract level of representation. The PF specification of Present is as a null affix: /+ø/. We see this clearly in (42), where the present-tense form of the verb *fish* is /fɪʃ/. The reason we posit T-to-V lowering here, although it does not affect the surface phonological form since the affix is null, is that *do*-insertion is obligatory in main-clause interrogatives and in negative clauses:

(51) a.   Do fish fish fish?
     b.   Fish do not fish fish.

So *do* is inserted here to satisfy the affixal property of Present Tense, even though no affix is phonologically realised.

There is a further complication involving Present Tense. Where the subject is third singular, Present is realised as /+z/. In fact, we could say that there is a separate Agreement head which is realised in this way in this context (as in (18a) of Chapter 1), or we could combine Tense and Agreement features on T and add (52) to (45a):

(52)   PF: /+ø/; /+z/ __ /[Person:3, Number: Sg]

Again, disjunctive ordering will force /+z/ in the more specified context where the features [Person: 3] and [Number: Sg] are present, while /+ø/ is the elsewhere form. For English, this choice between a separate Agreement (or Agr) head or (52) may be somewhat moot. In languages with richer tense and agreement inflection (e.g. Italian, as we saw in Chapter 1), distinguishing Tense and Agr as separate heads may be advantageous. As we also mentioned in Chapter 1, it may be desirable to 'line up' English and Italian verb forms as much as possible, which would entail postulating a separate Agr head in English.

The +*z* realisation of Present behaves exactly like Past +*d*, both in relation to *do*-insertion (applying where T-to-V lowering is blocked by an intervening head in the contexts in (49) and (50)) and in relation to the phonological assimilation rule, which changes /z/ to /s/ following a voiced obstruent (cf. *knots* /nɒts/ vs *nods* /nɒdz/) and inserts an epenthetic vowel when the root ends in a coronal fricative or affricate as in *fishes* (/fɪʃɪz/). Furthermore, a few verbs show stem allomorphy with +*z*: *do* becomes /dʌz/, not /duːz/, and *says* is pronounced /sɛz/ by many speakers (see Section 2.2).

What we see in the contrasting PF realisations of T (and of D in (42) and (43)) is simply differences in the lexical specifications of functional heads: Present (aside from third singular) happens to be null, just as *fish* happens to start with /f/; these are simply matters of lexical arbitrariness (i.e. why we need the lexicon in the first place). Copies resulting from movement are different: here we have a productive rule of copy deletion, as we have seen in our examples of all three movement types. Since copy deletion removes phonological content, we take it to be a PF process. We now have three PF processes: T-to-V lowering, *do*-support and copy deletion. In addition we have the morphological processes of lexically conditioned stem allomorphy forming the irregular past tenses of verbs like *sing* and *catch*, and the regular phonological assimilation rules applying to the affixes +*d* and +*z*. It is important to see that these rules must apply in a particular order, or ungrammaticality will result.

We can easily see that there is an **intrinsic ordering** of T-to-V lowering and copy deletion in that the former creates the context for the latter to apply; this is known as **feeding order**. Furthermore, lowering clearly creates the context for the irregular past-tense forms and for the assimilation rules applying to +*d* and +*z*; it therefore feeds and precedes those rules. Finally, if *do*-insertion is a 'repair' rule which applies when lowering fails in order to satisfy the affixation requirements of +*d*, +*z* and +*ø*, then it must also follow T-to-V lowering. *Do*-support seemingly applies where lowering does *not* apply; these rules are in **bleeding order** as lowering removes the context for *do*-insertion. *Do*-support also prevents the formation of irregular past tenses, and as we saw, *do* itself has an irregular past form and so must feed, and therefore precede, that rule. It also clearly precedes the assimilation rules. So it seems clear that we have the following partial ordering of the PF operations we have been considering:

(53)   T-to-V lowering > *do*-insertion > irregular past-tense formation > assimilation

It remains to be seen how copy deletion is ordered in relation to (53). We have already mentioned that it must follow T-to-V lowering. How is it ordered in relation to *do*-insertion? The account we gave above of (46) provides the answer. Let us look again at (46).

(46)

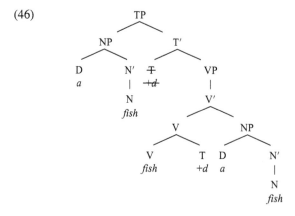

Here, if *do*-support precedes copy deletion, *do* will be inserted in T, giving rise to the ungrammatical **A fish did fished a fish*; here *do*-insertion would in fact bleed copy deletion, since *did* is not a copy of +*d* (alternatively, copy deletion could delete +*d* giving the equally ungrammatical **A fish do fished a fish*).

Let us now look again at the result of narrow-syntactic T-to-C raising of +*d*, repeated from (50):

(50′)

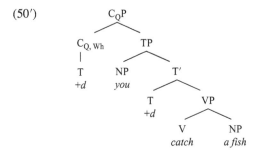

(50′) differs from (50) in that the copy of +*d* in T has not been deleted. If T-to-V lowering precedes copy-deletion, and T-to-C movement, as a syntactic rule, precedes all the rules in (53), then (50′) is the representation which is the input to PF. Following (53), we can in fact apply T-to-V lowering here, giving a form such as *[v [v catch] +d]* in the V position (see again (46)). If copy-deletion precedes *do*-support, the copy of +*d* in the original T position will disappear and there will be no head in between the moved T in C and V. However, this is not a problem since T-to-V lowering has already applied; if T-to-V lowering were allowed to apply iteratively it could then lower T from C to V, bleeding *do*-insertion, so we see that this is not a possibility. Copy deletion must in any case precede the other rules in (53), irregular past-tense formation and assimilation, as it will then delete the occurrence of +*d* attached to V and bleed these rules, guaranteeing that where *do* is inserted in C the verb always appears uninflected. So we arrive at the following ordering of the PF-rules:

(54)   T-to-V lowering > copy deletion > *do*-insertion > irregular past-tense for-
         mation > assimilation

Evidence from child language is relevant here. It has been observed that children sometimes 'repeat' the auxiliary in inversion contexts at early stages of language acquisition, producing examples like (55):

(55) a.   *Can* its wheels *can* spin?
     b.   *Is* the steam *is* hot?
     c.   *Was* that *was* Anna?

We could account for this by saying that, at the relevant stage of first-language acquisition, children have not fully acquired copy deletion, at least in the T-to-C context. Very strikingly, the same applies with *do*-support, examples like (56) being attested:

(56)   *Did* the kitchen light *did* flash?

We predict that (56) would arise from failure of copy-deletion of the occurrence of *do*+*d* in the original T position in (50′). This form is then input to past-tense formation, and *did* results. Failure of deletion of the lowest copy of T, the one attached to V, would give rise to examples like (57):

(57)   ***Did*** the light (did) flash*ed*?

These are also attested in the spontaneous speech of children acquiring English.

A further environment for *do*-support is VP-ellipsis, as in (58), repeated from Section 3.4:

(58)   John ate the cake and Mary did eat the cake too.

Here, as we argued in Section 3.4, the VP *eat the cake* is elided. One approach to English VP-ellipsis is to treat it as PF deletion. We interpret the elided VP as *eat the cake* because it is present at LF but absent at PF (a good example of understanding more than we hear). If VP-ellipsis is a PF operation, we can ask how it is ordered in relation to the operations we have been looking at here. The answer is clear from the presence of *do*-support in (58): ellipsis bleeds T-to-V lowering by deleting V and thereby feeds *do*-insertion by creating the context where *do* is required to meet the affixal requirement of +d in T. The order of operations is shown in (59):

(59) a.   ... and [TP Mary [T′ [T +d] [VP eat the cake]]] (S-structure)
      b.   ... and [TP Mary [T′ [T +d] [VP eat the cake]]] (VP-ellipsis)
      c.   ... and [TP Mary [T′ [T do+d] [VP eat the cake]]] (*do*-insertion)
      d.   ... and [TP Mary [T′ [T did] [VP eat the cake]]] (past-tense formation)

Because T-to-V lowering doesn't apply in (59), copy deletion doesn't apply.

If VP-ellipsis followed T-to-V lowering, the result would be (60):

(60)   John ate the cake and Mary too.

(Here the interpretation where Mary eats the cake is the relevant one, not the one where John eats Mary; see Section 3.4.) The sentence in (60) could be derived in the following way:

(61) a.   ... and [TP Mary [T′ [T +d] [VP eat the cake]]] (S-structure)
      b.   ... and [TP Mary [T′ [T +d] [VP [eat] + d] the cake]]] (by T-to-V lowering)
      c.   ... and [TP Mary [T′ [T +d] [VP [eat] + d] the cake]]] (by copy deletion)
      d.   ... and [TP Mary [T′ [T +d] [VP [eat] + d] the cake]]] (by VP-ellipsis)

Example (60) is in fact grammatical, but it is does not involve VP-ellipsis. As we saw in Section 3.4, (60) is the result of T′-deletion, which can apply with other auxiliaries as in (62) and so is not connected to *do*-support:

(62) a.   (John can speak Mandarin) and Mary [T′ can speak Mandarin] too.
      b.   (John has written a novel) and Mary [T′ has written a novel] too.

The T′-deletion operation can derive the string in (60) independently of VP-ellipsis and the operations in (61), but not vice versa.

We conclude that the ordering among the PF operations we have been considering is the following:

(63)   VP-ellipsis > T-to-V lowering > copy deletion > *do*-insertion > irregular
          past-tense formation > assimilation

It seems natural to suppose that the more purely phonological operation of assimilation should be the last of the series, while operations more similar to syntax, e.g. T-to-V lowering, which is a form of head-movement, should occur earlier. Similarly, the more morphological operation of irregular past-tense formation, i.e. stem allomorphy, perhaps naturally occurs in between. Furthermore, as we have already observed, T-to-V lowering must precede copy deletion. The place of VP-ellipsis and *do*-insertion must be as given here, given the evidence we have seen, but there is no clear theoretical ground for this.

In this section I have gone into some detail concerning a small number of PF operations which apply in English, in order to illustrate the workings of this component of the grammar and its interactions with narrow-syntactic rules, the lexicon and both phonological and morphological rules. We can see that the relevant rule systems are highly intricate. But a very important point, which we have already stressed, is that these rules do *not* interact with semantics, i.e with Logical Form. Now it is time to look at that component of the grammar.

8.7   Logical Form (LF)

As we said in Section 8.2, Logical Form (LF) is the level of representation which forms the input to the semantic component. It is important to see that LF itself is not the semantic representation: it is a syntactic representation (a phrase marker) which can be readily converted into a representation from which, on standard assumptions, truth conditions can be read and hence the meaning deduced. As we have seen, the architecture of the grammar in (1) involves a split into two paths after S-structure, one leading to PF, the other to LF. Since the PF path, which we looked at in the previous section, exclusively represents what we actually hear, the derivation from S-structure to LF is sometimes referred to as 'covert'; we are not directly presented even with LF strings, instead we must deduce them from various forms of indirect evidence mainly, since we are concerned with the input to semantics, concerning possible and impossible interpretations of various kinds.

In Section 6.7, we gave a very brief introduction to the semantic notions of quantifier and variable. There we saw that an NP like *every student* doesn't refer to a single individual (the way proper names like *Goona* and *Vurdy* do); instead, owing to the nature of the determiner *every*, this kind of NP is a quantified expression. Such NPs refer to sets of entities and relate them in various ways to the set denoted by a predicate, such as *likes pizza*. *Every student* in (64) says that every member of the set of students is also in the set denoted by the predicate, the set of pizza-likers:

(64)   Every student in our class likes pizza.

With a quantifier like *every* (a universal quantifier), this is a subset relation. We went on to give the quasi-logical representation for (64) in (65):

(65)   For every x, if x is a student in our class, then x likes pizza (or 'if x is in the set of students in our class, then x is in the set of pizza-likers').

Here x is a variable, ranging over individuals in the domain of discourse. To get the full meaning of (64), we have to 'plug in' individuals for x (technically, we assign values to the variable) and then see if that individual, say individual 23 = $John_{23}$, individual 5 = *the man next door*$_5$, individual 666 = *the pet shop boy*$_{666}$, etc., is a member of the set of students and a member of the set of pizza-likers. As long as we don't find any individuals which are in the set of students and not in the set of pizza-likers, then the sentence is true. What is crucial here is that the two occurrences of the variable x in 'if x is a student, then x likes pizza' always have the same value. In logic and semantics, these variables are said to be bound by the quantifier, and so as we compute the semantics of the quantifier, plugging in values for the variables, the two variables always have the same value.

We next compare related quantified expressions like (64) to wh-questions like (66):

(66)   Which course$_i$ does Goona like t$_i$?

The crucial observation is that *which* is also quantificational rather than referential: the answer to the question could be 'none of them', showing that *which course* doesn't have to pick anything out in the domain of discourse. Like *every student*, *which course* applies to a set of entities (courses) and asks for the identity of a member of that set such that Goona likes it. In quasi-logic:

(67)   For which x, x a course, does Goona like x ?

In this we observed an important semantic similarity between wh-elements and quantifiers: both instantiate operator-variable structures. The operator (or quantifier) applies to a set of entities and specifies the subpart of that set we are dealing with (in the case of wh-operators, find a member). The variable tells us where in the structure you would 'plug in' the specified constant in relation to the predicate so as to compute its relation to the predicate and see if the sentence is true or false. So, in relation to (67), we plug in different courses in the variable in object position as values of x, and ask if Goona is a member of the set of x-likers. Again, it is crucial that the two x's following 'which x' in (67) always have the same value. So, we concluded that these variables are semantically bound by the wh-word and that the rightmost x in (67) corresponds to the trace/copy of wh-movement. So we arrived at the important conclusion that syntactic binding, c-command and coindexation correspond exactly to the semantic binding involved in interpreting the wh-quantification. This is an important conclusion for LF, as it means that wh-movement creates a syntactic configuration which can be interpreted at LF as one kind of quantificational structure, subject to the general semantic rules for interpreting such structures.

We said above that it is vital for this system of interpreting quantifier-variable relations that in expressions like (65) and (67) each x should be 'filled in' with the same value. The variables that have this property are said to be in the scope of the quantifier. So all the x's in both (65) and (67) are in the scope of *every* or the wh-operator. In **predicate logic**, (65) could be written as follows:

(68) $\forall x \, [\, \text{student}(x) \rightarrow \text{likes-pizza}(x) \,]$

Here the symbol $\forall$ is the universal quantifier, meaning roughly 'every' or 'all', and the arrow indicates the 'if–then' implication relation, so (68) restates (65). The important point is that, by convention, the scope of the quantifier is indicated by the brackets following it; all and only occurrences of x inside that bracket are in the scope of the quantifier, i.e. are interpreted as bound by it. This is a convention developed by logicians.

If we now look at (66) and (67) in the light of these logical conventions, we can say that the interrogative C ($C_{Q, \, Wh}$) which triggers wh-movement to its Specifier thereby does two things. First, as we saw in our discussion of wh-movement in Chapter 5, it determines the position of the wh-operator by triggering wh-movement, thereby creating a copy in the original position. Second, it determines the scope of the wh-phrase. We can directly connect these two points by the following postulate:

(69)   A quantified phrase has scope over the portion of phrase structure it c-commands at LF which contains a variable that it binds.

Let us look again at our original example of wh-movement from Chapter 5:

(70)

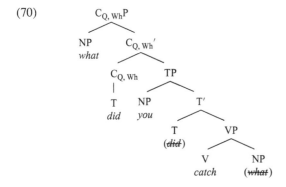

Here $C_{Q, \, Wh}$ triggers movement of *what* from the object position to SpecC$_{Q, \, Wh}$P. The Projection Principle requires the presence of the copy in object position. This copy is deleted at PF by the general copy-deletion rule we discussed in the previous section, but given that PF and LF do not interact, it remains at LF. In fact, it is interpreted as the variable bound by the wh-operator. The variable is in the scope of the operator since it is c-commanded by the operator. This is guaranteed by the general fact that narrow-syntactic movement always targets a c-commanding position (we saw in the previous section that PF-movement need not have this property); furthermore, the fact that the variable is bound by the wh-operator results from the definition of binding as c-command combined with coindexing (see Chapter 6, (37)). Hence, (70) can be read at LF as 'for which thing x, you caught x' (glossing *what* as 'which thing x'), and this can be read by interpretative rules for quantifier-variables along the lines sketched above and in a little more detail in Section 6.7.

Since it is $C_{Q, Wh}$ which triggers wh-movement to its Specifier, this element effectively determines the scope of wh-operators. We saw this in Section 7.6 in relation to the different matrix verbs in the following examples:

(71) a.   We wonder what you bought.
            ?*What did you wonder (that) I bought?

      b.   *I think what you bought.
            What did you think (that) I bought?

      c.   I remember what you bought.
            What did you remember (that) I bought?

As we observed there, the scope of the interrogative, i.e. the wh-operator, is determined by the c-selection properties of the main verbs: *wonder* selects $C_{Q, Wh}$ and so the operator only moves to the lower SpecC′ and has scope just over the embedded clause; *think* cannot c-select $C_{Q, Wh}$ and so in (71b) it is the matrix $C_{Q, Wh}$ which determines the movement and scope domain of the wh-operator, and *remember* optionally c-selects $C_{Q, Wh}$, and so either possibility is available. C-selection correlates with s-selection here, in that *wonder* obligatorily s-selects a question, *think* obligatorily s-selects a statement and *remember* s-selects either. We see in general, then, that the movement and scope domains of wh-operators coincide in English.

However, we also saw in Section 7.6 that there are languages in which wh-phrases do not move. Mandarin Chinese is probably the best-known example. As we saw in Section 7.6, the same scope and selection facts as in (71) hold in Mandarin, although the wh-phrase does not move overtly. Here are the relevant examples once again:

(72) a.   Zhangsan   xiang-zhidao [cp Lisi mai-le   shenme].
            Zhangsan   wonder   Lisi buy-PERF what
            'Zhangsan wonders what Lisi bought.'

      b.   Zhangsan   yiwei [cp Lisi mai-le   shenme] ?
            Zhangsan   think   Lisi buy-PERF what
            'What does Zhangsan think that Lisi bought?'

      c.   Zhangsan   jide [cp   Lisi mai- le   shenme] ?
            Zhangsan   remember Lisi buy- PERF what
            'Zhangsan remembers what Lisi bought.' **Or**
            'What did Zhangsan remember that Lisi bought?'

We also saw evidence, from sentential particles, that C can bear the Q and wh-features. So the question arises of how the wh-operator is interpreted in Mandarin, a question we left open in Section 7.4.

The covert derivation to LF allows us to give a very simple answer to this question: the Mandarin sentences in (72) have different structures at LF, where *covert* wh-movement operations parallel to those that take place overtly in languages like English create the required operator-variable structures. So, a simple wh-question in Chinese such as (73a) has the S-structure in (73b) and the LF in (73c):

(73) a.   Lisi mai-le   shenme?
             Lisi buy- PERF what
             'What did Lisi buy?'

   b.

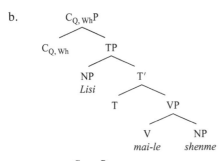

   c.

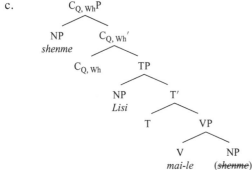

(Since the sentential particles marking the clause as Q or wh are final in Mandarin – see examples (30) and (31b) in Chapter 7 – we should perhaps place C in final position, but I leave this complication aside here.) Thanks to the operation of covert wh-movement, at LF Mandarin wh-questions are interpreted just like their English counterparts in terms of scope and variable-binding. The LFs of the two languages are close to uniform, while their S-structures (and PFs) appear quite different; this is in line with the fact that the interpretation of quantifiers, including wh-quantifiers, and variables is cross-linguistically uniform.

Covert wh-movement can distinguish the interpretations of the sentences in (72). The indirect question readings in (72a,c) result from wh-movement to the intermediate SpecC', and the direct question readings in (72b,c) result from wh-movement to the root SpecC'. So we can treat the Mandarin c-selection restrictions seen in (72) in the same way as those in English in (71).

So, in a nutshell: *Mandarin has wh-movement*. But this movement is covert, taking place after the derivation has split into the PF and LF paths. Since it only takes place on the LF path, we hear the Mandarin wh-phrases *in situ*, but we understand them in their moved positions. Thus, both languages feature wh-movement; the only difference lies in the point of the derivation at which the operation takes place. This difference is regulated by a parameter of the kind described in Section 7.6. A consequence of this is that if Mandarin has covert wh-movement, then we might expect it to have covert island phenomena comparable to the overt ones of English seen in Section 5.6. I will not go into this question here, but return to it in Volume II.

Are there any cases of covert movement in English? If we take seriously the idea that LF represents quantifier-variable relations in terms of binding (coindexation and c-command) of a variable created by movement, then we should extend our account of wh-questions to sentences containing quantifiers like *every*, as in (64) and (65), repeated here:

(64)   Every student likes pizza.

(65)   For every x, if x is a student, then x likes pizza (or 'if x is in the set of students, then x is in the set of pizza-likers').

If (65) approximates the LF of (64), then *every student* raises and its copy is interpreted as a variable bound by it. So (64) has the LF in (74):

(74)

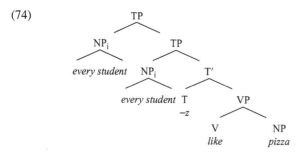

Here *every student* adjoins to TP (this is the standard kind of X′-adjunction which we saw in Chapter 4, extended from the X′ to the XP-level). As in all cases of narrow-syntactic movement, it c-commands and is coindexed with its copy and therefore binds it: the copy is thus interpreted as a variable. Thus (74) can be interpreted as in (65) or, more formally, as in (68). The operation adjoining *every student* to TP here is known as Quantifier Raising, or QR.

This approach allows us to capture **quantifier-scope ambiguities** of the kind illustrated by (75):

(75)   Every student dreads some lecture.

This sentence has two interpretations. In one, *every student* has scope over *some lecture*, so the interpretation is 'for every student x, there is some lecture y such that x dreads y'. The dreaded lecture could be a different one in each case (e.g. Goona dreads Syntax, Vurdy dreads Phonetics, Pete dreads Semantics, etc.). In the second reading, *some lecture* has scope over *every student*, so the meaning is 'there is some lecture x such that for every student y, y dreads x', i.e. one lecture so dreadful that all students dread it (clearly this cannot be a Syntax lecture …). The first reading is the wide-scope reading for *every student* (it's also the 'surface scope' reading, in that the linearly first quantifier has wider scope). The second reading is the wide-scope reading for *some lecture* (it is also known as the 'inverse scope' reading as the scope relations don't follow surface linear precedence).

If scope is determined by c-command, then we can disambiguate (75) by applying QR in different orders where there is more than one quantified NP. Thus the first reading of (75) (wide scope for *every student*) is represented in (76a), while the second reading (wide scope for *some lecture*) is represented in (76b):

(76) a.

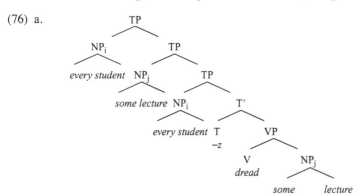

b.

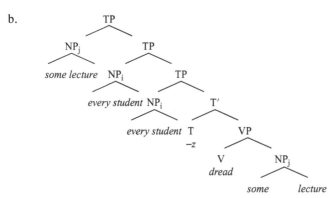

The postulate in (69) that scope reduces to c-command determines that *every student* has scope over *some lecture* in (76a) and *some lecture* has scope over *every student* in (76b). These representations can then be input to logical representations of the kind seen in (68) as necessary, in order to derive the semantic interpretations.

We also see covert wh-movement in certain contexts in English. This occurs in multiple questions (which we saw briefly in Section 5.3), illustrated in (77):

(77)   Who wrote which songs?

Here we assume the subject wh-phrase *who* has moved from SpecT' to SpecC' (recall the discussion of this in Section 5.4). The object wh-phrase *which songs* has clearly not moved. In English, the rule for multiple questions is that where there is more than one wh-phrase in the clause only one can move (this isn't true in all languages, e.g. Russian and other Slavic languages have multiple wh-movement). Nonetheless, *which songs* must bind a variable in (77) in order to be properly interpreted as a quantifier. Moreover, it interacts with *who*: the natural answer pairs people and songs (e.g. Paul wrote *Hey Jude*, John wrote *I am the Walrus*, George wrote *Here Comes the Sun*, etc.). This is known as the **pair-list interpretation** of multiple questions.

We can account for this by proposing that in multiple questions the wh-phrases combine (by a rule known as Absorption) to form a complex operator, giving an LF representation of the kind in (78):

(78)   [$_{CP}$ [who$_i$, which songs$_j$] [$_{TP}$ x$_i$ wrote x$_j$]

The interpretation of (78) is 'for which x, x a person, and for which y, y a song, x wrote y', which naturally elicits a pair-list answer of the kind seen in the previous paragraph. As with covert wh-movement in Mandarin, the postulation of covert movement in English leads to the prediction of covert island effects; we will come back to this in Volume II.

The final LF phenomenon we will look at here is **reconstruction**. This is illustrated in (79):

(79)   [$_{NP}$ Which joke about himself$_i$] does Donald$_i$ dislike --- most ?

This sentence is grammatical. It involves wh-movement of the complex wh-NP from the object position marked by the dash (for convenience). There is clearly nothing unusual about the wh-movement here, but the wh-phrase contains the anaphor *himself*. Recall from Chapter 6 that anaphors are subject to Principle A of the binding theory, which requires them to be bound in their binding domain. Binding involves c-command by and coindexation with the antecedent. But here the anaphor inside the moved wh-phrase is not c-commanded by an antecedent. Furthermore, it is clear that the antecedent is *Donald*, as the coindexation indicates. Assuming that the binding principles apply at S-structure or LF, i.e. after wh-movement has taken place, this example appears to be a problem for Principle A of the binding theory.

The idea that movement leaves a copy provides a solution to this problem. The full representation of (79) at S-structure is (80):

(80)   [$_{NP}$ Which joke about himself$_i$] does Donald$_i$ dislike [$_{NP}$ which joke about himself$_i$] most ?

The lower copy is deleted at PF, giving (79). But, again thanks to the independence of PF and LF, we can retain the copy at LF. In that context, the anaphor *himself* satisfies Principle A: it is c-commanded by its coindexed antecedent *Donald* within its binding domain (which is TP, the smallest XP containing the anaphor and a subject as well as a finite T; see (41) of Chapter 6). So LF looks at the copy for satisfaction of Principle A. In fact, since the occurrence of the anaphor inside the moved wh-phrase in (80) would otherwise violate

Principle A, it may be that copy deletion deletes this copy at LF (but not the whole wh-phrase, as we need an operator here).

This concludes our very brief introduction to LF. We have seen three examples of covert movement, i.e. movement that takes place after the derivation splits into its PF and LF branches at S-structure and whose effects therefore cannot be directly 'heard': wh-movement in Mandarin, QR in English and wh-movement in multiple questions in English. Finally, we looked at reconstruction in relation to copies and copy deletion. All of these operations are motivated by the need to create LF representations which can be directly fed into semantic interpretation.

8.8 Conclusion

To end this chapter, let us look once more at the overall architecture of the grammar given in (1):

(1)

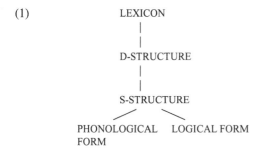

The lexicon is a list of lexical items with an associated specification of syntactic category, c- and s-selection features, a phonological representation and a specification of the item's semantics. Functional items are also listed in essentially the same way, although functional items may be phonologically null (presumably not a possibility for lexical items) and may have rather simple c-selection specifications. If all lexical specifications can be reduced to features, then the Projection Principle requires them to hold at all levels of representation.

D-structure is the level of syntactic representation generated by PS-rules in line with X'-theory. Lexical and functional items are inserted at this level in conformity with the Projection Principle; c- and s-selection properties must therefore be respected. This directly determines what appears in X'. To the extent that they have direct structural correlates, arguments bearing particular thematic roles may appear in specific positions at this level, e.g. Agents always occupy an external-argument position.

S-structure is derived from D-structure by movement rules: head-movement, NP-movement and wh-movement. These operations all share the central property of substituting an element of type X into a c-commanding position of type X, where X ranges over head position, grammatical-function position (or A-position, e.g. SpecT') and wh-position (or A'-position, such as SpecC'). Movement leaves a copy in the original position. Wh-movement is subject to island constraints of various kinds. At S-structure the derivation divides and follows two separate paths, one to PF and one to LF. The derivations of these interface levels are therefore independent of one other and cannot interact directly.

Phonological Form, PF, takes S-structure as its input and gives a phonological representation as its output. As such a great deal of syntactic information, including much (but almost certainly not all) hierarchical structure, is lost. Unlike in narrow syntax (the derivation from D-structure to S-structure and S-structure to LF), 'downward' movements such as T-to-V lowering in English are allowed. The operations at PF appear to be ordered in a partially intrinsic fashion, with more syntactic operations such as head-movement (lowering) taking precedence over deletion operations such as copy-deletion and ellipsis, as well as repair operations like *do*-insertion, which in turn precede morphological stem allomorphy rules and phonological assimilation rules.

Logical Form, LF, takes S-structure as its input and derives a representation which can directly feed the semantic interpretation proper. The operations in the derivation from S-structure to LF are covert, in the sense that they do not interact with phonology, given the architecture in (1). We saw examples of covert wh-movement and Quantifier Raising. We also saw that copy deletion may not have to apply as it does in PF and may, in fact, affect only parts of copies. Copies left by wh-movement and Quantifier Raising are interpreted as variables.

This concludes our overview of the architecture of grammar. Of the five levels in (1), two are interface levels (PF and LF) and one must be posited in order to account, at the very least, for arbitrary idiosyncrasies of a given language, namely the Lexicon. The other two levels, D-structure and S-structure, are 'internal' to the grammar. In part they reflect purely syntactic properties; in part they act as a bridge between the other levels, with D-structure particularly close to the lexicon and S-structure closer to PF and LF. The core mechanisms at these levels have been our principle focus in earlier chapters.

Exercises

1.   There are at least four kinds of *have* in English, shown in (a–d):

   a.   John has written a book.   [perfect *have*]
   b.   John has to write a book.   [modal *have (to)*]
   c.   John has many books.   [possessive *have*]
   d.   John has his students proofread his books.   [causative *have*]

   Which of these requires or allows (i) subject-auxiliary inversion, (ii) negation with *n't*, (iii) contraction to *'ve*? What can we conclude about the position(s) the different kinds of *have* can occupy? There is some dialectal variation concerning the possessive and modal forms.

You may also want to try replacing *have* with *(have) got*; here again there is some dialectal variation. Try to formulate and analyse the data based on your own judgements.

2.   Modals have complex and intriguing semantic properties and have been the object of a great deal of study. One central idea in many analyses of modal semantics is that they involve quantification over possible worlds. So, (ia) can be approximately glossed as in (ib), and (iia) as (iib):

(i) a.   I may have lost my keys.
    b.   In some possible world (consistent with what I know), I have lost my keys.

(ii) a.   I must have lost my keys.
     b.   In all possible worlds (consistent with what I know), I have lost my keys.

'Possibility' modals like *may* involve existential quantification over possible worlds and 'necessity' modals like *must* involve universal quantification. If modals have quantificational properties, the question of their scope, and possible scope ambiguities, arises. What are the scopal relations between the modal and negation in the following examples?

(iii) a.   John cannot come along today.
      b.   Confronting the enemy cannot be avoided.
      c.   You mustn't drink and drive.
      d.   You needn't drink and drive.

(*Can* is a possibility modal, *need* is a necessity modal.) If c-command relations at LF determine scope, what LF representations do these examples have?

3.   There is a scope ambiguity in example (i):

(i)   What did everyone buy for Bill?

Explain the ambiguity and give the relevant LF representations. What does this tell us about the nature of QR?

4.   Describe the derivation of the following sentence:

(i)   How many students were arrested?

Give the D-structure, S-structure, PF and LF representations and describe how the later levels are derived from the earlier ones. At PF, describe how the forms *were* and *arrested* are derived. At LF, bear in mind the implicit agent ('by someone or other').

Further Reading

Most of the textbooks cited as Further Reading in earlier chapters discuss the organisation of the grammar (from slightly varying perspectives) and various more advanced topics not covered here. On some of the specific topics covered here (the lexicon, passives, *do-support* and affix lowering), see the following:

Adger, D. 2003. *Core Syntax*. Oxford: Oxford University Press, Chapter 3.5 (on thematic roles) and 5.5 (on *do*-support).

Carnie, A. 2002. *Syntax: A Generative Introduction*. Oxford: Blackwell, Chapters 8 (on the lexicon), 9 (on head-movement and *do*-support) and 10 (on passives and related matters).

Larson, R. 2010. *Grammar as Science*. Cambridge, MA: MIT Press, Unit 13 (on the lexicon).

Freidin, R. 2012. *Syntax: Basic Concepts and Applications*. Cambridge: Cambridge University Press, Chapter 7.2 (on *do*).

Radford, A. 2016. *Analysing English Sentences*. Cambridge: Cambridge University Press, Chapter 5.10 (on *do*-support).

Sportiche, D., H. Koopman & E. Stabler. 2014. *An Introduction to Syntactic Analysis and Theory*. Oxford: Wiley, Chapter 6.8 and 6.9 (on the lexicon).

Tallerman, M. 1998. *Understanding Syntax*. London: Routledge, Chapter 7.1 (on passives).

Conclusion

In the foregoing chapters, I have tried to present the core elements of the theory of syntax. We began with the basic notions of categories and constituents, and how to find them (Chapter 2). Then we saw how PS-rules can generate the well-formed structures, creating phrase markers which we can represent either as tree diagrams or as labelled bracketings. We saw how to justify the proposed rules and the structures they generate using constituency tests (Chapter 3). Next, we introduced X′-theory, as a simpler, more general and more abstract format for PS-rules (Chapter 4). In Chapter 5, we introduced movement rules, concentrating on wh-movement (how it works and where it is unable to apply, i.e. islands). Chapter 6 introduced the interpretative rules of binding theory, along with the very important structural relation of c-command and the related notion of variable binding; here we also made the distinction between A- and A′-positions. In Chapter 7, we looked a little beyond English and introduced the important notion of parameter, giving several examples from a small range of languages along with some data from the *World Atlas of Language Structures*. Finally, Chapter 8 introduced the architecture of grammar we adopt, namely the 'Y-model', so-called because the derivation looks like an inverted Y, splitting at S-structure into PF and LF. This led to a discussion of certain PF rules and the important idea of covert movement in the derivation to LF.

There are many questions that we can raise concerning the model of syntax described here, even while remaining within a broadly Chomskyan conception of grammar and the language faculty (and of course, if we move beyond that conception, still more questions arise). One very important question is whether our assumption that constituency relations (dominance, constituency and c-command) are primary and dependency relations (subject, object, predicate) secondary, defined in terms of constituency, is justified. It has often been claimed that syntactic descriptions based on constituency work well in languages like English which have fairly fixed word order and rather little inflectional morphology, especially case morphology, while many languages have much freer word order and appear to mark relations like subject, object, etc. morphologically (often with case); such languages appear to lend themselves less well to a constituency-based approach to syntactic analysis and more naturally to a dependency-based one. Clearly, this question is partly a cross-linguistic one, and something we were unable to properly investigate in our brief comparative discussion in Chapter 7. It is of central importance for syntactic theory though.

A further set of questions concerns clause structure. In Chapter 5, we proposed that the tripartite division of the clause into CP, TP and VP, repeated in (1), corresponds to different domains, and each domain plays a characteristic role in building up the clause:

(1)

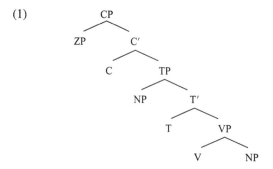

CP is the discourse domain, notably featuring clause-typing features like Q and wh (and associated movement operations). TP is the domain of the 'inflectional' functional categories Tense, Agreement, Mood and possibly PerfP and ProgP, the latter playing a role in the English auxiliary system. VP is the domain of argument structure: all internal arguments are realised here, while subjects/external arguments are somewhat distinct from other arguments (they are not c-selected, many languages including English requiring a subject position no matter what the argument structure of the verb is, and predication seems to be a central relation). We touched on the possibility that external arguments are first inserted in SpecV′ and raise to SpecT′, but we have not developed this possibility at all. We mentioned in Chapter 1 and in Chapter 5 that TP may be expanded into a range of further categories (Mood, Agreement, Aspect, etc.) and in Section 8.6 saw some motivation for a negation phrase, NegP. Can the other domains be similarly expanded? What are the principles determining this and what are the limits to such expansions? Can the nature or degree of expansion vary across languages? A further very major question is whether anything comparable can be said of other categories, notably nominals.

Another area of grammar we did not develop here is A-movement. Passive is clearly a central example. A further case of A-movement is seen in the alternation found with verbs like *break* mentioned in Section 5.3 and repeated here:

(2) a.   The vase broke.
    b.   John broke the vase.

The sentence in (2a) bears a resemblance, both syntactic and semantic, to the passive *The vase was broken*. It seems natural to propose that the Theme argument *the vase* moves from the object position to the subject position. Finally, there are raising verbs like *seem*, which show the alternation in (3):

(3) a.   It seems that the world is round.
    b.   The world seems to be round.

In (3b), *the world* arguably raises from the lower subject position to the higher one.

A very general question, which we only addressed rather sketchily, is what causes movement to happen. We said that a wh-feature on C triggers wh-movement, although we did not go into detail as to how or why this happens, and we didn't mention any kind of trigger for head-movement or A-movement. There is much more to say on these points, most of it of a rather technical nature. Related to this is the question of what underlies the fact that wh-movement is (mainly) overt in English but covert in Mandarin, that V raises to T in French and German but not in English, and T raises to all main-clause Cs in German but only in certain clause types (mainly interrogatives) in English and French. These last observations suggest that the triggers for movement should be parametrised in some way.

The Head Parameter clearly has great potential for accounting for typological generalisations about cross-linguistic word-order variation, as we saw in Section 7.4. However, the nature of disharmonic languages like German and Mandarin needs clarification. Further, while the other parameters we have looked at here mainly involve the presence or absence of movement (head-movement and wh-movement, and we mentioned that there are languages which lack passives and therefore possibly NP-movement), the Head Parameter seems to concern X'-theory rather than movement. Again, the question arises as to the range of possible parametric variation: which rule systems can be parametrised?

Finally, there are two very large theoretical questions. First, we have seen that there are two main rule systems: PS-rules (X'-theory) and movement. We have treated these as quite distinct and we have treated movement as substitution into positions created by X'-theory. But we also saw two examples where movement created new adjunction structures: T-to-V lowering in Section 8.6 and Quantifier Raising in Section 8.7. Can movement also create structure? If so, how different are our two rule systems really? As a related question, we saw that lexical insertion involves substituting a lexical item for a categorially matching head generated by PS-rules (e.g. substituting *fish*$_N$ for N). But the noun *fish* has a feature N, so if we simply place it in a structure it creates its own N-node. If we could do this, would we need to say that lexical insertion takes place all at once at D-structure? Nothing in the lexical entries themselves or in the formulation of the Projection Principle requires this. Since D-structure is an internal level, as we observed at the end of Chapter 8, perhaps it would then not be strictly necessary. This, in turn, would raise the question of whether we need the other internal level, namely S-structure: perhaps it is enough to simply say that the derivation splits into its PF and LF paths at some point, nothing more. All of these questions are interrelated and form the central object of research in post-1990 generative grammar; collectively they form a large part of the minimalist programme for linguistic theory. They are addressed in depth in Volume II, but the groundwork laid here is essential for understanding their scope and import.

In our conclusion to Chapter 1, after the discussion of the fish sentences in both English and Italian, which was intended as a demonstration simultaneously of tacit native-speaker competence in understanding strange sentences never heard before and of how similar and different two languages such as English and Italian might be, in response to the question 'what are the properties of individual I-languages and what are the properties of UG that underlie them?' I pointed out that 'this must involve the operations that are capable of producing the kinds of structures we saw in relation to the fish-examples'. Well, now we have a pretty good idea of what those operations are: PS-rules in the form of X′-theory, movement rules, interpretative rules such as binding theory, parameters distinguishing English and Italian, and derivations giving the PFs we observe and the LFs we understand, manipulating lexical items whose syntactic manifestations are regulated by the Projection Principle. We have also just seen some of the theory-internal questions our expositions have raised. Then, of course, there is the overarching and crucial question of how children acquire all this and how much of it is given by the genetic endowment (UG), how much is parametrised, how parameter settings are acquired and what is attributable to third factors.

There is clearly much to do, but we have made a solid start. As Lao Tzu said 'The journey of a thousand miles begins with one step.' We might have made more than one step here, but we do have quite a journey ahead of us.

Glossary

A-position an XP-position which is a grammatical-function position, e.g. SpecT′, the subject position.

A′-position an XP-position which is not a grammatical-function position, e.g. SpecC′, the landing site for wh-movement.

A-binding a **binding** (*q.v.*) relation in which the antecedent occupies an **A-position** (*q.v.*).

acceptability judgements given by native speakers regarding well-formedness, ambiguity, etc., of sentences in their language are acceptability judgements rather than grammaticality judgements. Sentences generated by the rules of the grammar are grammatical; those judged well-formed by native speakers are acceptable. Grammaticality is a matter of competence, while performance factors such as memory and processing interfere with acceptability judgements. A famous example of grammatical but unacceptable sentences is **centre-embedding** (*q.v.*).

accusative one of the case forms found in Latin, Sanskrit and many other languages. It typically marks the **direct object** (q.v.) of the verb.

Adjective a **lexical category** (*q.v.*) whose typical semantic value is to describe a quality or property. Adnominal adjectives modify nouns directly, occupying a position inside NP, as in *red bus*. Predicative adjectives modify subjects from within the predicative constituent (AP or VP), as in *the bus is red*.

adjunct optional, usually modificational, material, which is not **c-selected** (*q.v.*), e.g. *on Monday* in *I ate a pizza on Monday*.

adjunction (transformation) the transformational (or movement) operation which creates a new position attached to the target of movement. Opposed to **substitution** (*q.v.*), which is movement to an already existing position.

Adverb a **lexical category** (*q.v.*) whose typical semantic value is to describe the manner in which an eventuality takes place, or the speaker's beliefs or attitudes towards that eventuality. There are numerous subtypes of adverb, including speaker-oriented (e.g. *frankly*), subject-oriented (e.g. *cleverly*) and manner adverbs (e.g. *quickly*), as well as adverbs of time, place and reason.

Agent the 'doer' of an action described by a verb of the relevant type, e.g. *Mary* in *Mary ate her dinner*. The Agent corresponds to the subject of an active clause.

anaphor according to the **binding principles** (*q.v.*), an NP subject to Principle A, e.g. **reflexive** and **reciprocal pronouns** (*q.v.*).

antecedent (of an **anaphoric** (*q.v.*) or **pronominal** (*q.v.*) expression), the nominal to which the anaphoric/pronominal nominal is semantically connected.

arbitrary implicit argument an argument with arbitrary reference is a special kind indefinite, often with a generic, plural, human interpretation, such as *they* in *They eat pasta in Italy*. The implicit argument of a passive is the 'understood' external argument in cases where there is no *by*-phrase as in *Pasta is eaten in Italy*.

argument structure the property of a lexical item which determines the distribution of its **thematic roles** (*q.v.*) so that the predicate and the clause can be fully interpreted regarding who is doing what to whom.

Basque a language spoken by approximately 750,000 people in north-western Spain and south-western France. Basque is of great interest to linguistics, since it is probably the best-known example of a language isolate, a language that has no proven historical relation with any other known language.

behaviorist psychology an approach to psychology dominant in the English-speaking world in the first half of the twentieth century and which still has many adherents. The approach rejects introspection and regards observable behavior, and various methods for conditioning that behavior, as central to psychological research. On this view, language is a set of habits that can be acquired through conditioning.

binding principles the three principles which determine the anaphoric relations which **anaphors** (*q.v.*), pronouns and **R-expressions** (*q.v.*) enter into.

binding the chief way to establish anaphoric relations, defined as **c-command** (*q.v.*) combined with **coindexing** (*q.v.*); **A-binding** (*q.v.*) is regulated by the **binding principles** (*q.v.*), while operator-variable binding involves binding of a variable by an **operator** (*q.v.*) in an **A′-position** (*q.v.*).

bleeding order the order of two rules, A and B, such that A applies before B and removes the structural environment for the application of B, preventing B from applying. For example, English T-to-V lowering in PF removes the context for *do*-insertion.

branch a line connecting two **nodes** (*q.v.*) in a **tree diagram** (*q.v.*).

C(ategorially)-select part of the **lexical entry** (*q.v.*) of a lexical item which specifies the syntactic category of the item's complement (if any). For example, transitive verbs have the c-selection frame __ *NP*, indicating that they take a single NP **complement** (*q.v.*).

C(onstituent)-command the configuration relation defining relative structural prominence between syntactic positions. The relation plays a fundamental role in many aspects of syntax, including, notably, **binding**.

case a class of inflectional endings (typically) which attach to nouns in many languages to mark the grammatical function of an NP in a clause.

categorial feature a class of features (N, V, etc.) defining **lexical categories** (*q.v.*) and **functional categories** (*q.v.*).

category a class of words sharing the same distribution, morphological markings and (roughly) semantic properties, e.g. noun, verb, etc. Roughly corresponds to the traditional notion of 'art of speech'. Standardly divided into **lexical** (*q.v.*) and **functional categories** (*q.v.*).

centre-embedding relative clauses formed on an object which are embedded in subject position and therefore follow the head noun and precede the verb of the main clause. If, as is possible with object relatives in English, no relative marker is present, the string *N N V V* results with one relative clause, e.g. *the mouse the cat caught died*. Adding a further relative of the same kind on the second N gives rise to sentences which are very hard to process and often judged unacceptable, although they must be grammatical, e.g. *the mouse the cat the dog chased caught died*.

classifiers markers of noun classes with an approximate semantic basis, typically along the lines of animacy, shape and other properties. Very common in the languages of East Asia, including Mandarin and Japanese, e.g. *san-ge xuesheng* 'three Classifier student', i.e. 'three students'.

clause a minimal sentence, containing a subject and a predicate. Not all clauses can stand alone: infinitives generally cannot (e.g. *John to be the best* in *I believe John to be the best*).

clefting a syntactic operation which emphasises (or focuses) a constituent XP by placing it in the frame *It was XP that S*, where S contains a gap corresponding to the neutral position of XP. A standard **constituency test** (*q.v.*) in English.

coindexing a notation for indicating anaphoric relations between NPs (and possibly heads). Each referential NP has a constant index, written *i, j, k* ..., and quantifiers are associated with variable indices. Combined with **c-command** (*q.v.*), gives rise to **binding** (*q.v.*).

complement a general term for a **c-selected** (*q.v.*) **internal argument** (*q.v.*) of a head X.

competence the tacit knowledge an adult has of their language. Competence is usually contrasted with performance, which refers to the actualisation of competence in behaviour.

Complex NP Constraint (CNPC) an **island constraint** (*q.v.*) which bans **wh-movement** (*q.v.*) out of an NP containing a CP which modifies or is the complement of the head noun.

conjugation morphological classes of verbs; in Latin and the Romance languages, the three or four morphological classes formed by theme vowels.

constituency tests manipulations of syntactic structure which can only apply to XPs (often a subclass of XPs), designed to validate proposed constituent structure and associated **Phrase-Structure rules** (*q.v.*). The tests include movement or permutation operations, substitution of **pro-forms** (*q.v.*), **ellipsis** (*q.v.*), **coordination** (*q.v.*) and **fragments** (*q.v.*).

constituency the fundamental syntactic relation, specified by **Phrase-Structure rules** (*q.v.*) and indicated by **dominance** (*q.v.*) relations in **tree diagrams** (*q.v.*).

constituent a **category** (*q.v.*) A is a constituent of another category B just where a continuous set of **branches** (*q.v.*) can be traced from A to B going consistently 'upward' in the **tree diagram** (*q.v.*); the inverse of **dominance** (*q.v.*).

constituent structure the core set of relations in syntax, generated by **Phrase-Structure rules** (*q.v.*) and represented equivalently by labelled bracketings or **tree diagrams** (*q.v.*).

constructed languages (conlangs) languages which have been deliberately constructed for one purpose or another rather than developing naturally by historical generation-to-generation transmission.

coordination the combination of two words or phrases with *and* (canonically). Can serve as a **constituency test** (*q.v.*) for XPs.

copy the occurrence of a moved category which remains in the original, pre-movement position after movement has taken place. Copies are usually deleted by the **copy-deletion rule** (*q.v.*).

copy-deletion rule the rule which deletes **copies** of movement.

dative one of the case forms found in Latin, Sanskrit and many other languages. It typically marks the **indirect object** (q.v.) of the verb.

D(eep)-structure the level of syntactic representation where c-selection and s-selection specifications of lexical entries are directly realized in phrase structure. D-structure is generated by **Phrase-Structure rules** (*q.v.*), but no movement applies prior to this level.

declarative the clause type used for making statements, opposed to interrogative, imperative and exclamative, among others.

definite article marks an NP as definite (*the* in English). A definite NP refers to something which is taken to exist and to be known to both speaker and hearer in the context. The definite article also implies exhaustive reference to the members of the set of entities denoted by the noun.

direct object an NP which typically marks the 'undergoer' of an action described by the verb, and forms part of the VP with the verb.

disjunctive ordering the principle of ordering two rules A and B such that the rule with the more specific structural description precedes the more general one. The more general rule may be the **elsewhere** (*q.v.*) case.

distribution (as a test for categories) a way of identifying and distinguishing categories according to the syntactic positions they are able, and unable, to appear in, i.e. how a given category is distributed across the overall set of syntactic positions the grammar makes available. NPs, for example, are almost the only category able to appear both in subject position and as the complement of a preposition.

dominance the inverse of **constituency** (*q.v.*): a **category** (*q.v.*) A dominates another category B just where a continuous set of **branches** (*q.v.*) can be traced from A to B going consistently 'downward' in the **tree diagram** (*q.v.*).

do-**support** the phenomenon peculiar to English which involves the obligatory appearance of the meaningless dummy auxiliary *do* in main-clause interrogatives, negative clauses and **VP-ellipsis** (*q.v.*) contexts where no other auxiliary (modal, *have* or *be*) is present. The phenomenon is discussed in detail in Section 8.6.

echo questions wh-questions (*q.v.*) in which the **wh-phrase** (*q.v.*) is not moved, but appears *in situ*, typically associated with an interpretation of surprise or disbelief on the part of the speaker.

E-language external or extensional conceptions of language. Opposed to **I-language** (*q.v.*). Examples of E-language are texts, corpora, or in fact any occurrence of language which is not I-language. The everyday concepts of languages such as English, French, etc. are E-language concepts, since they are largely social, cultural and historical.

ellipsis elided categories are 'understood', i.e. they are present in the semantic interpretation (in some way) but absent in the phonological representation (i.e. silent). Can be used as a **constituency test** (*q.v.*) for XPs. A prominent type of ellipsis in English is **VP-ellipsis** (*q.v.*).

elsewhere the default, non-specified or minimally specified context for the application of a rule; for example +*d* for English Past Tense.

endocentric a phrasal category which has a **head** (*q.v.*). According to the **X′-schema for PS-rules** (*q.v.*) all categories are endocentric.

ethnolect a language variety associated with a specific ethnic group. It may be a distinguishing mark of social identity, both within the group and for outsiders. Probably the best-studied ethnolect is Afro-American Vernacular English (AAVE).

evidential markers clausal markers which indicate the speaker's commitment to the evidential basis for what is asserted by the clause: typical evidentials mark direct vs indirect knowledge, witnessed or not witnessed by the speaker, etc.

exocentric a phrasal category which has no **head** (*q.v.*). According to the **X′-schema for PS-rules** (*q.v.*) no categories are exocentric.

Experiencer a thematic role designating the sentient being affected by an emotion or psychological state, one of the arguments of a **psych-verb** (*q.v.*).

external argument the s-selected argument of a head which appears outside the maximal projection of that head. External arguments are never c-selected. Agents are always external arguments, but external arguments are not always Agents.

feeding order the order of two rules, A and B, such that A applies before B and creates the structural environment for the application of B, making it possible for B to apply. For example, movement rules feed copy deletion by creating the environment in which copy deletion applies.

finite finite clauses contain a tense-marked verb or auxiliary. Main clauses are typically finite; **declarative** (*q.v.*) main clauses always are.

first person the type of personal pronoun or person inflection on a verb used to refer to the speaker or (in the plural) a group including the speaker, *I/me/we/us* in English.

fragment a piece of a sentence, often occurring in the answer to a question, possibly derived from one or more applications of **ellipsis** (*q.v.*). Can be used as a **constituency test** (*q.v.*) for XPs.

fronting a syntactic operation which places a constituent XP at the beginning of the sentence; the remainder of the sentence contains a gap corresponding to the neutral position of XP. A standard **constituency test** (*q.v.*) in English.

functional categories the subclass of **categories** (*q.v.*) that represent grammatical rather than lexical information. Functional categories tend to have rather few members, which are frequently phonologically reduced, affixal, or silent, and to be closed classes. Some seem to lack a semantic value, others have complex or rather abstract semantics. Examples include auxiliaries, complementisers and determiners.

gender a grammatical category distinguishing classes of nouns. As mentioned in the Introduction, in many languages, including Italian and the other Romance languages, gender is grammatical, not semantic; in other words, it has no connection with biological or social definitions. In Italian, all nouns have masculine or feminine gender, and this has no semantic basis at all in many cases: 'sun' is masculine, 'moon' is feminine; 'sincerity' is feminine, 'feminism' is masculine; 'violence' is feminine, 'socialism' is masculine and so on. Nouns are arbitrarily assigned to two distinct morphological classes.

generate technically a way to enumerate the members of a set, e.g. the members of the set of grammatical sentences of English. **Phrase-Structure rules** (*q.v.*) generate constituent structure. The term gives its name to the theory of grammar adopted here, **generative grammar** (*q.v.*).

generative grammar the theory of language put forward by Noam Chomsky. Generative grammars recursively enumerate the set of well-formed expressions in a language, along with their structural descriptions. The well-formed sentences of the language are akin to the theorems of a deductive system, and the rule systems that specify them are akin to rules of inference. The theory of generative grammar aims to provide an account of the human **language faculty** (*q.v.*) by specifying the class of humanly attainable grammars.

generic a use of NPs, typically as subjects, to express general statements, e.g. *Fish live in water*. The most natural case is with bare **indefinite** (*q.v.*) plurals, as here, but singular definites can also be generic: *The fish is an aquatic animal*. Generics are usually taken to denote **natural kinds** (*q.v.*).

Germanic a branch of **Indo European** (*q.v.*) spoken natively by a about 515 million people mainly in north-western Europe. All Germanic languages are derived from Proto Germanic, one of the daughters of Indo European.

harmonic word-order patterns word-order sequences in which all, or at least the clear majority, of phrasal categories show a consistent value for the **Head Parameter** (*q.v.*). Japanese is an example of a harmonically **head-final** (*q.v.*) language, French of a harmonically **head-initial** (*q.v.*) one. Languages with mixed patterns are disharmonic; a well-known example is German, as discussed in Section 7.5.

head a lexical item, functional or lexical, of category X which combines with a complement and forms an intermediate X′ **projection** (*q.v.*) of the same category.

Head Parameter the **parameter of variation** (*q.v.*) determining whether the head X precedes or follows its complement in X′. Where the choice is 'precede', XP is **head-initial**, where the choice is 'follow', XP is **head-final**.

head-final (order/language) the case where the **Head Parameter** (*q.v.*) is set to 'follow'. Where all or most XPs show this setting the pattern is **harmonic** (*q.v.*).

head-initial (order/language) the case where the **Head Parameter** (*q.v.*) is set to 'precede'. Where all or most XPs show this setting the pattern is **harmonic** (*q.v.*).

head-movement a movement operation which copies a head into another head position, as in English subject-auxiliary inversion.

idiolect a language variety characteristic of an individual. It is extremely plausible that all individual idiolects are different in one respect or another.

I-language the internal, intensional, individual conception of language. **Generative grammar** (*q.v.*) aims to provide a theory of I-language by providing a theory of the **language faculty**, which makes individual I-languages possible.

immediate constituency a **category** (*q.v.*) A is an immediate constituent of another category B just where a continuous set of **branches** (*q.v.*) can be traced from A to B going 'upward' in the **tree diagram** (*q.v.*), and there is no category C such that C intervenes between A and B, i.e. there is no **node** (*q.v.*) C such that B is a constituent of C and A is not a constituent of C; the inverse of **immediate dominance** (*q.v.*).

immediate dominance a **category** (*q.v.*) A is immediately dominates another category B just where a continuous set of **branches** (*q.v.*) can be traced from A to B going 'downward' in the **tree diagram** (*q.v.*), and there is no category C such that C intervenes between A and B, i.e. there is no **node** (*q.v.*) C such that C dominates B and C does not dominate A; the inverse of **immediate constituency** (*q.v.*).

indefinite indefinite NPs are marked by the indefinite article *a(n)* in English, where the head noun is a count noun: *a cat is on the mat*. Indefinite mass nouns have no singular article: *milk is good for you*. Generally, indefinite NPs have none of the properties of NPs marked with the **definite article** (*q.v.*) and so may be used with no commitment to the existence, the familiarity or the exhaustive reference of the set denoted by the noun.

indicative mood the mood used to express statements that the speaker believes to be factually correct. In many languages, the indicative contrasts with the subjunctive (used to express various degrees of doubt, unlikelihood, unreality, etc.), but in Modern English this contrast barely survives in the verb-inflection system. Modern English more readily employs modal auxiliaries in these situations: *John may/might/could/should be home by now*.

indirect object an NP or PP which typically marks the goal or beneficiary of the action described by the verb, and forms part of the VP with the verb.

Indo European a large family of languages spoken across western and southern Eurasia. Most, but not all, of the languages of Europe, Northern India and Iran are Indo European. The Indo-European family is divided into several branches or sub-families: Albanian, Anatolian, Armenian, Balto-Slavic, Celtic, **Germanic** (*q.v.*), Hellenic, Indo-Iranian, Italic and Tocharian.

infinitival clause in English, clauses marked with the infinitive *to*, a subset of non-finite clauses, those which lack a tense-marked verb or auxiliary (see **finite**)

inflectional endings one way of forming complex words, which involves adding a bound morpheme at the end of a root to indicate grammatical information such as tense on verbs or case on nouns. English has a rather impoverished set of inflections compared to many other Indo-European languages.

interface levels those levels of representation which connect **narrow syntax** (*q.v.*) to non-syntactic parts of the grammar. **Phonological Form (PF)** (*q.v.*) connects narrow syntax to phonology and **Logical Form (LF)** (*q.v.*) connects it to semantics.

Interlingua a constructed language 'developed between 1937 and 1951 by the American International Auxiliary Language Association (IALA). It ranks among the most widely used IALs and is the most widely used naturalistic IAL [footnote omitted] – in other words, those IALs whose vocabulary, grammar and other characteristics are derived from natural languages, rather than being centrally planned. Interlingua literature maintains that (written) Interlingua is comprehensible to the hundreds of millions of people who speak Romance languages [footnote omitted], though it is actively spoken by only a few hundred' (https://en.wikipedia.org/wiki/Interlingua, accessed 14/9/21).

internal argument the **c-selected** (*q.v.*) argument(s) of a head X which form its **complement(s)** (*q.v.*) inside X'. Agents are never internal arguments.

interpretative rule rules which specify relations between syntactic constituents which affect semantic interpretation, distinct from both **Phrase-Structure** (*q.v.*) and **movement rules** (*q.v.*). **Binding** of various kinds is a prominent example.

intervention the case where a syntactic relation between A and B may be blocked if there is a third element 'in between' A and B. Very frequently defined in terms of **c-command** (*q.v.*), i.e. C intervenes between A and B where A c-commands C and B, C c-commands B and C does not c-command A; see (31) of Chapter 6.

intrinsic ordering the order of two rules, A and B, such that one can only precede the other. For example, the **feeding order** (*q.v.*) of movement rules and copy deletion is a case of intrinsic ordering, as there are no copies to delete before movement applies.

island constraints a class of restrictions on **wh-movement** (*q.v.*) including the **Complex NP Constraint** (*q.v.*), the **Left Branch Constraint** (*q.v.*) and **wh-islands** (*q.v.*). Island constraints do not permit wh-movement to move a **wh-phrase** (*q.v.*) from a position inside the island to a position outside it.

labelled bracketing in syntax, one of the standard ways of displaying constituent structure, along with tree diagrams (which are equivalent).

language acquisition the process by which people acquire the ability to speak and understand a language. First-language acquisition takes place in early childhood. From the perspective of **generative grammar** (*q.v.*), first-language acquisition involves the development of the **language faculty** (*q.v.*) on the basis of the **three factors of language design** (*q.v.*).

language faculty whatever cognitive structure underlies our ability to acquire our native language, to store the knowledge so acquired in the mind/brain and to put it to use in production and comprehension. In **generative grammar** (*q.v.*), **Universal Grammar** (*q.v.*) is the theory of the genetic endowment underlying the human language faculty.

Left Branch Constraint (LBC) an **island constraint** (*q.v.*) which prevents a **wh-phrase** (*q.v.*) moving off a left branch, e.g. SpecN' in English possessives.

lexical category a **category** (*q.v.*) whose head is a substantive lexical item, e.g. a noun, verb or adjective. Lexical categories are open classes, i.e. it is possible to invent new members and seemingly always have a phonological form, sometimes quite a complex multisyllable one. Opposed to **functional categories** (*q.v.*).

lexical entry the specification in the lexicon of all and only the idiosyncratic properties of a lexical item. Lexical entries are discussed in more detail in Section 8.3.

lexical insertion the operation which places lexical items in **D-structure** (*q.v.*). As presented in Section 8.4, this is an operation which substitutes a lexical item into a head position at that level.

Lexicon the mental dictionary, in which, in principle, all and only idiosyncratic information about individual lexical items is listed. This information includes at least a specification of s-selection, c-selection, phonological and semantic properties.

Linnean taxonomy a system of biological classification based on the system established by the eighteenth-century Swiss biologist Carl Linnaeus. Linnaeus introduced the system of two-part Latin names for species such as *Homo sapiens* for humans and *felix catus* for domestic cats.

Logic the study of the laws of valid inference, relevant for **semantics** (*q.v.*), since sound inferences are truth-preserving, and truth provides a way to elucidate meaning in truth-conditional semantics.

Logical Form (LF) the level of representation which converts the syntactic representation into a representation which can be the input to the semantic representation.

marked the marked value of an asymmetric opposition is the more complex term of that opposition. **Parameters of variation** (*q.v.*) may have marked and unmarked values, or perhaps a combination of parameter settings may give rise to a marked system, as suggested in Section 7.4 for the rarer sentential word orders.

maximal projection the phrasal projection of a **head** (*q.v.*) X and the intermediate projection X′. Can be defined as the projection of X immediately dominated by Y ≠ X.

morphology the study of the internal structure of complex words.

movement rule one kind of **transformational rule** (*q.v.*) which copies categories into a c-commanding position.

multiple questions questions featuring more than one **wh-phrase** (*q.v.*). In English, since only one wh-phrase can move per clause, the other(s) must remain *in situ*.

narrow syntax the collective term for the 'internal' syntactic levels of representation, **D-structure** (*q.v.*) and **S-structure** (*q.v.*), which do not interface with non-syntactic parts of the grammar.

natural kind 'To say that a kind is *natural* is to say that it corresponds to a grouping that reflects the structure of the natural world rather than the interests and actions of human beings. We tend to assume that science is often successful in revealing these kinds; it is a corollary of scientific realism that when all goes well the classifications and taxonomies employed by science correspond to the real kinds in nature', *Stanford Encyclopedia of Philosophy* (https://plato.stanford.edu/entries/natural-kinds/#SemNatKinTer, accessed 14/9/21).

Navajo a Southern Athabaskan language spoken by 170,000 people primarily in the Southwestern United States.

negative concord the phenomenon, found in French and many other languages, whereby the co-occurrence of two negative morphemes in a sentence does not give rise to a double negation but rather to single negation, also found in many varieties of non-standard English.

node a position in a **tree diagram** (*q.v.*) from which either at least one **branch** (*q.v.*) emanates 'downwards' (a **non-terminal node** (*q.v.*)) or a site of **lexical insertion** (*q.v.*).

nominative one of the case forms found in Latin, Sanskrit and many other languages. It typically marks the **subject** (q.v.) of a sentence.

non-terminal node a node (*q.v.*) in a **tree diagram** (*q.v.*) from which at least one **branch** emanates 'downwards' and hence which **dominates** (*q.v.*) at least one other **node** (*q.v.*).

Noun Phrase (NP) a phrase which contains a noun or pronoun and occupies the same syntactic positions as a noun or pronoun (subject, direct object, object of preposition, etc.).

NP-movement the operation which moves an object NP into the subject position in passives.

number the inflectional category which distinguishes singular from plural, marked on nouns in many languages, and on verbs in quite a few (in English, only in the present); some languages, e.g. Mandarin, have no obligatory number marking (either on nouns or verbs).

operator roughly equivalent to **quantifier** (*q.v.*), a category which binds a variable from an **A′-position** (*q.v.*), giving rise to quantificational interpretation. Wh-phrases are a typical example.

operator-variable structures a syntactic configuration in which an **operator** (*q.v.*) or **quantifier** (*q.v.*) binds a variable from an **A′-position** (*q.v.*), giving rise to a quantificational interpretation.

pair-list interpretation the usual interpretation of multiple wh-questions, in which the answers associated with each wh-phrase are paired, e.g. *John drank beer and Paul drank whisky* in answer to *Who drank what?*

parameters of variation a way to define and analyse syntactic variation among languages. A given grammatical system (I-language) may be seen as the set of parameter values characteristic of that system, combined with the invariant aspects of Universal Grammar.

Patient the **thematic role** (*q.v.*) of the argument that is affected by the action described the verb, e.g. *her dinner* in *Mary ate her dinner*.

performance putting **competence** (*q.v.*) into practice in production and comprehension; performance involves competence, combined with short-term memory, attention and other non-linguistic cognitive capacities.

person the inflectional category which disambiguates between first, second and third, marked on pronouns in very many languages, and on verbs in many languages (in English only in the third-person singular of the present).

Phonological Form (PF) the level of representation which converts a syntactic representation (**S-structure** (*q.v.*), given the standard architecture seen in (1) of Chapter 8) into a representation which can be input to phonological and phonetic rules and representations.

phonology the branch of linguistics dealing with how speech sounds are organized in linguistic systems.

phrasal category in **syntax** (*q.v.*), a unit of organization of words, intermediate between the word level and the sentence level; phrasal categories are non-root, non-terminal nodes (see Chapter 3).

phrasal stress the accent (marker of phonological prominence through pitch, loudness, length or some combination of these) which falls on the designated most prominent syllable in a phonological phrase (often close to a syntactic XP), as in *Oxford Róad*.

phrase marker synonymous with **tree diagram** (*q.v.*) or labelled bracketing, the means of displaying **constituent structure** (*q.v.*).

Phrase-Structure (PS) rules rules which **generate** (*q.v.*) **constituent structure** (*q.v.*). The recursive nature of these rule systems accounts for the fact that natural languages make infinite use of finite means.

pied-piping a case of **wh-movement** (*q.v.*) where the moving **wh-phrase** (*q.v.*) takes along other parts of a constituent to which it belongs in its pre-movement position.

postposition the category P is postpositional if it has the **head-final** (*q.v.*) value of the **Head Parameter** (*q.v.*); if **head-initial** (*q.v.*) it is prepositional. Strictly speaking, P should be taken as the abbreviation for the order-neutral term 'adposition'.

predicate logic the branch of logic which breaks propositions (roughly, logical-semantic representations of sentences) down into predicates and arguments; a key aspect of predicate logic is its ability to represent quantification.

predicate traditionally seen as the part of a sentence which describes a property or action of the subject, typically corresponding to VPs, PPs or APs, although NPs can be predicates too.

Preposition a **lexical category** (*q.v.*) typically denoting a location or path and taking an NP complement. Unlike other lexical categories, Prepositions are closed-class items.

Preposition stranding of the complement of a preposition without associated **pied-piping** (*q.v.*) of the preposition. Found in English (e.g. in *Who did you talk to?*) but cross-linguistically rare.

prescriptive grammar 'the establishment of rules defining preferred or correct usage of language … such normative practices often suggest that some usages are incorrect, inconsistent, illogical, lack communicative effect, or are of low aesthetic value, even in cases where such usage is more common than the prescribed usage' (https://en.wikipedia .org/wiki/Linguistic_prescription, accessed 14/9/21).

present tense a form of the verb which, in English, is just the root in all persons except the third-person singular, where it is marked by -*s*. The present tense situates the event or situation described by the sentence in the present time.

pro-form a reduced form of an XP that can substitute for that XP in the appropriate context. Pronouns are pro-NPs, *do so* can function as a pro-VP and *so* as a pro-AP.

progressive a verbal aspect indicating, roughly, ongoing action. Formed by adding -*ing* to the verb and marking tense and agreement inflection on the auxiliary *be*, as in *John was singing*.

projection the occurrences of the category of a **head** (*q.v.*) which contain further material in addition to the head: the X′ projection contains the head and its lexically specified complement, and the **maximal projection** (*q.v.*) XP contains the X′ projection and the **Specifier** (*q.v.*).

Projection Principle the principle which conditions **lexical insertion** (*q.v.*) and holds lexical properties constant through the syntactic derivation by requiring these properties to hold at all levels. A particular formulation is given in (25) of Chapter 8.

pronoun an underspecified NP, bearing a particular anaphoric relation to its **antecedent** (*q.v.*), if there is one.

proposition a semantic representation of a sentence, which bears a truth value.

psych-verbs a class of verbs denoting psychological, mental or emotional events or states, typically having an **Experiencer** (*q.v.*) and a Theme, or Cause, argument. At first sight, the two arguments both seem able to appear as either subject or object, depending on the verb, as in *John fears snakes* (Experiencer-Theme) vs *Snakes frighten John* (Theme-Experiencer).

quantifier a category involved in expressions of generality which are not predicated of individuals; a quantifier binds a variable in an **A-position** (*q.v.*) from an **A′-position** (*q.v.*).

quantifier-scope ambiguities ambiguities involving at least two quantifiers in which the different interpretations result from the apparent logical scopal relations between the quantifiers, as in *Every student bought some new book*, where there could be a different book for each student or each student could have bought the same book.

R(eferring)-expression NPs with independent semantic content, subject to **Binding Principle** C (*q.v.*).

reciprocal pronoun a class of pronouns subject to **Binding Principle A** (*q.v.*), e.g. *each other*. Owing to their semantics, reciprocals always require a plural antecedent.

reconstruction the case where movement, typically wh-movement, distorts the c-command relations required for binding interpretations, e.g. of reflexives inside complex fronted wh-phrases. Postulating that movement always leaves copies offers a good account for many such phenomena.

recoverability a condition on elided (deleted) constituents: there must be a way to 'recover' their content such that they can be 'understood', i.e. accessible to semantic interpretation.

recursion the property of **Phrase-Structure rules** (*q.v.*) that allows them to apply to their own output and thereby create an unbounded number of well-formed sentences.

reflexive pronoun a class of pronouns subject to **Binding Principle A** (*q.v.*), e.g. *himself*. In English, all reflexives end in -*self*.

relative clause a complex modifier of a noun or NP which contains a disguised sentence, as in *[the person [*RelativeClause* who I met yesterday]*.

root the **node** (*q.v.*) in a **tree diagram** (*q.v.*) from which all the other nodes emanate. As such, the root **dominates** (*q.v.*) every category in the tree diagram, and every category in the tree diagram is a **constituent** (*q.v.*) of the root.

S(urface)-structure the level of syntactic representation derived from **D-structure** (*q.v.*) by movement rules, after which the derivation divides into the two distinct paths to **Phonological Form** (*q.v.*) and **Logical Form** (*q.v.*).

scope the domain over which a quantifier/operator acts, typically by binding variables. Scope is defined in terms of c-command: a quantifier/operator has scope over the constituents it c-commands.

second-person pronoun the type of personal pronoun used to refer to an addressee, *you* in English. English does not distinguish the singular and plural of this person, neither does it make politeness distinctions indicating the status of the addressee, as many other languages do.

semantics the study of meaning, particularly sentence meaning.

sign language language(s) transmitted through the visual-gestural rather than the oral-aural medium, mostly used by deaf communities; sign languages are now known to be languages in every sense of the word, having all the salient structural properties of oral-aural languages.

sociolect a variety of language used by a particular socioeconomic class.

Specifier the category (itself a **maximal projection** (*q.v.*)) which combines with the intermediate X′ projection to form the maximal projection. Specifiers are typically, but not only, modifiers in a rather broad sense.

string-vacuous movement movement of a category in such a way that the constituent structure is changed, but the linear order of terminals is not. The best-known example is **wh-movement** (*q.v.*) of subjects in English, as in *Who left?*

strong crossover the configuration where a wh-phrase moves 'over' a pronoun, which is unable to take it as its antecedent. Falls under **Binding Principle** C (*q.v.*); see Section 6.7.

structural description the precise description of the structure of a syntactic object, usually a sentence. The standard form of such a description is in terms of **constituent structure** (*q.v.*) generated by **Phrase-Structure rules** (*q.v.*) and **transformational rules** (q.v.).

Subject an NP which typically marks the **Agent** (q.v.) of an action described a VP.

substitution (transformation) a movement rule copying a category into a position which has been created by the **Phrase-Structure rules** (*q.v.*). Both **NP-movement** (*q.v.*) and **wh-movement** (*q.v.*) substitute into Specifier positions (SpecT′ and SpecC′ respectively).

syntax the study of the structure of sentences.

terminal node a **node** (*q.v.*) in a **tree diagram** (*q.v.*) which **dominates** (*q.v.*) no other node; the site of lexical insertion.

thematic role lexico-semantic properties of predicates which designate the way in which their arguments participate in the eventuality they describe. An important component of **argument structure** (*q.v.*).

third-person plural the third-person plural pronoun in English is *they/them/their*. Generally used to refer to a group of known individuals who are neither the speaker nor the addressee(s), although it may also be used as an arbitrary pronoun (*they eat pasta in Italy*) or as a singular pronoun to avoid reference to gender. In many languages, verbs have special forms for the third-person plural distinct from other verb forms; English does not, however.

three factors in language design the three elements that together constitute the adult language faculty: (i) the genetic endowment (Universal Grammar), (ii) the primary linguistic data which acts as the input to language acquisition, (iii) third factors of a general cognitive nature.

Topic typically an XP that has undergone **fronting** (*q.v.*). Topics generally stand for 'old' or known information, something already talked about or given in the context.

trace a cover term for a position from which movement takes place. More precisely, **copies** (*q.v.*) occupy these positions.

transformational rule syntactic rules which map **phrase markers** (*q.v.*) into other phrase markers. Deletion and **movement rules** (*q.v.*) are types of transformations.

tree diagram one of the standard ways of displaying **constituent structure** (*q.v.*), along with labelled brackets. Synonymous with **phrase marker** (*q.v.*).

truth conditions the standard way of understanding sentence meaning; the central idea is that to know the meaning of a declarative sentence is to understand what the world would have to be like for the sentence to be true.

unbounded dependency the property of **wh-movement** (*q.v.*) which gives the appearance of movement across arbitrarily long stretches of material.

Undergoer a further thematic role, almost synonymous with **Patient** (*q.v.*).

Universal Grammar (UG) the initial state of the language faculty, assumed to be genetically endowed. The first factor in language design.

universal quantifier a quantifier, written $\forall$ in **predicate logic** (*q.v.*), corresponding roughly to *every*, *each* or *all* in English. Its semantics involves set-inclusion, i.e. *Every A is B* means that all members of A are included in B but not necessarily vice versa.

verb second the syntactic constraint operative in German (see Section 7.5) and other Germanic languages, but not English, which requires that the finite verb or auxiliary be preceded by exactly one XP in declarative main clauses.

Volapük a conlang created by the German Catholic priest Johann Martin Schleyer in 1879–80. It was later displaced by Esperanto.

VP-ellipsis a kind of **ellipsis** (*q.v.*) which affects VPs. Quite common in English, and a good **constituency test** (*q.v.*) for VPs.

V-to-T Parameter the parameter which determines whether the lexical verb V raises to T to combine with tense-agreement marking. Positive in French and German; negative in English.

Warlpiri an Australian language spoken by about 3,000 people Australia's Northern Territory. It is a member of the Pama–Nyungan family.

weak crossover a further configuration where a wh-phrase moves 'over' a pronoun, like **strong crossover** (*q.v.*). In this case, though, the crossed-over pronoun does not **c-command** (*q.v.*) the variable bound by the wh-phrase. The effect of unacceptability is weaker than in the case of strong crossover, hence the name.

wh-islands an **island constraint** (*q.v.*) which prevents **wh-movement** (*q.v.*) out of a CP whose Specifier is already filled by a **wh-phrase** (*q.v.*).

wh-movement the operation which moves a **wh-phrase** (*q.v.*) to a SpecC′ position, leaving a **copy** (*q.v.*) in the original position. Can be used as a **constituency test** (*q.v.*). A very important operation, which later chapters look at in detail.

wh-movement parameter the parameter which determines whether wh-phrases move to SpecC′ in wh-questions. Positive in English; negative in Mandarin.

wh-phrase an XP either consisting just of a wh-word (e.g. *who*, *what*, etc.) or having a wh-word in its Specifier (e.g. *which man*, *how big*, etc.).

wh-question an interrogative CP with **wh-movement** (*q.v.*) to its Specifier.

word stress the accent (marker of phonological prominence through pitch, loudness, length or some combination of these) which falls on the designated most prominent syllable in a phonological word (often close to a syntactic head X), as in *Óxford Street*.

X′-schema (for PS-rules) the category-neutral template that restricts PS-rules to the three given in (2) of Chapter 3. This makes the PS-rules highly abstract but also tightly constrained.

Index

A-binding, 151–3
A-movement, 216–17
A-positions, 151–3
acceptability
  and grammaticality, 35–6, 55
  native-speaker competence, 12, 217–18
  pro-form test, 84–5
  relative clauses, 27–8
accusative, 105, 131
accusative objects, 39
accusative singular, 39
active–passive pairs, 102–4
Adjective Phrase (AP)
  constituency tests, 69–75
  syntactic diagnostics, 40
adjectives
  internal arguments, 184–5
  lexical categories, 36
  morphological diagnostics, 39
adjunction transformations, 121
adjuncts, 65, 95–6
adpositions, 36–7
adverbs, 39
  lexical categories, 36
  word order, 159
Agent (argument structure), 102
agreement
  functional categories, 37–8
  wh-movement, 109–11
anaphors, 131–41
antecedent–anaphor relations, 132–41
antecedents, 63–71
arbitrary implicit argument, 193–4
argument structure, 102–104, 184–5
artificial languages, 4–7
auxiliaries, 39–42
  child language, 201
  subject-auxiliary inversion, 90, 101–2
  types of movement rules, 100–4
  wh-movement, 109–11
  X′-theory, 89–90

binding, 130
  anaphors, 132–41
  the binding principles, 144–6

coindexing, 131–2
  pronouns, 130–2, 142–3
  R-expressions, 143–4
  variables, principle C and movement, 146–53
bleeding order, 200
body language, 6–7
bracketing see labelled bracketing
branches (tree diagrams), 46
building rules, 100
building structure, 119
  see also Phrase-Structure rules

case (in English), 130–1
case marking, 39
Catalan, 8
categorial features, 86
categories, 36
  identification of, 44
  lexical and functional, 36
  morphological diagnostics for, 38–9
  phonological diagnostics, 42
  and semantics, 42–3
  syntactic diagnostics, 39–42
causative reading, 107–8
centre-embedding, 27–30
child language, 201
Chinese
  V-to-T movement, the Head Parameter and
    wh-movement, 175–6
  wh-movement, 172–4, 206–8
classifiers, 157
clause structure, 216
clause type, 110–11
clauses, 23–4
  wh-movement, 109–11
  X′-theory and functional categories,
    87–95
clefting, 61–3
cognitive perspective on language, 9–12
coindexing, 131–2, 134
competence
  native speakers, 12, 217–18
  and performance, 30
complement-clause structure, 57–9
Complementiser Phrase (CP), 94–5, 110

complements
    Phrase-Structure rules, 82–7
    wh-movement, 114–15
Complex NP Constraint (CNPC), 124–5
computer-programming languages, 5
conjugation, 18–19
constituency, 46–7, 215
constituency tests, 59–75, 87–95
constituent-command (c-command), 135–9
    intervention, 139–40
    movement, 147
constituent structure, 36
    hierarchical relations, 45–7
    phrasal constituents, 44–5
constructed languages, 6
coordination, constituency tests, 61, 68, 71
copy-deletion rule, 101–2
copy, head-movement, 101–2
culture, language as part of, 4

D-structure (deep structure), 180, 187–90, 211–12
    Logical Form (LF), 203–11
    Phonological Form (PF), 195–203
dative singular, 39
declarative, 39–42, 58–9, 100–1, 110–11
declension, 39
definite article, 17–18
deletion rules, 100
dependency relations, 215
determiners, 37–8
dialects, 8–9
disjunctive ordering, 185–6
distributional tests, 39–42
do-support, 92–3
dominance, hierarchical relations, 46–7

E-language, 10–12, 31
echo questions, 106
ellipsis
    constituency tests, 61, 66–8, 72
    X'-theory, 84–6, 89–90
endocentric phrases, 81–2
English
    comparison with Italian, 17–22, 31–2, 217–18
    as cultural concept, 4
    defining Standard English, 8–9
    emergence of Standard English, 8
    'good' English vs native speech, 7–8
    history of language, 4–5
    tacit knowledge, 15
    theory of syntax, 153–4, 156
    V-to-T movement, the Head Parameter and
        wh-movement, 175–6
'English speakers' as term, 12
Esperanto, 6
ethnolects, 9
evidential markers, 157

exocentric phrases, 81–2
Experiencers, 181–2
external arguments, 181–2, 184–5

feeding order, 200
fictional languages, 6
finite subordinate clauses, 58–9
first person, 130–1
fish
    lexical entries, 186–7
    six- and seven-fish sentences, 25–30
    and some relative clauses, 22–5
    tacit knowledge, 15–22
formal theory, 11
fragments, 61
    constituency tests, 68, 69
    X'-theory, 89–90
French
    V-to-T movement, the Head Parameter and
        wh-movement, 175–6
    verb positions, 157–60
fronting, 61–2, 65
functional categories, 36, 157

gender (in English), 130–1
gendered nouns, 20–21
generic reading of NP, 21–2
German
    dialects, 4–5
    syntax in, 165–71
    V-to-T movement, the Head Parameter and
        wh-movement, 175–6
grammar, architecture of, 179, 211–2
    D-structure, 180, 187–90
    the lexicon, 179–87
    Logical Form (LF), 180, 203–11
    a model of grammar, 179–80
    Phonological Form (PF), 180, 195–203
    S-structure, 180, 190–5
    see also Universal Grammar (UG)
grammaticality
    and acceptability, 35–6
    binding theory, 131–2
    competence, 27–8
    Phrase-Structure rules, 52–5, 75–6
    recursion, 55–9
    structural descriptions, 51
    syntactic categories, 44
    wh-movement, 107–108, 113–14

harmonic word-order patterns, 163
head-final, 163, 172
head-initial pattern, 162
head-movement, 101–2
    across five languages, 175–6
    S-structure, 190–5
    'target head', 119–20

head of the phrase, 81
Head Parameter, 163, 217
hierarchical relations
    constituent structure, 45–7
    X′-theory, 86
Homo sapiens, 4

I-language, 10–11
    linguistic theory, 31–2
    and performance, 30
    in relation to syntax, 35
    Universal Grammar, 156–7
idiolects, 9
immediate constituency, 46–7
immediate dominance, 46–7
indefinite interpretation of NP, 21–2
indicative mood, 18–19
indices, coindexing, 131–2, 134
indirect questions, 58–9, 112–18
Indo-European dialects, 5
infinitival clauses, 58–9
inflectional endings, 16
interface levels, 180
intermediate projection, 86
internal arguments, 181–2, 184–5
interpretative rules, 130
    anaphors, 131–41
    the binding principles, 144–6
    pronouns, 130–2, 142–3
    R-expressions, 131, 143–4
    variables, principle C and movement,
        146–53
intervention, c-command, 139–40
intransitive verbs, 107–108
intrinsic ordering, 200
island constraints, 124–5
Italian, comparison with English, 17–22, 31–2,
    217–18

Japanese
    head-final, 172
    V-to-T movement, the Head Parameter and
        wh-movement, 175–6
    word order, 161–3, 169–70

labelled bracketing, 16, 19
    hierarchical relations, 45–7
    Phrase-Structure rules, 52–5
    structural descriptions, 51
language
    as concept vs individual languages, 3–4
    natural vs artificial, 4–7
    perspectives on, 7–9
    theory of syntax, 153–4
    see also syntax beyond English
language acquisition, 10
language design, 10

language faculty, 10
language instinct, 10
Left Branch Constraint (LBC), 123–4
lexical categories, 36
the lexicon, 179–87, 211
lingua franca, 6
linguistics
    scientific approach, 1–3
    sub-disciplines, 1
Linnean taxonomy, 4
local rules, 118–22
logic
    computer-programming languages, 5
    predicate logic, 204–5
Logical Form (LF), 180, 203–11
    S-structure, 194–5, 211–12

marked options (word order), 163
maximal projection, 86
modals, 92–3
modifiers, Phrase-Structure rules, 82–7
mood
    functional categories, 37–8
    wh-movement, 109–11
morphological diagnostics, 38–9
morphology, 1
movement, causes of, 217
movement, characterisation of, 127, 146
movement rules, 100
    conclusions about, 217
    nature of, 118–22
    S-structure, 190–5
    types of, 100–4, 119–20, 126–7
    variables, principle C and movement, 146–53
    see also wh-movement
multiple questions, 106–7
music, as a language, 6–7

N′-ellipsis, 85–6
narrow syntax, 194–5
native-speaker competence, 12, 217–18
'natural kind', 17–18
natural languages
    scientific approach, 9–12
    vs artificial, 4–7
negation rule, 90
negative concord, 7
nodes (tree diagrams), 46
nominative case marking, 39, 131
nominative singular, 39
Noun Phrase (NP)
    binding, 147–8
    centre-embedding, 28–9
    fish, 17–18, 26–7
    generic vs indefinite interpretation, 17–18
    NP-movement, 102–4
    phrasal constituents, 45

Phrase-Structure rules, 55–9
possible and impossible PS-rules, 79–80
pro-forms, 63–71
R-expressions, 143–4
syntactic diagnostics, 40
wh-movement, 61, 109–11, 122–5
X'-theory, 82–4
nouns
  fish, 15–22
  internal arguments, 184–5
  lexical categories, 36
  lexical entries, 186–7
  morphological diagnostics, 38–9
  semantic criteria, 42–3
NP-movement, 102–4
  existence of parameter, 174
  kinds of NP positions, 151
  S-structure, 190–5
  structure of, 120
  target of, 121
number (in English), 130–1

operator-variable structures, 149
operators, 149

pair-list interpretation, 209–10
parameters of variation, 157
parts of speech, 42–3
passives
  languages without, 174
  NP-movement, 101–2, 120, 151, 193
Patient (argument structure), 102
performance
  and competence, 30
  relative clauses, 27–8
periphrastic tense, 168–9
permutation
  clefting, 62–3
  tests, 70–5
  X'-theory, 89–90
person, 130–1
  see also pronouns
philosophy of mind, 11
phonological diagnostics, 42
Phonological Form (PF), 180, 195–203
  S-structure, 194–5, 211–12
phonology, 1
phrasal category, 17–18
phrasal constituents, 44–5
phrasal stress, 42
phrase markers, 45–7
Phrase-Structure (PS) rules
  as building rules, 100
  conclusions about, 217
  constituency tests, 59–75
  D-structure, 187–90
  distinguishing from movement rules, 118–22

interpretative rules, 130
possible and impossible, 78–80
recursion, 55–9
as structural descriptions, 52–5, 75–6, 99
X'-theory, 80–7
X'-theory, adjuncts in, 95–6
X'-theory and functional categories, 87–95
pied-piping, 105–6
plurals
  English vs Italian, 20–1
  morphological diagnostics, 38–9
postpositions, 162–4
predicate, 22–3, 40
predicate logic, 204–5
preposition stranding, 105–6
Prepositional Phrase (PP)
  pro-forms, 63–71
  syntactic diagnostics, 40
prepositions
  external arguments, 184–5
  lexical categories, 36
  Phrase-Structure rules, 60–1
  word order, 162–4
present tense, English vs Italian, 18–20
Principle A, 151–3
Principle B, 149–51
Principle C, 146–53
pro-forms
  constituency tests, 61, 63–71
  X'-theory, 84–6, 95–6
progressive forms, 40
projection of categorial features, 86
Projection Principle, 187–90, 193–4, 205–6
pronouns
  constituency tests, 63–71
  interpretative rules, 130–2, 142–3
  second-person, 16, 17
propositions, X'-theory, 90
PS rules *see* Phrase-Structure rules
psych-verbs, 181–3

Q-feature, 114–15, 119–20
quantified expression, 148
quantifier-scope ambiguities, 208–9
quantifiers, 149, 186, 203–11

R-expressions, 131
  interpretative rules, 143–4
  proper-name subject, 148
reciprocal pronouns, 131
  see also anaphors
reconstruction, 210
recoverability, 65–6
recursion, 55–9
reflexive pronouns, 131
  see also anaphors
relative clause, 23–4, 27–30

S-structure (surface structure), 180, 190–5, 211–12
 Logical Form (LF), 203–11
 Phonological Form (PF), 195–203
satellite words, 21–2, 37
scientific approach to linguistics, 1–3, 9–12
second-person pronouns, 16, 17
semantics, 1, 42–3
sign language, 5–6
sociopolitical perspective, 8
sociolects, 9
Specifiers, Phrase-Structure rules, 82–7
Standard English, 8, 9
stress (phonology), 42
string-vacuous movement, 113
strong crossover, 151–2
structural descriptions
 constituency tests, 59–75
 grammaticality, 51
 Phrase-Structure rules, 52–5, 75–6, 99
 possible and impossible PS-rules, 78–80
 presentation of, 51
 recursion, 55–9
 syntactic representations, 29
subject-auxiliary inversion, 39–40, 90, 101–2, 114–15
subject-object-verb (SOV) word order
 French vs English, 157–60
 Japanese, 161–3
 X′-theory, 160–4
subject questions, 112–18
subject-verb-object (SVO) word order
 French vs English, 157–60
 German, 165–71
substitution, 121
substitution transformations, 121
syntactic diagnostics, 39–42
syntactic representations, 29
syntactic theory, goal of, 32
syntax
 as constituent structure, 35–6
 I-language, 35
 as sub-discipline, 1
syntax beyond English, 156
 approaching Universal Grammar, 156–7
 German, 165–71
 verb positions in French and English, 157–60
 wh-movement, 171–4
 word order and X′-theory, 160–4

T-to-C movement
 S-structure, 192
 subject-auxiliary inversion, 114–15
 target of, 122
 word order, 168–9
tacit knowledge, 15
 fish, 15–22

fish and some relative clauses, 22–5
 linguistic theory, 31–2
 six- and seven-fish sentences, 25–30
teleological perspective, 8, 9
tense
 functional categories, 37–8
 wh-movement, 109–11
TenseP (TP), 92–5, 110, 122–5
terminal nodes (tree diagrams), 46
thematic roles, 102, 180
third-person plural, 18–19
to, 92–3
Tolkien, J. R. R., 6
topic, fronting, 61–2
trace, head-movement, 101–2
transformations, 100
 see also movement rules
tree diagrams, 45–7
 local PS-rules, 118–22
 Phrase-Structure rules, 52–5
 structural descriptions, 51
truth conditions, 148

unbounded dependency, 117–18
Undergoer of the action (argument structure), 102
ungrammatical language see grammaticality
Universal Grammar (UG)
 competence, 12
 language acquisition, 10
 syntax beyond English, 156–7
universal quantifiers, 186

V-to-T movement, 171, 175–6
V-to-T parameter, 159–60, 167
Verb Phrase (VP)
 fish, 22–3, 26–7
 phrasal constituents, 45
 Phrase-Structure rules, 55–9
 possible and impossible PS-rules, 79–80
 syntactic diagnostics, 40
 VP-ellipsis, 66–8
 wh-movement, 61, 109–11, 122–5
 X′-theory, 82–4
verb positions, French and English, 157–60
verb second, 165
 see also subject-verb-object (SVO) word order
verbs
 English vs Italian, 18–19
 external arguments, 184–5
 fish, 15–22
 lexical categories, 36
 lexical entries, 186–7
 morphological diagnostics, 38–9
 semantic criteria, 42–3

weak crossover, 151–2
Weinreich, Max, 8

wh-islands, 124
wh-movement, 61–2, 104–12
  across five languages, 175–6
  binding, 147–8
  limitations, 122–5
  Logical Form (LF), 205–6
  long-distance, 112–18
  nature of, 118–22
  S-structure, 190–5
  syntax beyond English, 171–4
wh-phrase, 104, 120–1
wh-questions, 104
wide scope, 208–9
word order
  syntax beyond English, 160–4
  verb positions in French and English, 157–60
word stress, 42
World Atlas of Language Structures (WALS), 160,
  163–5, 171–4

'X′-schema' for PS-rules, 83
X′-theory, 80–7
  adjuncts in, 95–6
  conclusions about, 217
  functional categories, 87–95
  syntax beyond English, 160–4
  template for categories, 99
  Universal Grammar, 156–7

For EU product safety concerns, contact us at Calle de José Abascal, 56–1°,
28003 Madrid, Spain or eugpsr@cambridge.org.

www.ingramcontent.com/pod-product-compliance
Ingram Content Group UK Ltd.
Pitfield, Milton Keynes, MK11 3LW, UK
UKHW030900150625
459647UK00021B/2704